BUREAU FOR PARANORMAL RESEARCH AND DEFENSE

B.P.R.D. HELL ON EARTH: FLESH AND STONE

created by MIKE MIGNOLA

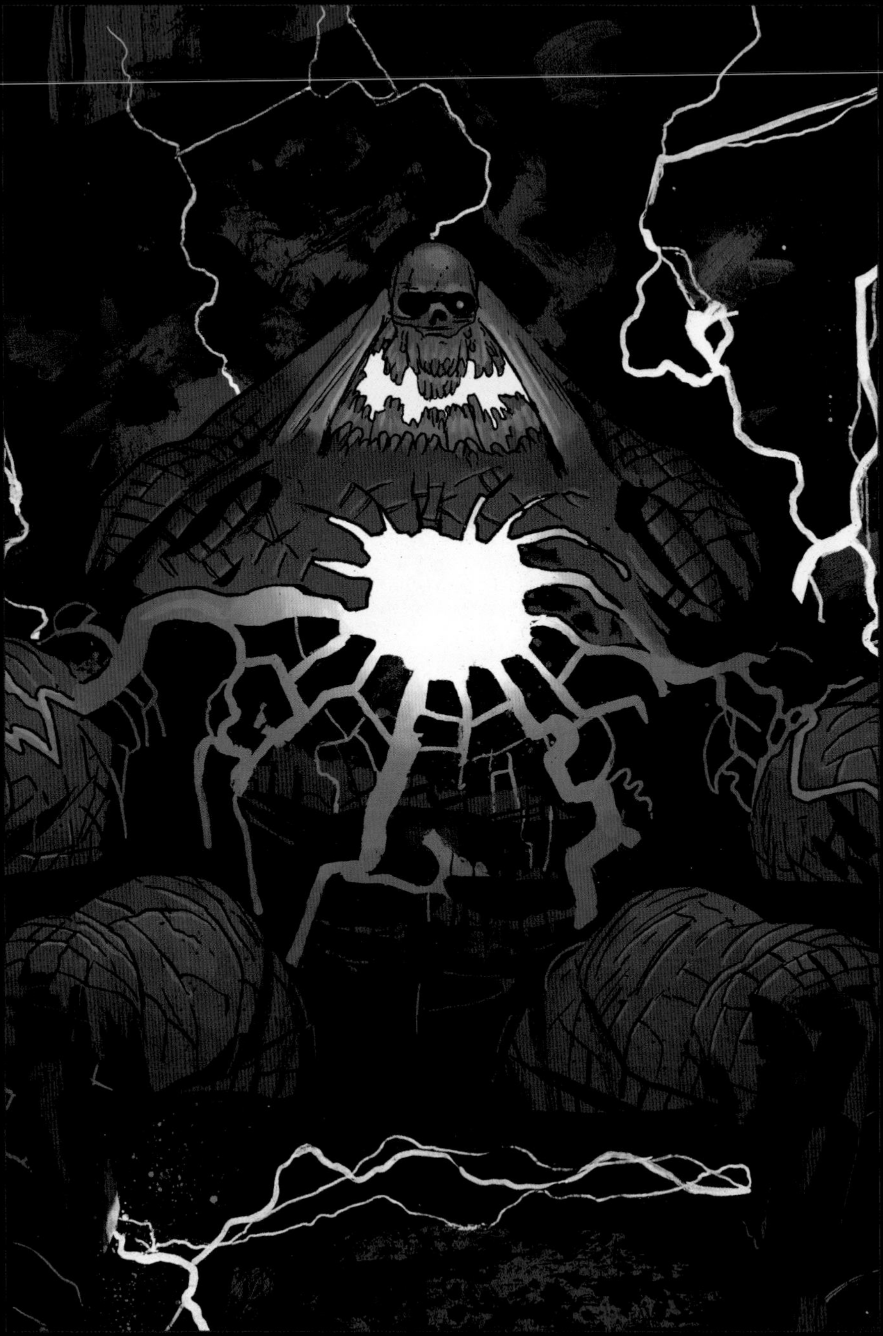

When the Black Flame attempted to raise a new race of man, Liz Sherman lit a fire that nearly cracked the world in two in order to destroy him. With Zinco's resurrection of a new and even more powerful Black Flame, Kate Corrigan finds herself in charge of a Bureau facing a worldwide crisis and the new threats that continue to crawl out of the earth, while Agent Abe Sapien remains AWOL.

MIKE MIGNOLA'S

B.P.R.D.™
HELL ON EARTH
FLESH AND STONE

story by **MIKE MIGNOLA** and **JOHN ARCUDI**

art by **JAMES HARREN**

colors by **DAVE STEWART**

letters by **CLEM ROBINS**

cover and chapter break art by **LAURENCE CAMPBELL**
with **DAVE STEWART**

publisher **MIKE RICHARDSON**

editor **SCOTT ALLIE**

associate editor **SHANTEL LaROCQUE**

collection designer **AMY ARENDTS**

digital art technician **CHRISTINA McKENZIE**

DARK HORSE BOOKS ®

Mike Richardson PRESIDENT AND PUBLISHER · Neil Hankerson EXECUTIVE VICE PRESIDENT
Tom Weddle CHIEF FINANCIAL OFFICER · Randy Stradley VICE PRESIDENT OF PUBLISHING
Michael Martens VICE PRESIDENT OF BOOK TRADE SALES · Scott Allie EDITOR IN CHIEF
Matt Parkinson VICE PRESIDENT OF MARKETING · David Scroggy VICE PRESIDENT OF
PRODUCT DEVELOPMENT · Dale LaFountain VICE PRESIDENT OF INFORMATION TECHNOLOGY
Darlene Vogel SENIOR DIRECTOR OF PRINT, DESIGN, AND PRODUCTION · Ken Lizzi GENERAL
COUNSEL · Davey Estrada EDITORIAL DIRECTOR · Chris Warner SENIOR BOOKS EDITOR · Cary
Grazzini DIRECTOR OF PRINT AND DEVELOPMENT · Lia Ribacchi ART DIRECTOR · Cara Niece
DIRECTOR OF SCHEDULING · Mark Bernardi DIRECTOR OF DIGITAL PUBLISHING

DarkHorse.com   Hellboy.com

B.P.R.D.™ Hell on Earth Volume 11: Flesh and Stone

This book collects B.P.R.D. Hell on Earth #125–#129.

Published by Dark Horse Books
A division of Dark Horse Comics, Inc.
10956 SE Main Street
Milwaukie, OR 97222

International Licensing: (503) 905-2377

First edition: September 2015
ISBN 978-1-61655-762-1

10 9 8 7 6 5 4 3 2 1
Printed in China

CHAPTER ONE

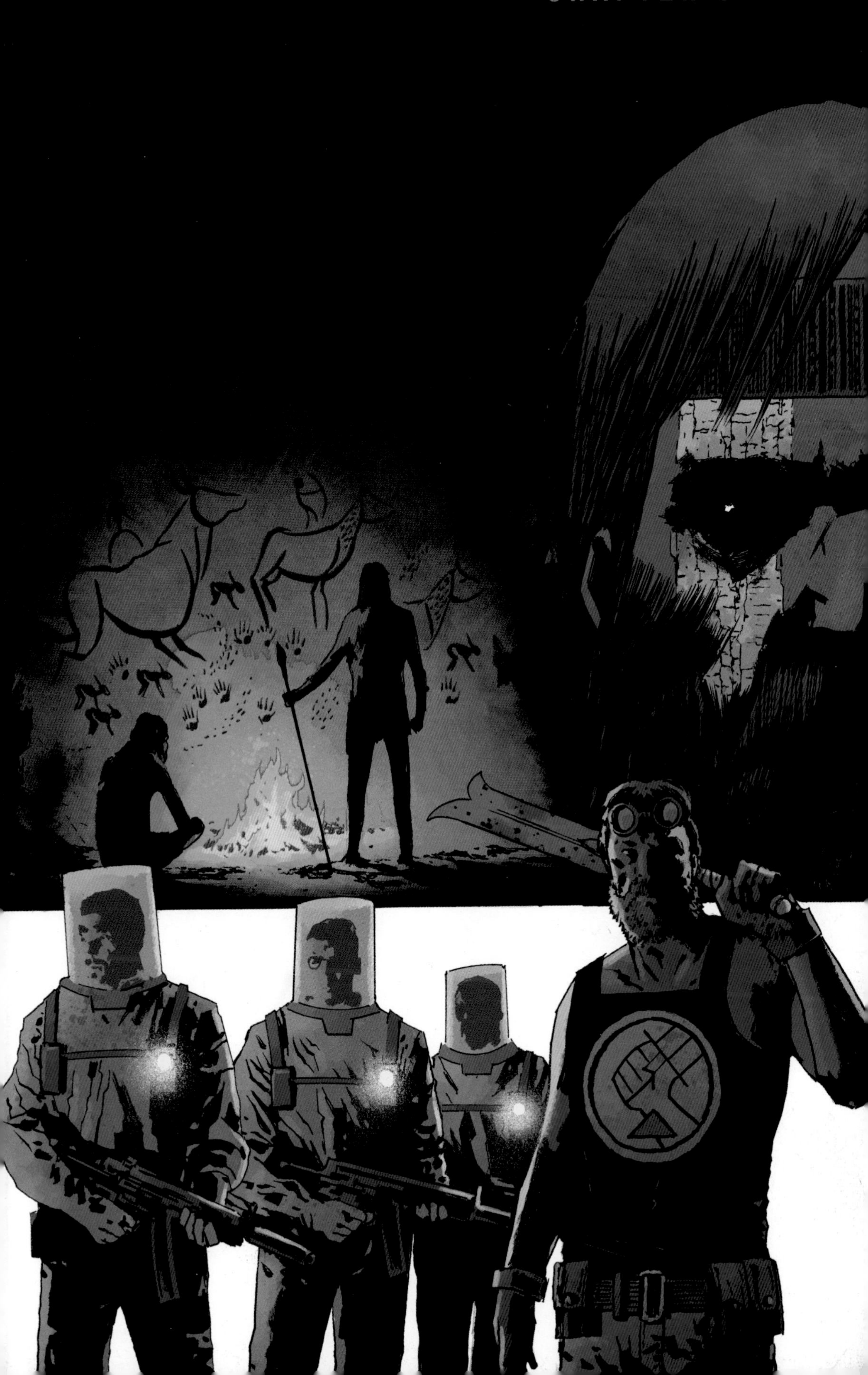

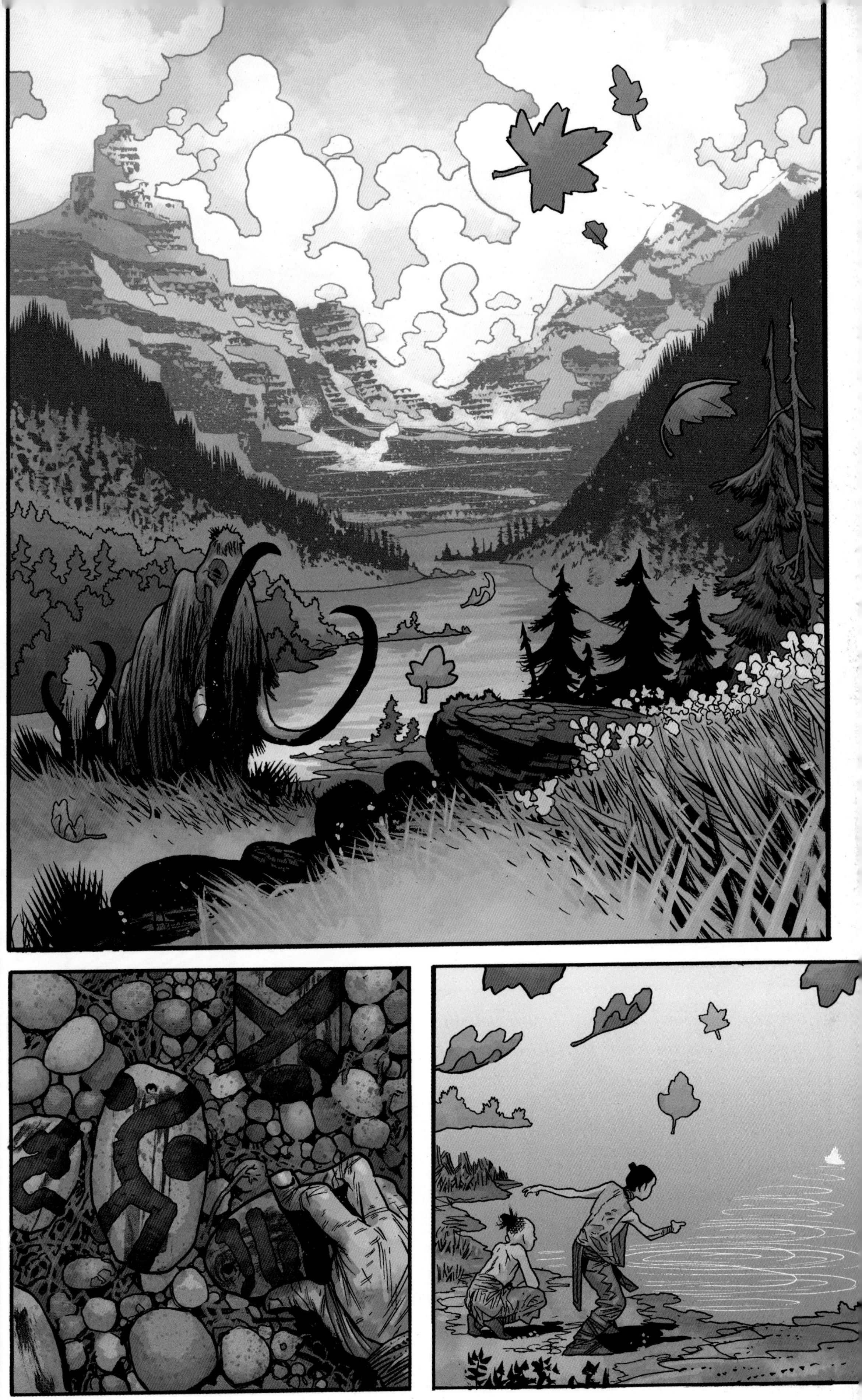

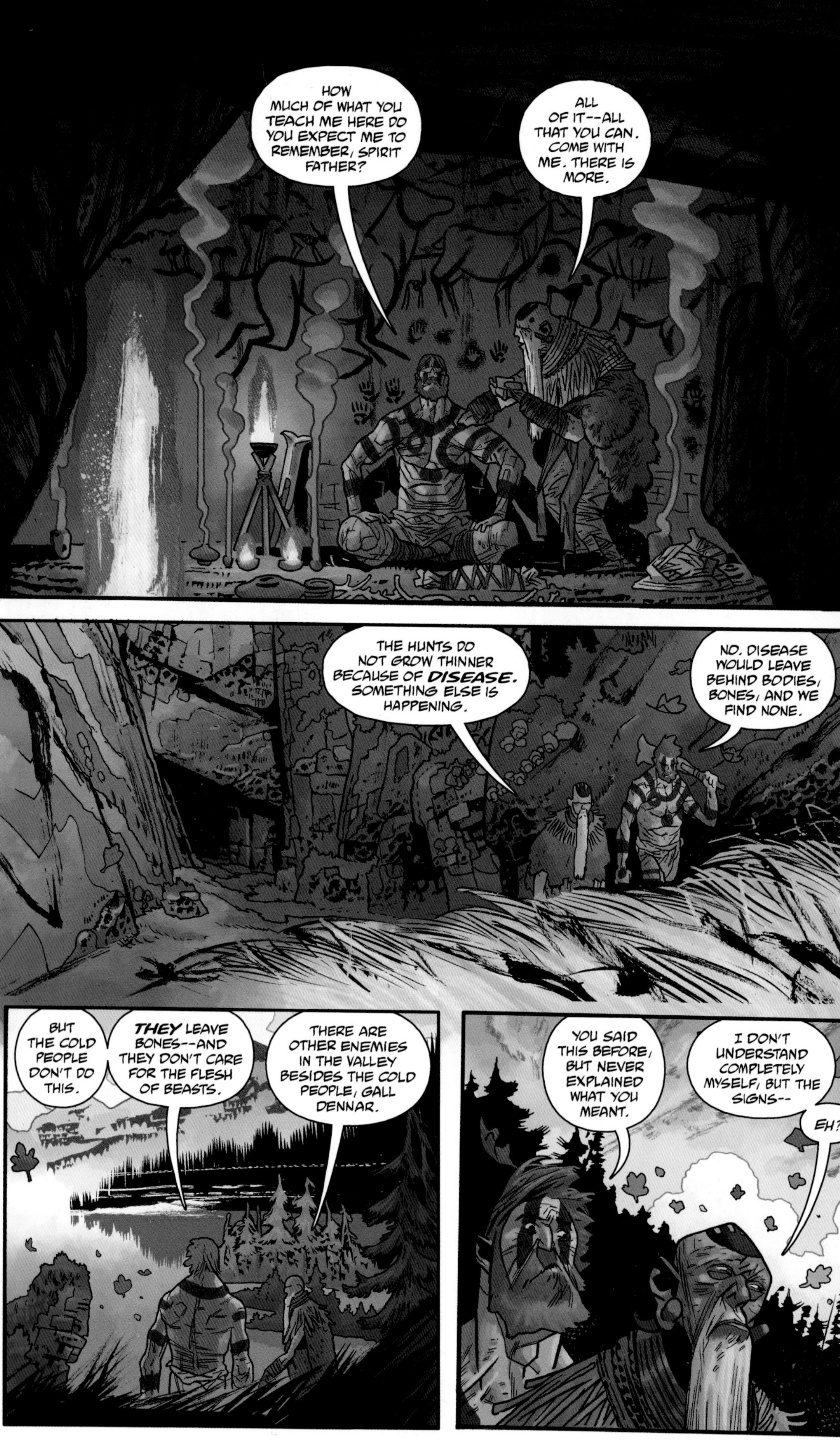
HOW MUCH OF WHAT YOU TEACH ME HERE DO YOU EXPECT ME TO REMEMBER, SPIRIT FATHER?
ALL OF IT--ALL THAT YOU CAN. COME WITH ME. THERE IS MORE.
THE HUNTS DO NOT GROW THINNER BECAUSE OF DISEASE. SOMETHING ELSE IS HAPPENING.
NO. DISEASE WOULD LEAVE BEHIND BODIES, BONES, AND WE FIND NONE.
BUT THE COLD PEOPLE DON'T DO THIS.
THEY LEAVE BONES--AND THEY DON'T CARE FOR THE FLESH OF BEASTS.
THERE ARE OTHER ENEMIES IN THE VALLEY BESIDES THE COLD PEOPLE, GALL DENNAR.
YOU SAID THIS BEFORE, BUT NEVER EXPLAINED WHAT YOU MEANT.
I DON'T UNDERSTAND COMPLETELY MYSELF, BUT THE SIGNS--
EH?

BOY! WHAT ARE YOU DOING?!

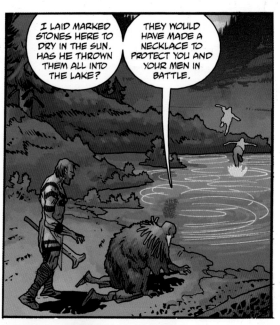

I LAID MARKED STONES HERE TO DRY IN THE SUN. HAS HE THROWN THEM ALL INTO THE LAKE?

THEY WOULD HAVE MADE A NECKLACE TO PROTECT YOU AND YOUR MEN IN BATTLE.

I HAVE TO GET THEM!

THEY ARE IMPORTANT FOR YOU TO SEE, TO KNOW! THEY ARE YOUR SUCCESS!

HOLD, SPIRIT FATHER.

THE WATERS OF THE LATE SEASON ARE COLD.

IF YOU FALL ILL, WHERE WILL THAT LEAVE US? STAY HERE AND GIVE ME YOUR BLESSING. YOUR BLESSINGS SERVE ME ALWAYS.

AND I CAN DO THE REST.

WAIT! YOU MUST WAIT UNTIL I PAINT MORE!

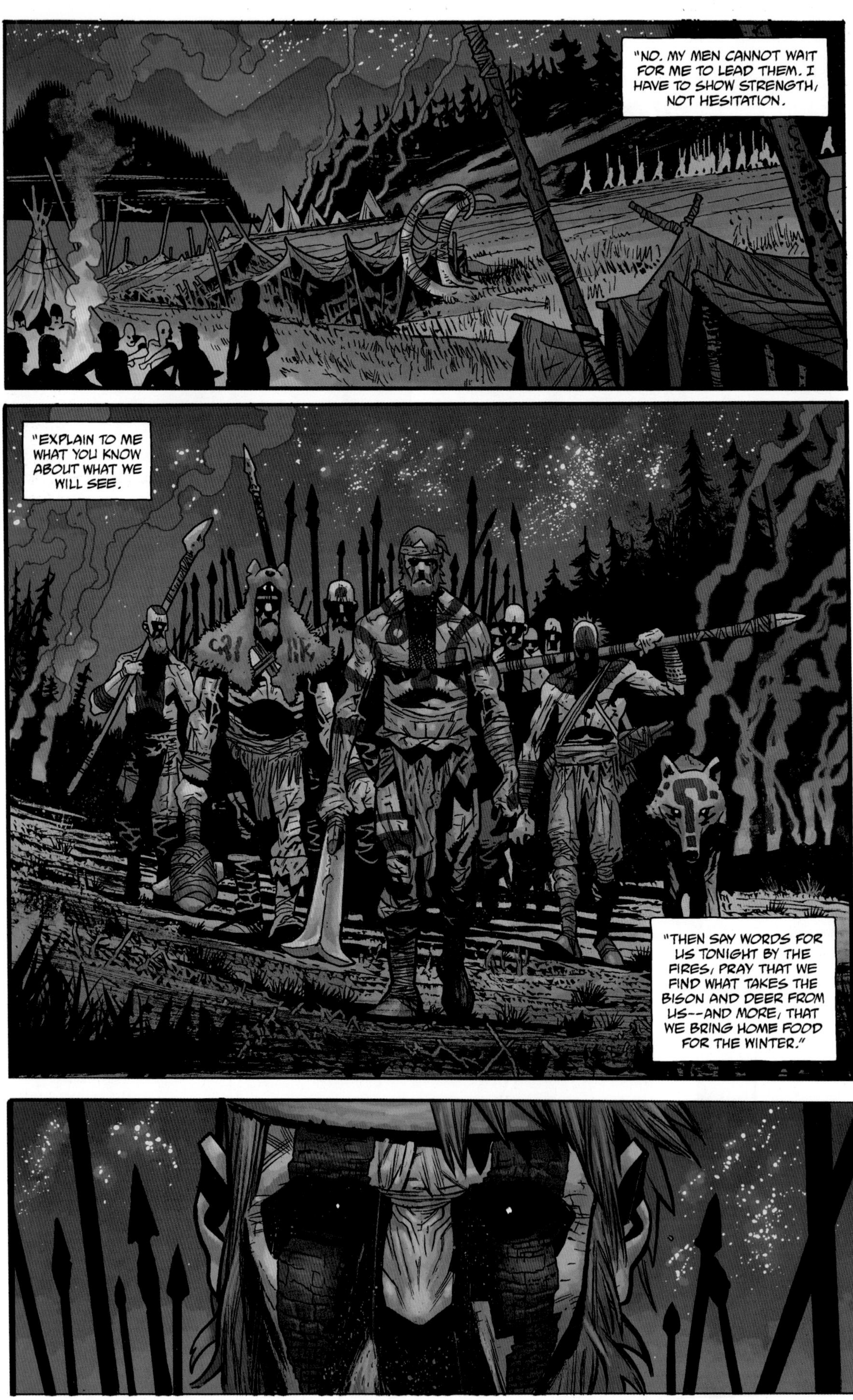
"NO. MY MEN CANNOT WAIT FOR ME TO LEAD THEM. I HAVE TO SHOW STRENGTH, NOT HESITATION.
"EXPLAIN TO ME WHAT YOU KNOW ABOUT WHAT WE WILL SEE.
"THEN SAY WORDS FOR US TONIGHT BY THE FIRES, PRAY THAT WE FIND WHAT TAKES THE BISON AND DEER FROM US--AND MORE, THAT WE BRING HOME FOOD FOR THE WINTER."

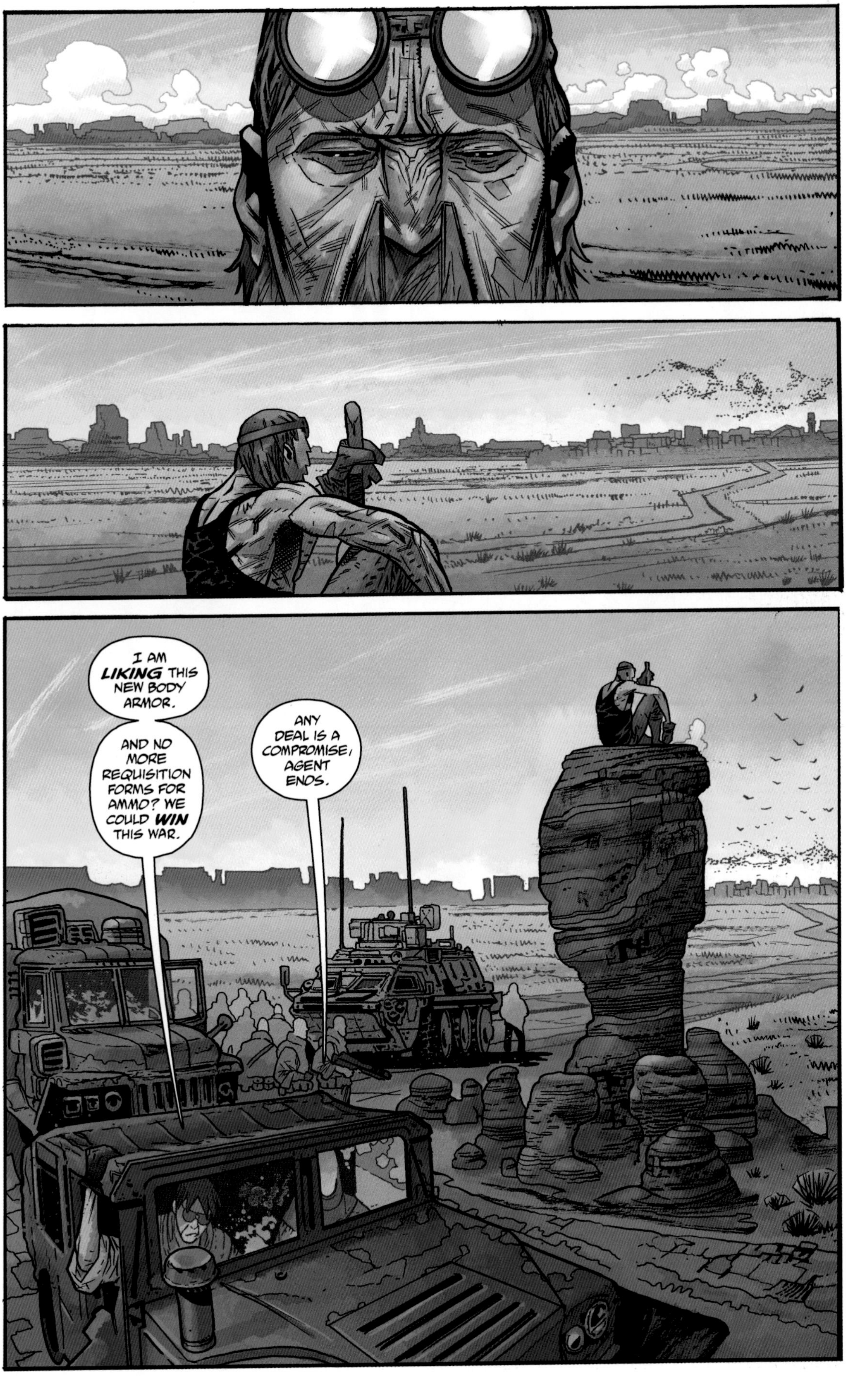
I AM LIKING THIS NEW BODY ARMOR.
AND NO MORE REQUISITION FORMS FOR AMMO? WE COULD WIN THIS WAR.
ANY DEAL IS A COMPROMISE, AGENT ENOS.

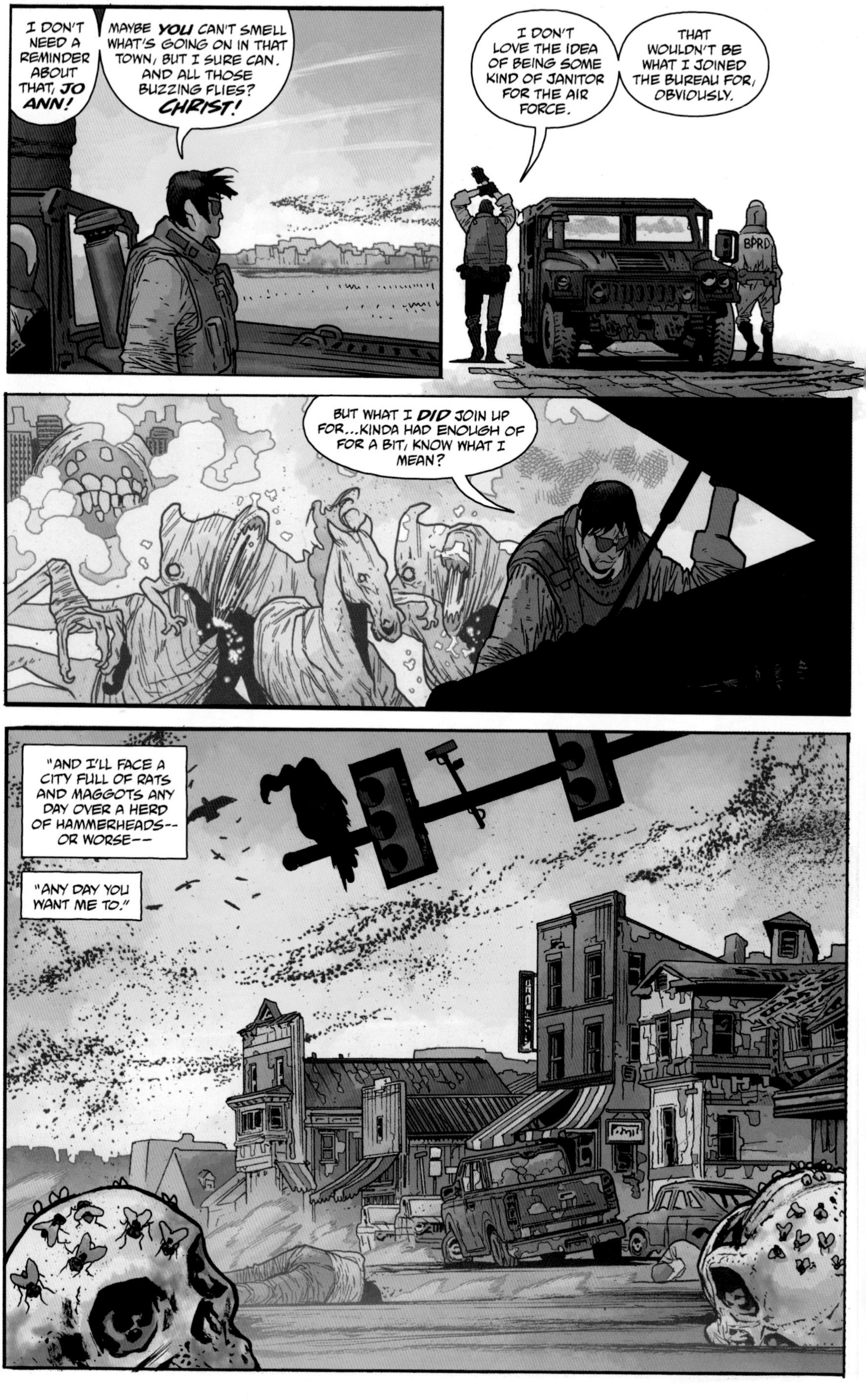
I DON'T NEED A REMINDER ABOUT THAT, JO ANN!
MAYBE YOU CAN'T SMELL WHAT'S GOING ON IN THAT TOWN, BUT I SURE CAN. AND ALL THOSE BUZZING FLIES? CHRIST!
I DON'T LOVE THE IDEA OF BEING SOME KIND OF JANITOR FOR THE AIR FORCE.
THAT WOULDN'T BE WHAT I JOINED THE BUREAU FOR, OBVIOUSLY.
BPRD
BUT WHAT I DID JOIN UP FOR...KINDA HAD ENOUGH OF FOR A BIT, KNOW WHAT I MEAN?
"AND I'LL FACE A CITY FULL OF RATS AND MAGGOTS ANY DAY OVER A HERD OF HAMMERHEADS-- OR WORSE--
"ANY DAY YOU WANT ME TO."

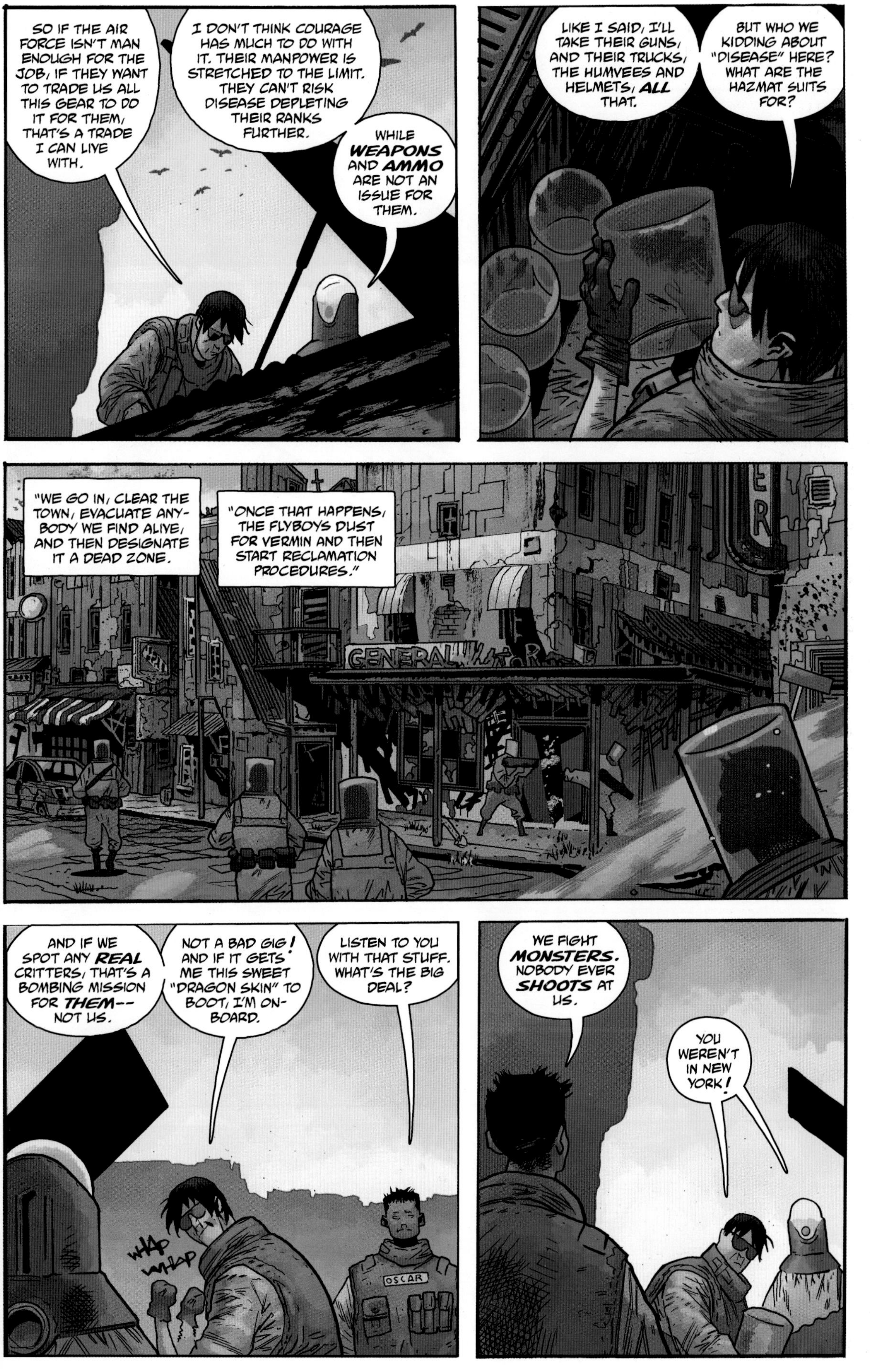
SO IF THE AIR FORCE ISN'T MAN ENOUGH FOR THE JOB, IF THEY WANT TO TRADE US ALL THIS GEAR TO DO IT FOR THEM, THAT'S A TRADE I CAN LIVE WITH.
I DON'T THINK COURAGE HAS MUCH TO DO WITH IT. THEIR MANPOWER IS STRETCHED TO THE LIMIT. THEY CAN'T RISK DISEASE DEPLETING THEIR RANKS FURTHER.
WHILE **WEAPONS** AND **AMMO** ARE NOT AN ISSUE FOR THEM.
LIKE I SAID, I'LL TAKE THEIR GUNS, AND THEIR TRUCKS, THE HUMVEES AND HELMETS, **ALL** THAT.
BUT WHO WE KIDDING ABOUT "DISEASE" HERE? WHAT ARE THE HAZMAT SUITS FOR?
"WE GO IN, CLEAR THE TOWN, EVACUATE ANYBODY WE FIND ALIVE, AND THEN DESIGNATE IT A DEAD ZONE.
"ONCE THAT HAPPENS, THE FLYBOYS DUST FOR VERMIN AND THEN START RECLAMATION PROCEDURES."
GENERAL
AND IF WE SPOT ANY **REAL** CRITTERS, THAT'S A BOMBING MISSION FOR **THEM**-- NOT US.
NOT A BAD GIG! AND IF IT GETS ME THIS SWEET "DRAGON SKIN" TO BOOT, I'M ON-BOARD.
LISTEN TO YOU WITH THAT STUFF. WHAT'S THE BIG DEAL?
WHAP WHAP
OSCAR
WE FIGHT **MONSTERS.** NOBODY EVER **SHOOTS** AT US.
YOU WEREN'T IN NEW YORK!

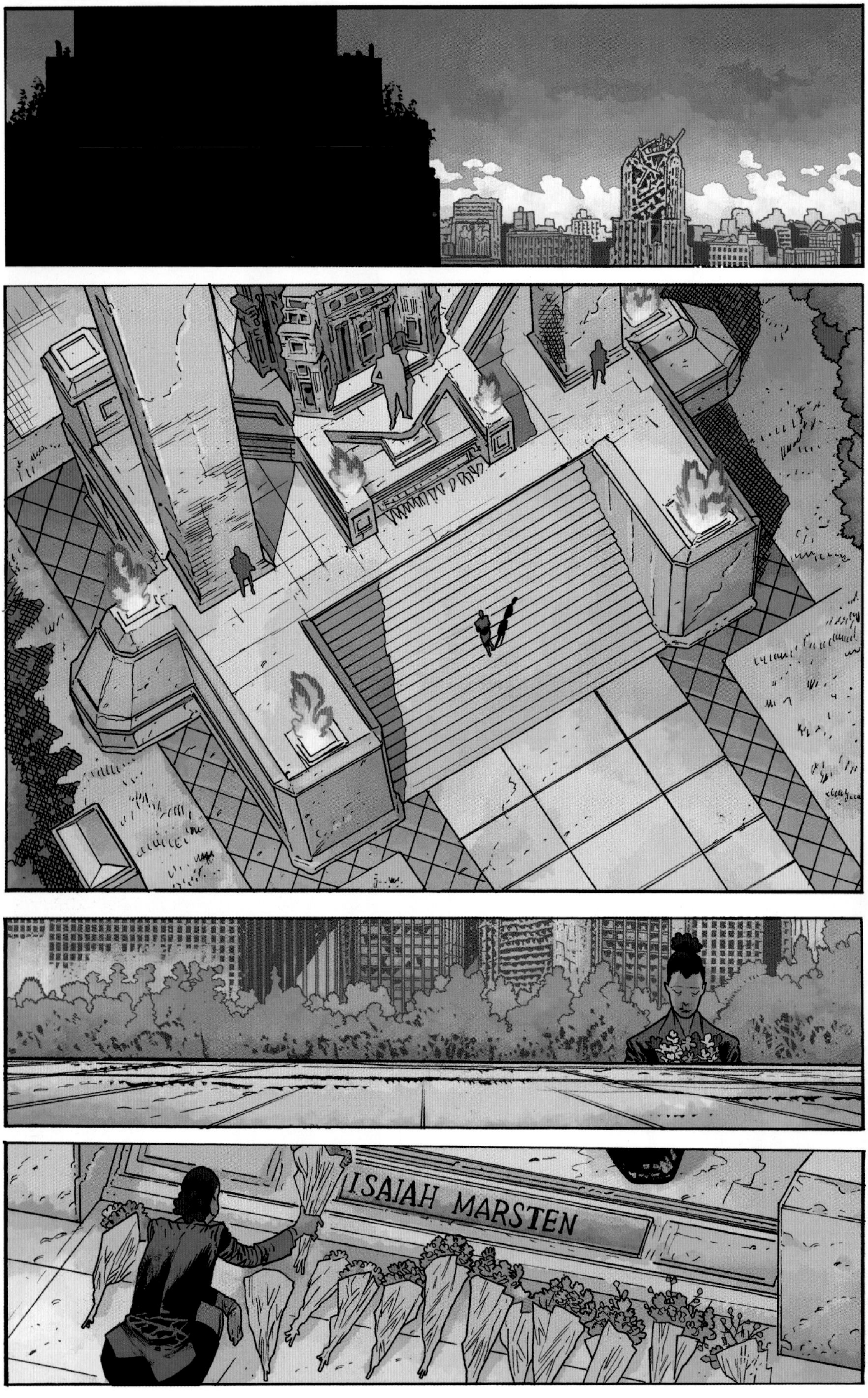
ISAIAH MARSTEN

HAS HE BEEN HERE TODAY?

NO, MA'AM. NOT YET.

THAT'S GOOD. I KNOW I'M LATE, BUT IT'S GETTING HARDER AND HARDER TO FIND SUITABLE WILD-FLOWERS.

YOU LET HIM KNOW I WAS HERE, WON'T YOU? TELL HIM *THOSE* ARE MY FLOWERS?

I ALWAYS DO, MA'AM.

THANK YOU, DENNIS. I'LL TRY TO BE EARLIER TOMORROW SO WE CAN TALK MORE.

YES, MA'AM!

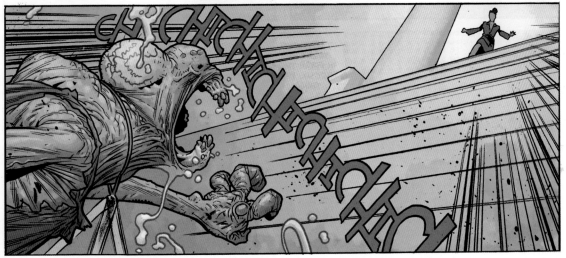

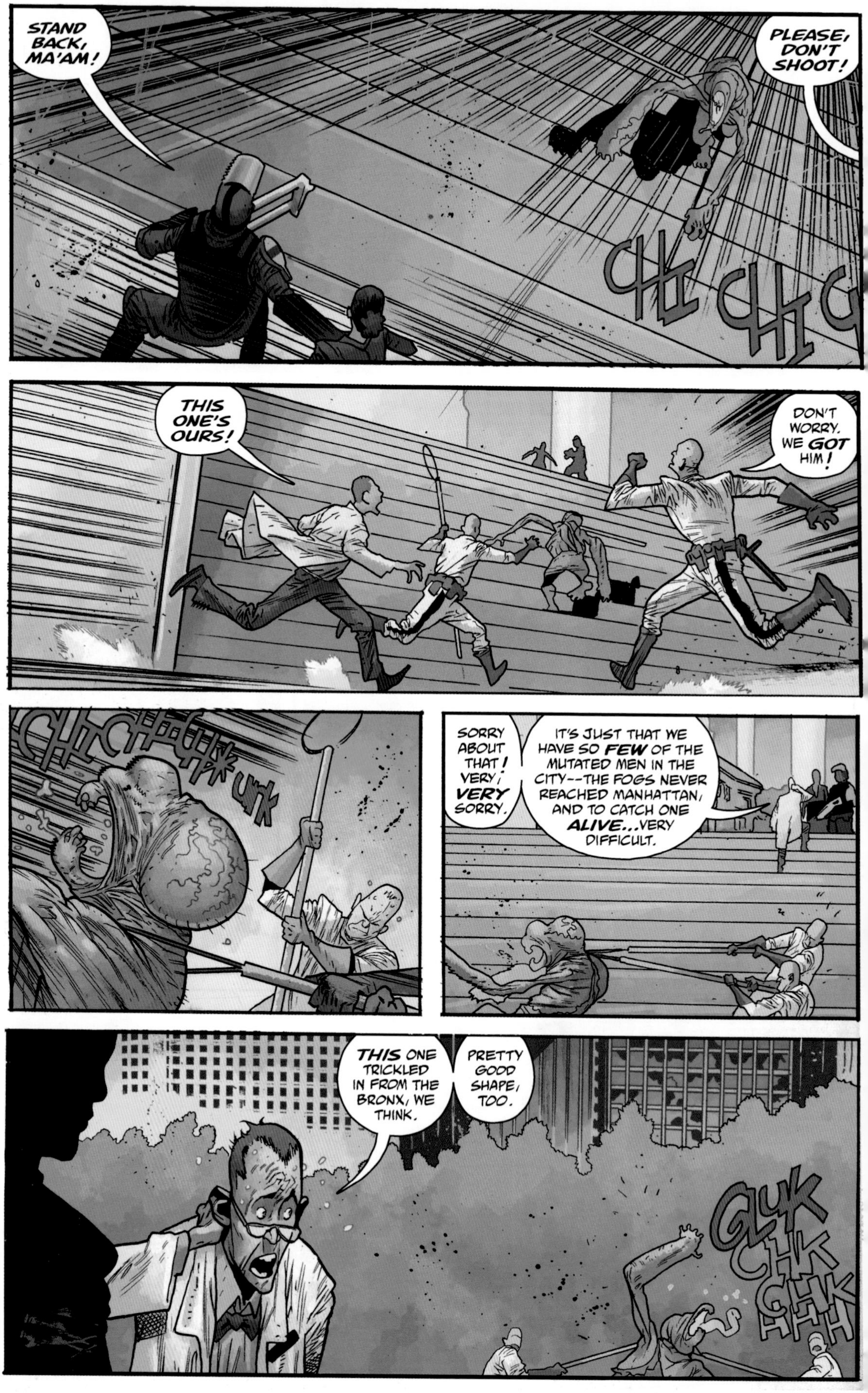
STAND BACK, MA'AM!
PLEASE, DON'T SHOOT!
CHI CHI CHI
THIS ONE'S OURS!
DON'T WORRY. WE GOT HIM!
CHICHICHICH UNK
SORRY ABOUT THAT! VERY, VERY SORRY.
IT'S JUST THAT WE HAVE SO FEW OF THE MUTATED MEN IN THE CITY--THE FOGS NEVER REACHED MANHATTAN, AND TO CATCH ONE ALIVE...VERY DIFFICULT.
THIS ONE TRICKLED IN FROM THE BRONX, WE THINK.
PRETTY GOOD SHAPE, TOO.
GLUK CHK CHK AHH

AND WHY WOULD YOU NEED A *LIVING MUTANT,* HIRSCH?

MA'AM.

I DON'T RECALL YOU OR ANYBODY ELSE FROM *RED* SUBMITTING PAPERWORK ABOUT THIS.

MA'AM.

EVELYN!

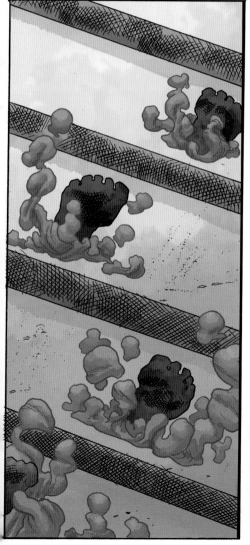

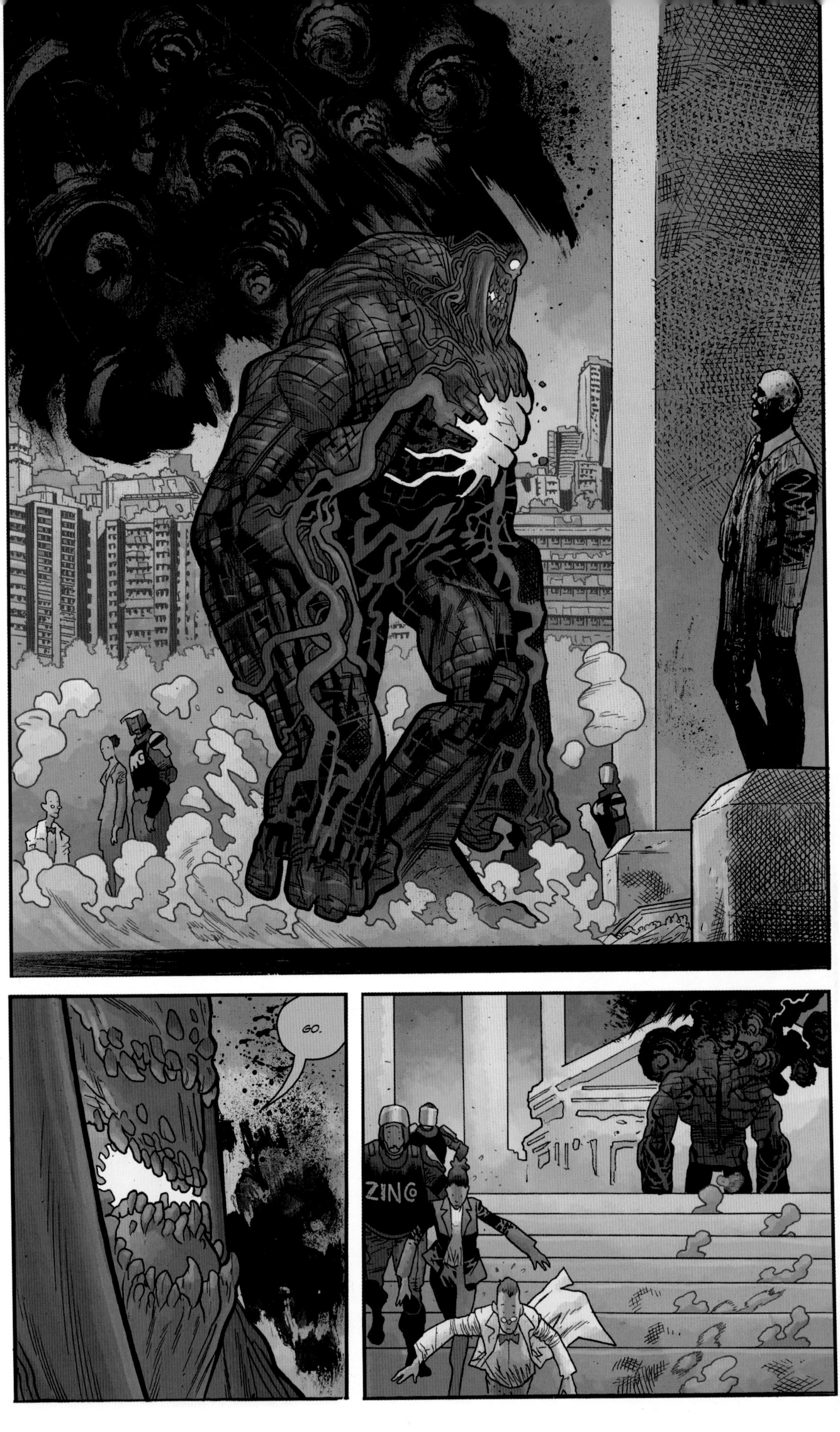
GO.
ZINC

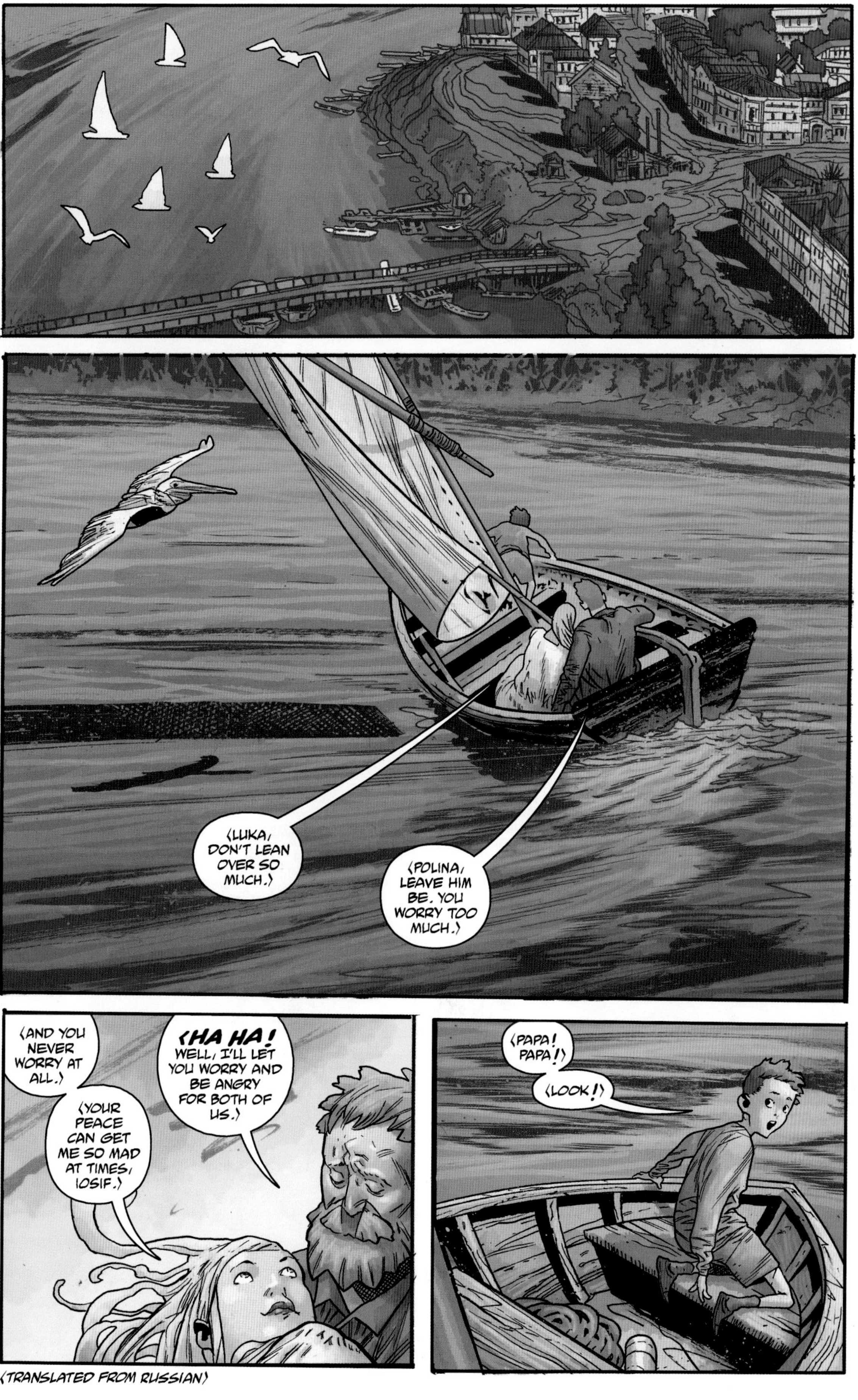
⟨LUKA, DON'T LEAN OVER SO MUCH.⟩
⟨POLINA, LEAVE HIM BE. YOU WORRY TOO MUCH.⟩
⟨AND YOU NEVER WORRY AT ALL.⟩
⟨YOUR PEACE CAN GET ME SO MAD AT TIMES, IOSIF.⟩
⟨HA HA! WELL, I'LL LET YOU WORRY AND BE ANGRY FOR BOTH OF US.⟩
⟨PAPA! PAPA!⟩
⟨LOOK!⟩

⟨TRANSLATED FROM RUSSIAN⟩

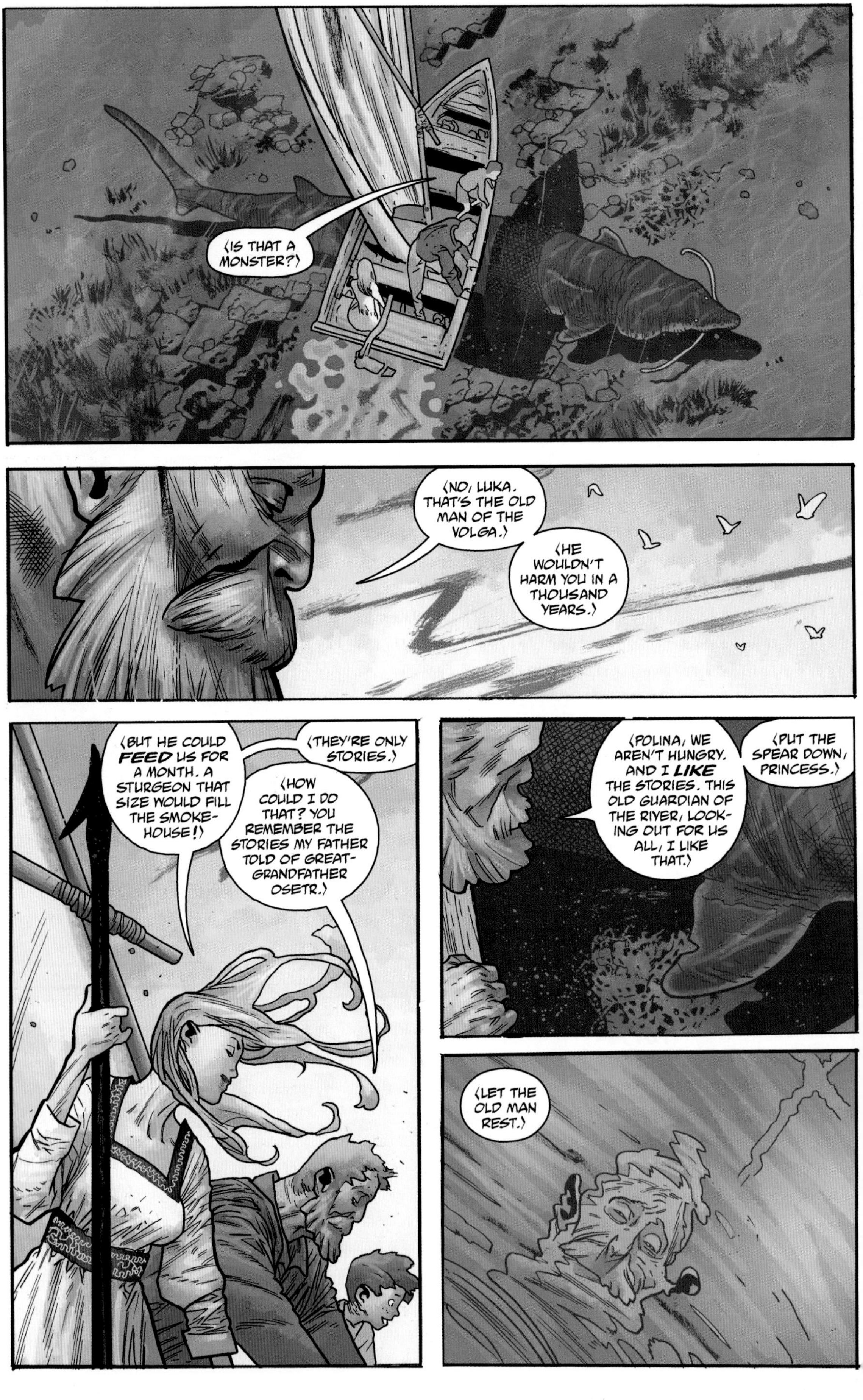
⟨IS THAT A MONSTER?⟩
⟨NO, LUKA. THAT'S THE OLD MAN OF THE VOLGA.⟩
⟨HE WOULDN'T HARM YOU IN A THOUSAND YEARS.⟩
⟨BUT HE COULD **FEED** US FOR A MONTH. A STURGEON THAT SIZE WOULD FILL THE SMOKE-HOUSE!⟩
⟨THEY'RE ONLY STORIES.⟩
⟨HOW COULD I DO THAT? YOU REMEMBER THE STORIES MY FATHER TOLD OF GREAT-GRANDFATHER OSETR.⟩
⟨POLINA, WE AREN'T HUNGRY. AND I **LIKE** THE STORIES. THIS OLD GUARDIAN OF THE RIVER, LOOKING OUT FOR US ALL, I LIKE THAT.⟩
⟨PUT THE SPEAR DOWN, PRINCESS.⟩
⟨LET THE OLD MAN REST.⟩

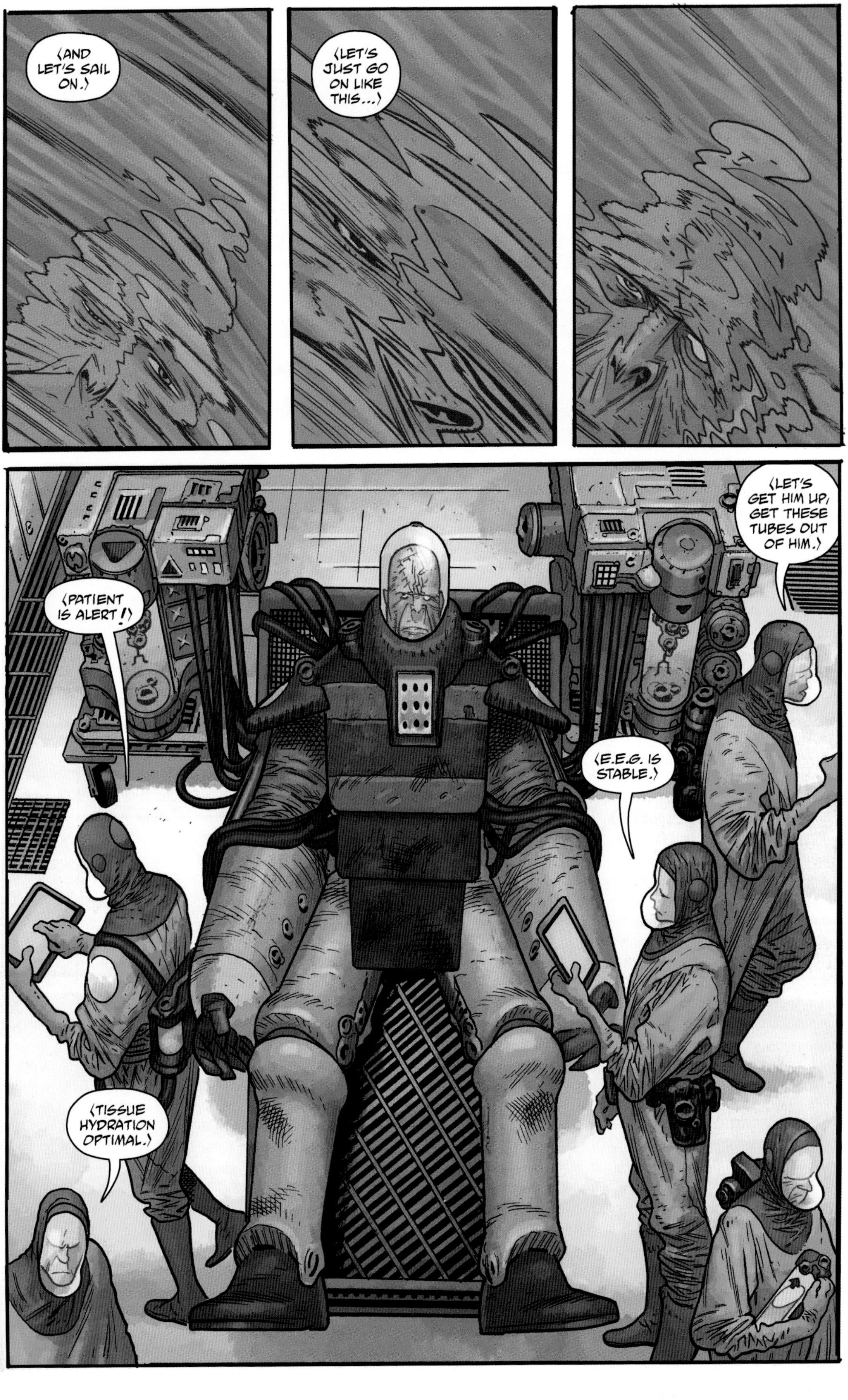
‹AND LET'S SAIL ON.›
‹LET'S JUST GO ON LIKE THIS...›
‹PATIENT IS ALERT!›
‹LET'S GET HIM UP, GET THESE TUBES OUT OF HIM.›
‹E.E.G. IS STABLE.›
‹TISSUE HYDRATION OPTIMAL.›

⟨DIRECTOR NICHAYKO, ARE YOU ALL RIGHT?⟩

⟨IT SEEMS SO, I SUPPOSE. I FEEL SO DIFFERENT, HOWEVER.⟩

⟨I IMAGINE THAT'S THE NEW CONTAINMENT SUIT WE DESIGNED FOR YOU.⟩

⟨AFTER THE DAMAGE YOUR LAST SUIT RECEIVED IN NEW YORK, WE NEEDED TO UPGRADE SOME NUTRIENT-DELIVERY SYSTEMS TO CORRECT FOR FLUID LOSS. IN THE PROCESS, THE MATERIAL FOR THE SUIT ITSELF IS OF HIGHER TENSILE--⟩

⟨SO THEN...I'M... ALIVE.⟩

⟨EH, BY YOUR UNIQUE STANDARDS, **YES.** THE MONITORS SHOW YOU DOING VERY WELL, IN FACT.⟩

⟨MY "UNIQUE STANDARDS."⟩

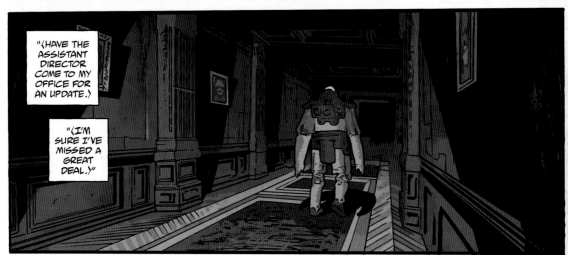

"⟨HAVE THE ASSISTANT DIRECTOR COME TO MY OFFICE FOR AN UPDATE.⟩

"⟨I'M SURE I'VE MISSED A GREAT DEAL.⟩"

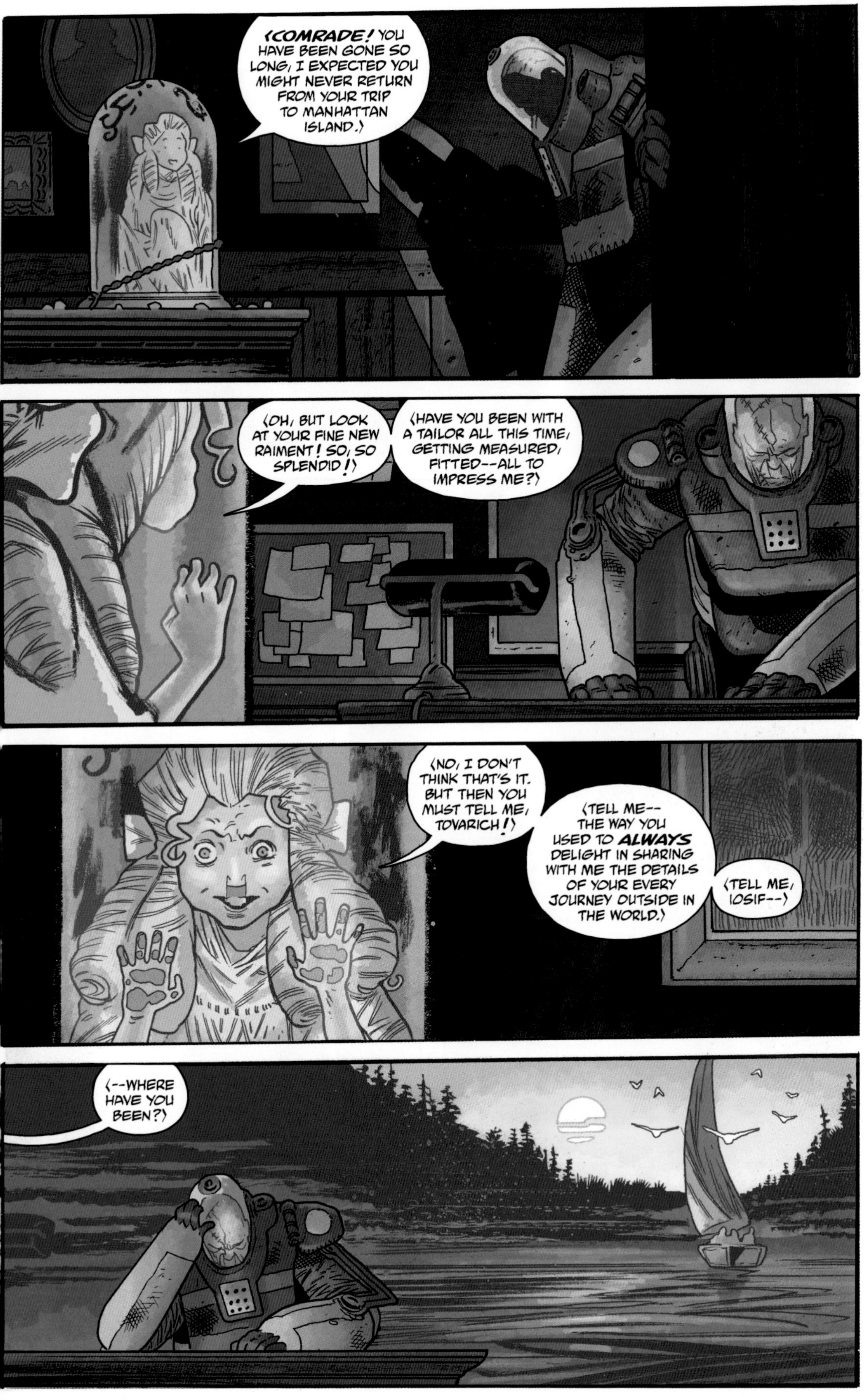
⟨COMRADE! YOU HAVE BEEN GONE SO LONG, I EXPECTED YOU MIGHT NEVER RETURN FROM YOUR TRIP TO MANHATTAN ISLAND.⟩
⟨OH, BUT LOOK AT YOUR FINE NEW RAIMENT! SO, SO SPLENDID!⟩
⟨HAVE YOU BEEN WITH A TAILOR ALL THIS TIME, GETTING MEASURED, FITTED--ALL TO IMPRESS ME?⟩
⟨NO, I DON'T THINK THAT'S IT. BUT THEN YOU MUST TELL ME, TOVARICH!⟩
⟨TELL ME-- THE WAY YOU USED TO ALWAYS DELIGHT IN SHARING WITH ME THE DETAILS OF YOUR EVERY JOURNEY OUTSIDE IN THE WORLD.⟩
⟨TELL ME, IOSIF--⟩
⟨--WHERE HAVE YOU BEEN?⟩

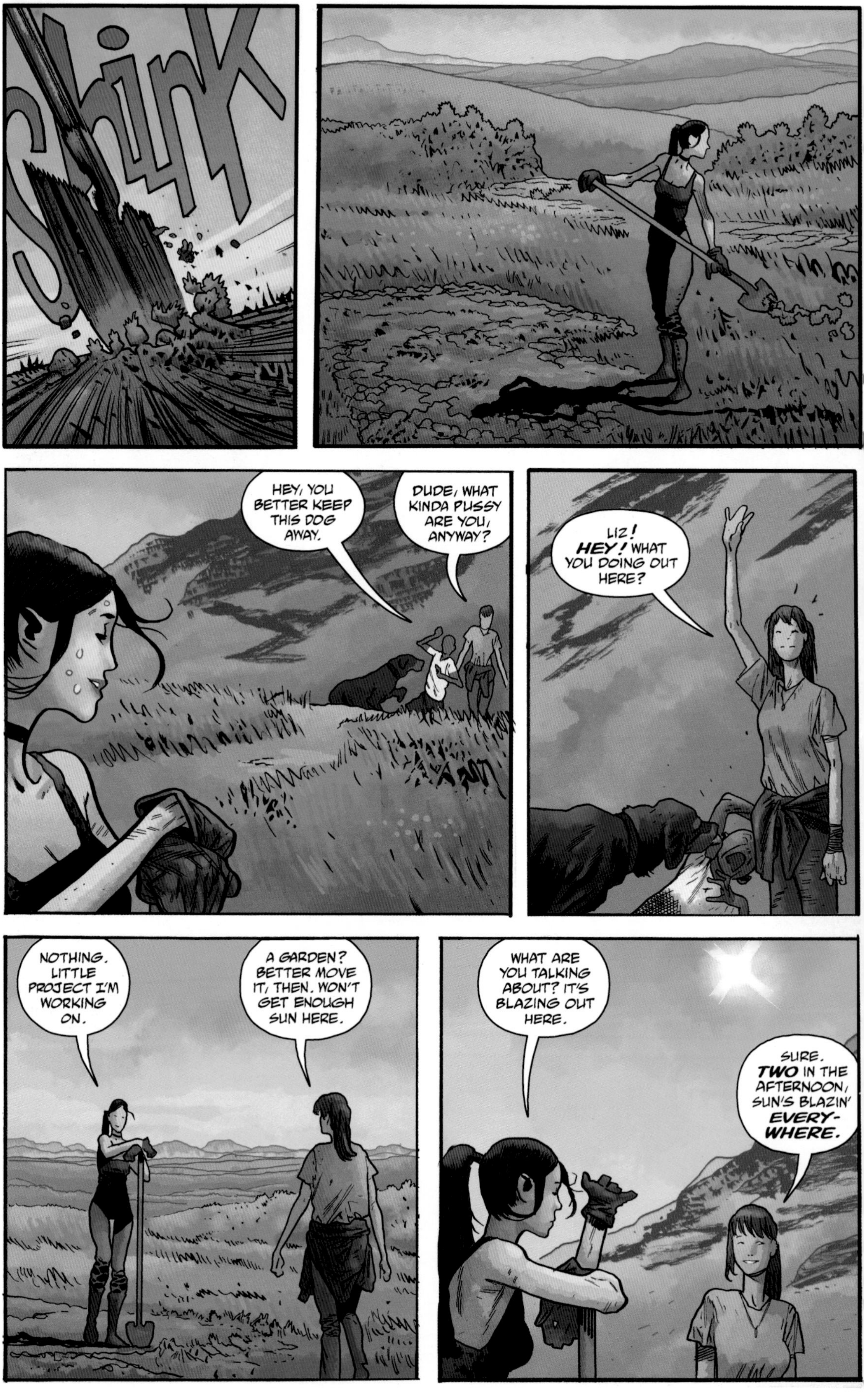
Shink
HEY, YOU BETTER KEEP THIS DOG AWAY.
DUDE, WHAT KINDA PUSSY ARE YOU, ANYWAY?
LIZ! HEY! WHAT YOU DOING OUT HERE?
NOTHING. LITTLE PROJECT I'M WORKING ON.
A GARDEN? BETTER MOVE IT, THEN. WON'T GET ENOUGH SUN HERE.
WHAT ARE YOU TALKING ABOUT? IT'S BLAZING OUT HERE.
SURE. TWO IN THE AFTERNOON, SUN'S BLAZIN' EVERY-WHERE.

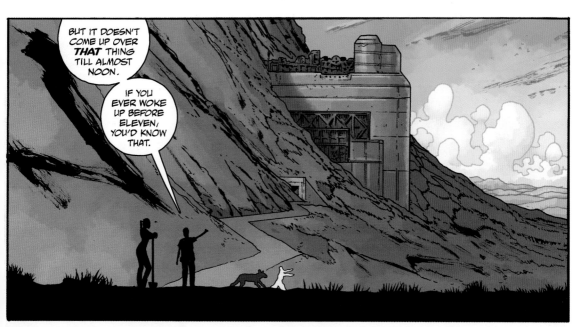

BUT IT DOESN'T COME UP OVER *THAT* THING TILL ALMOST NOON.

IF YOU EVER WOKE UP BEFORE ELEVEN, YOU'D KNOW THAT.

WHAT DO YOU KNOW ABOUT GROWING VEGETABLES?

VEGETABLES?! YOU KIDDIN'? I THOUGHT THAT WAS FOR FLOWERS.

YOU'LL NEED A BIGGER PLOT IF YOU WANNA DO THAT OUT HERE. MUCH BIGGER!

AND WHAT DO I KNOW? GROWING UP, WE GREW A LOT OF OUR OWN FOOD.

CUCUMBERS—— THOSE ARE EASY—— CARROTS, ONIONS, KALE, AND LATER SQUASH——

HEY. *HEY!!* COME GET YOUR DOG!

OOPS! GOTTA GO.

DON'T WORRY ABOUT IT, SHERMAN. I'LL BAIL YOU OUT *WHEN* YOU SCREW IT UP.

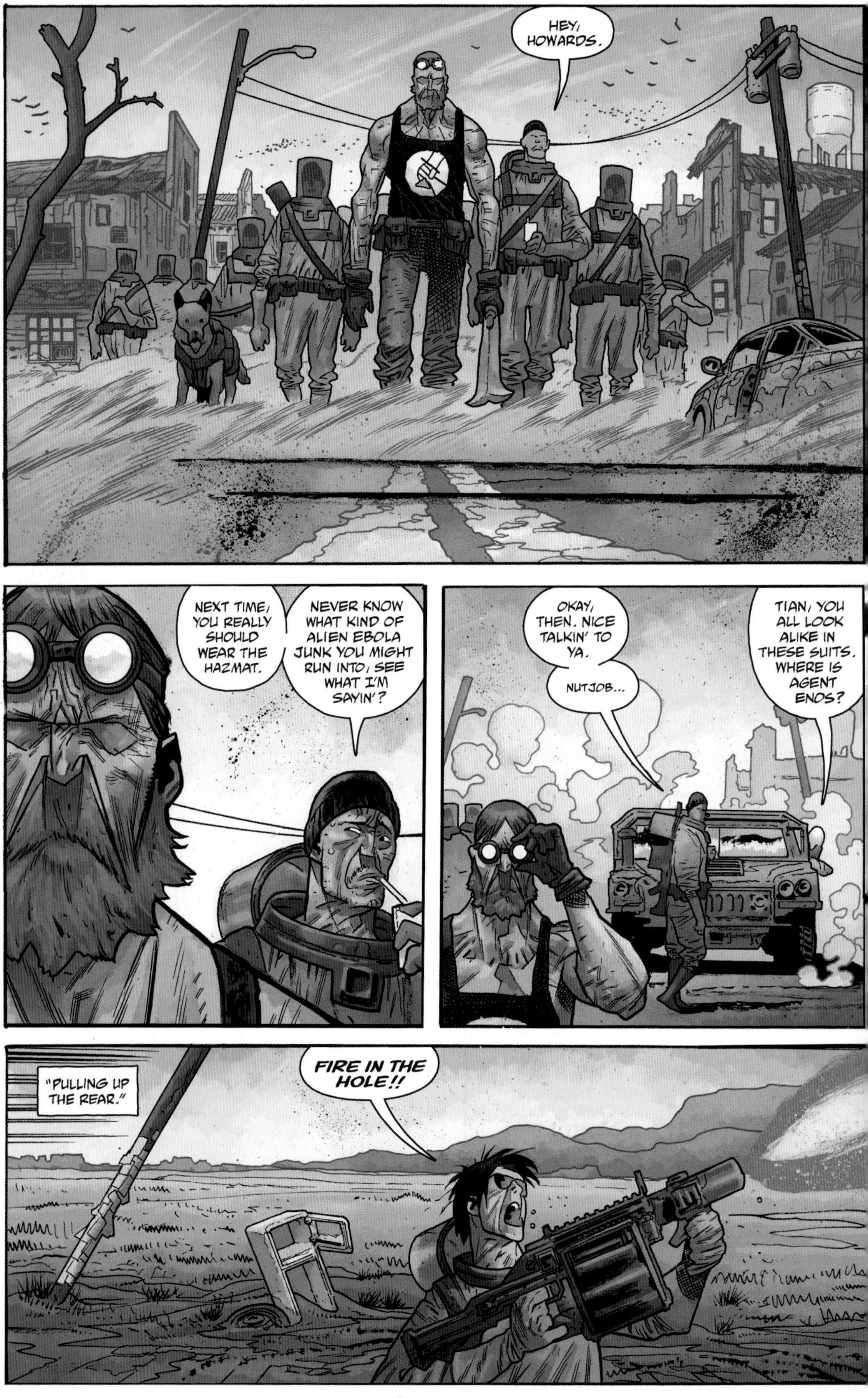
HEY, HOWARDS.
NEXT TIME, YOU REALLY SHOULD WEAR THE HAZMAT.
NEVER KNOW WHAT KIND OF ALIEN EBOLA JUNK YOU MIGHT RUN INTO, SEE WHAT I'M SAYIN'?
OKAY, THEN. NICE TALKIN' TO YA.
NUTJOB...
TIAN, YOU ALL LOOK ALIKE IN THESE SUITS. WHERE IS AGENT ENOS?
"PULLING UP THE REAR."
FIRE IN THE HOLE!!

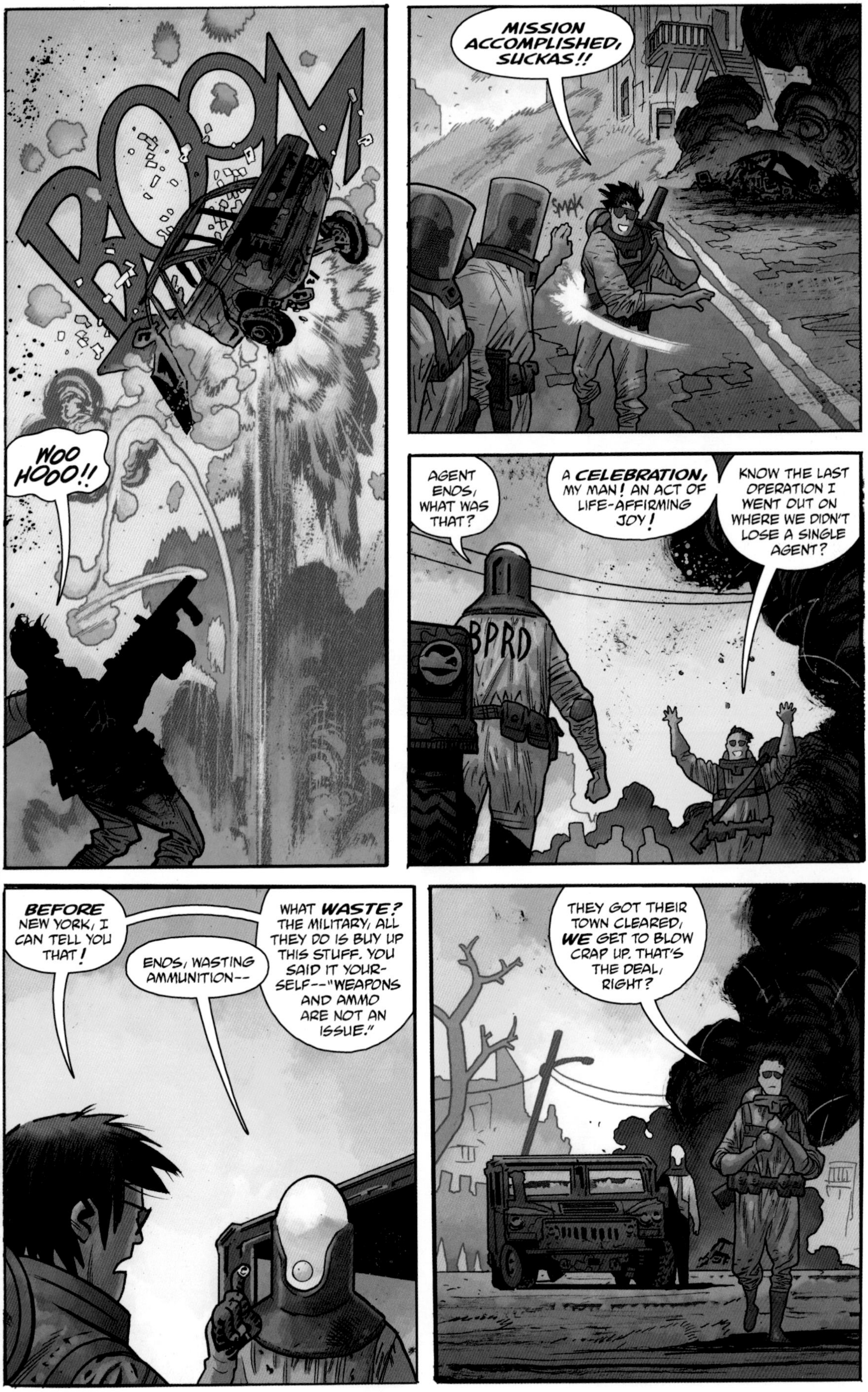
BOOOM
WOO HOOO!!
MISSION ACCOMPLISHED, SUCKAS!!
SMAK
AGENT ENOS, WHAT WAS THAT?
A CELEBRATION, MY MAN! AN ACT OF LIFE-AFFIRMING JOY!
KNOW THE LAST OPERATION I WENT OUT ON WHERE WE DIDN'T LOSE A SINGLE AGENT?
BPRD
BEFORE NEW YORK, I CAN TELL YOU THAT!
ENOS, WASTING AMMUNITION--
WHAT WASTE? THE MILITARY, ALL THEY DO IS BUY UP THIS STUFF. YOU SAID IT YOUR-SELF--"WEAPONS AND AMMO ARE NOT AN ISSUE."
THEY GOT THEIR TOWN CLEARED, WE GET TO BLOW CRAP UP. THAT'S THE DEAL, RIGHT?

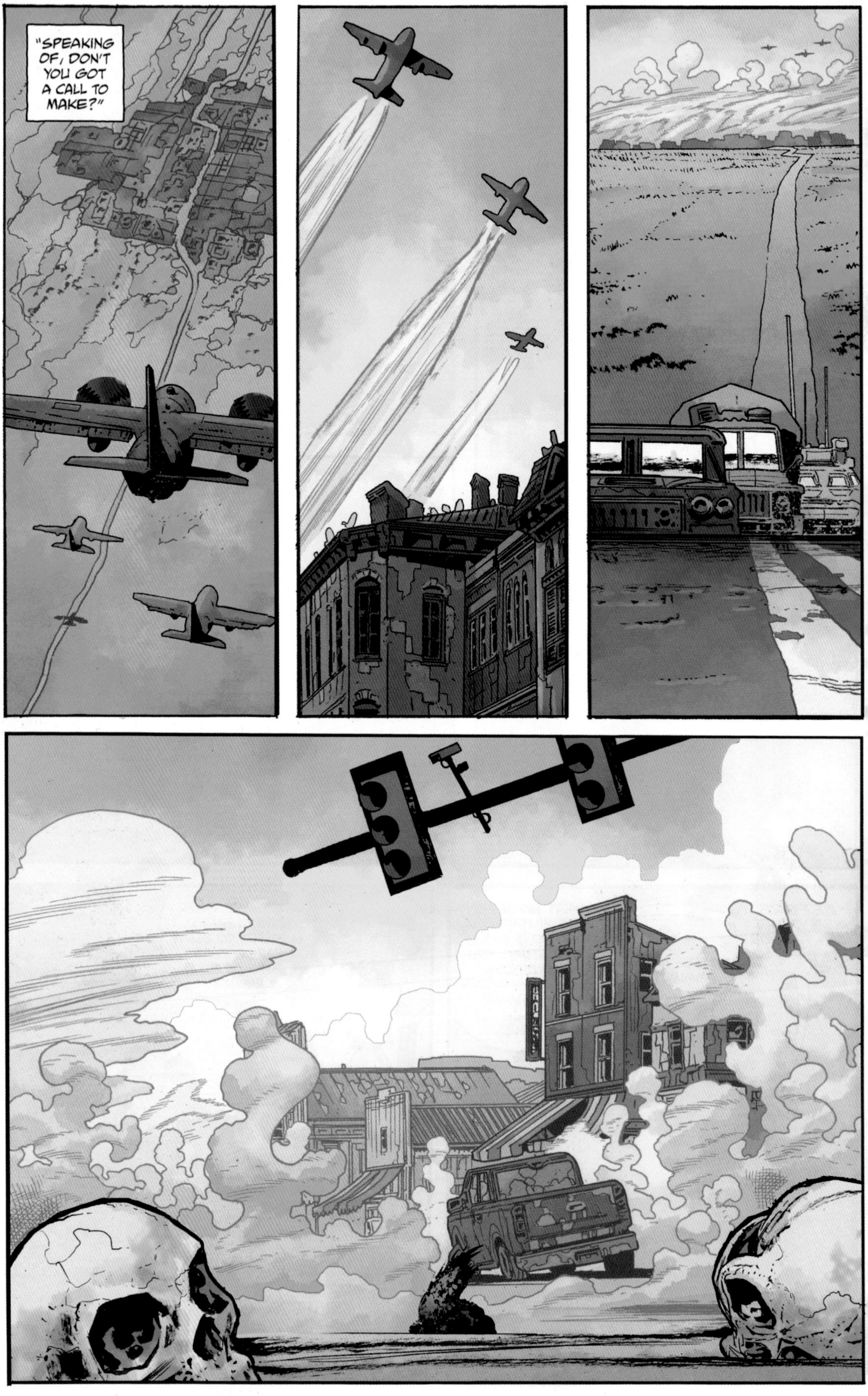
"SPEAKING OF, DON'T YOU GOT A CALL TO MAKE?"

CHAPTER TWO

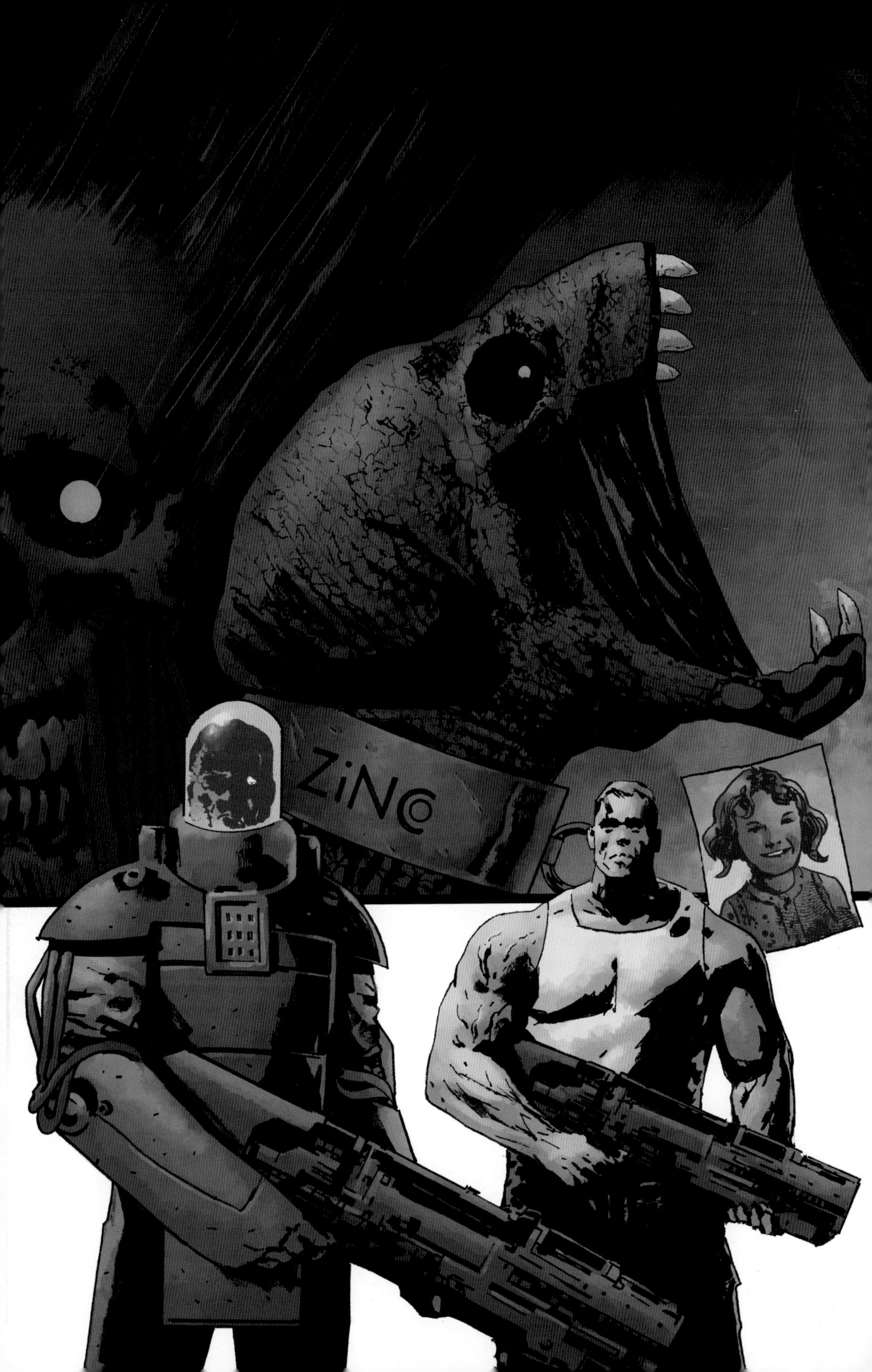
ZiNCo

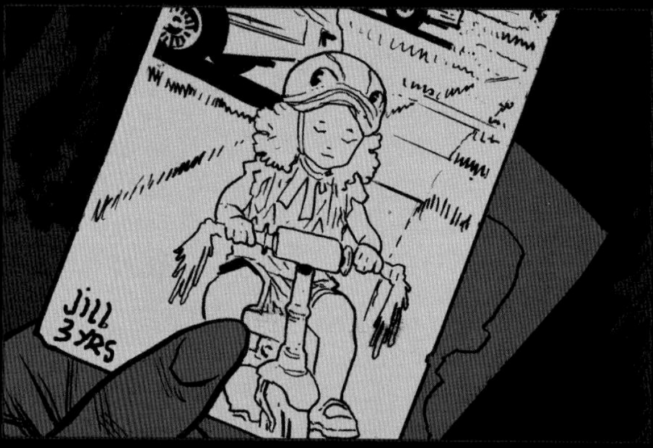
Jill
3 YRS

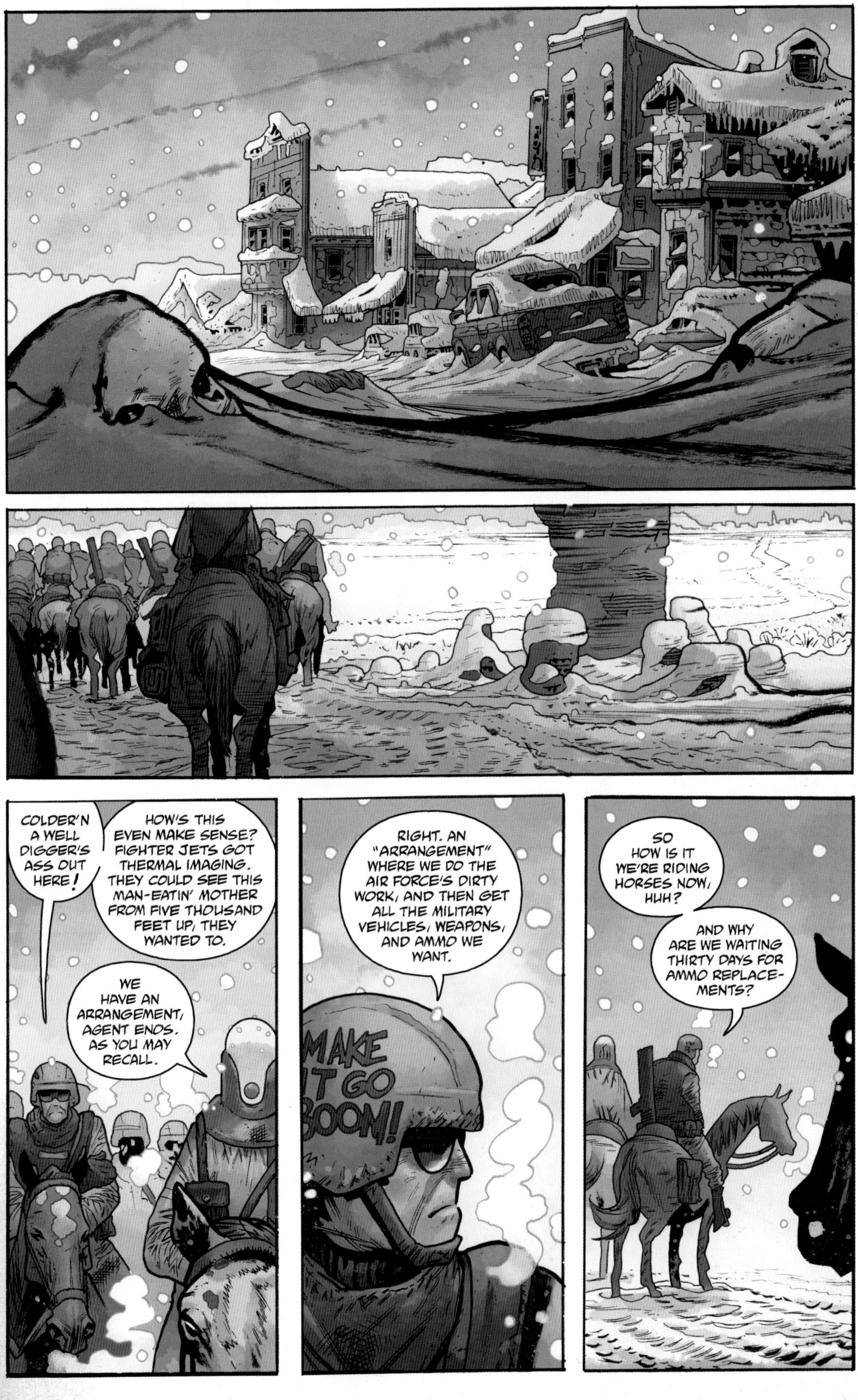
COLDER'N A WELL DIGGER'S ASS OUT HERE!
HOW'S THIS EVEN MAKE SENSE? FIGHTER JETS GOT THERMAL IMAGING. THEY COULD SEE THIS MAN-EATIN' MOTHER FROM FIVE THOUSAND FEET UP, THEY WANTED TO.
WE HAVE AN ARRANGEMENT, AGENT ENOS. AS YOU MAY RECALL.
RIGHT. AN "ARRANGEMENT" WHERE WE DO THE AIR FORCE'S DIRTY WORK, AND THEN GET ALL THE MILITARY VEHICLES, WEAPONS, AND AMMO WE WANT.
MAKE IT GO BOOM!
SO HOW IS IT WE'RE RIDING HORSES NOW, HUH?
AND WHY ARE WE WAITING THIRTY DAYS FOR AMMO REPLACE-MENTS?

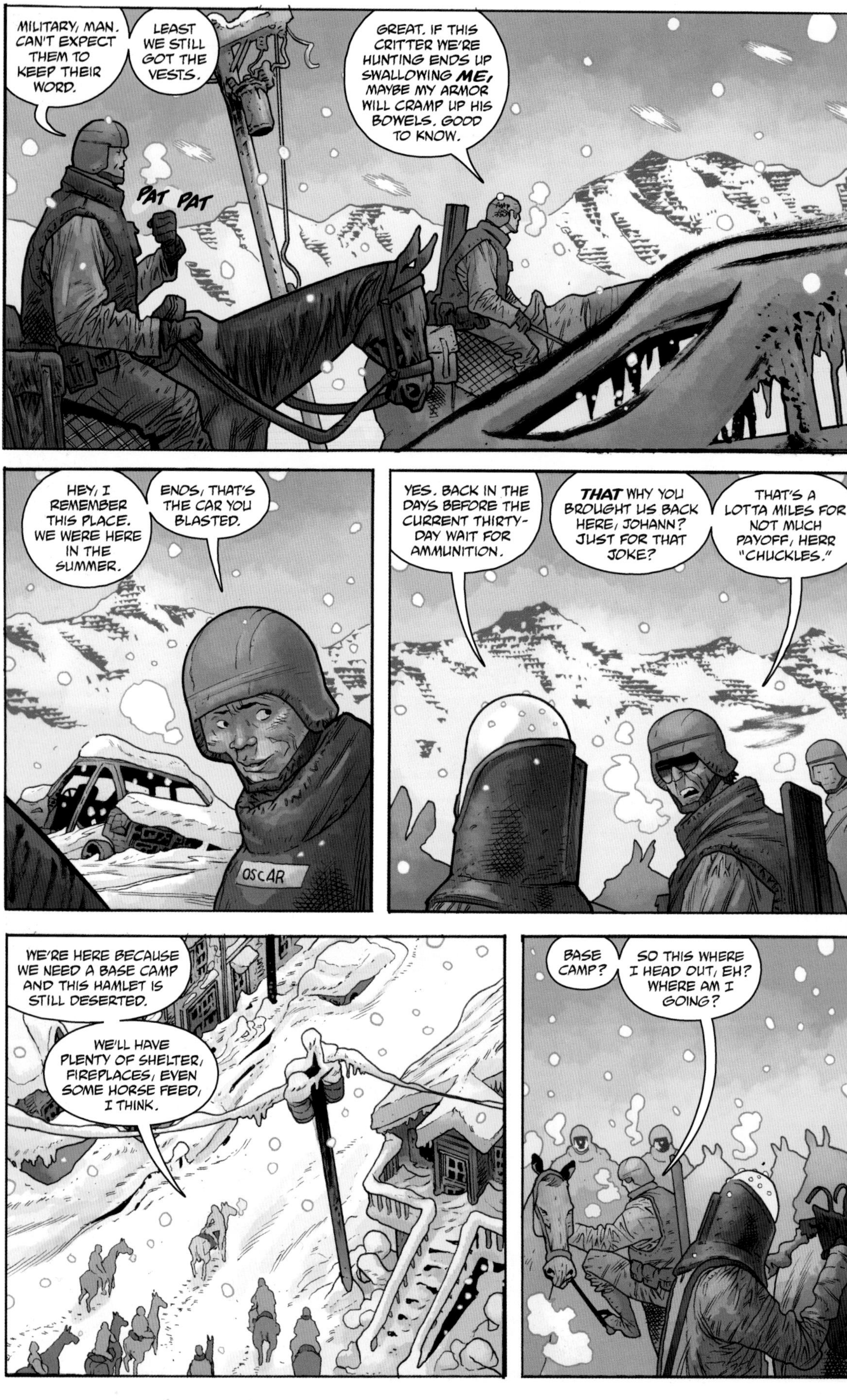

MILITARY, MAN. CAN'T EXPECT THEM TO KEEP THEIR WORD.
LEAST WE STILL GOT THE VESTS.
GREAT. IF THIS CRITTER WE'RE HUNTING ENDS UP SWALLOWING ME, MAYBE MY ARMOR WILL CRAMP UP HIS BOWELS. GOOD TO KNOW.
PAT PAT
HEY, I REMEMBER THIS PLACE. WE WERE HERE IN THE SUMMER.
ENOS, THAT'S THE CAR YOU BLASTED.
OSCAR
YES. BACK IN THE DAYS BEFORE THE CURRENT THIRTY-DAY WAIT FOR AMMUNITION.
THAT WHY YOU BROUGHT US BACK HERE, JOHANN? JUST FOR THAT JOKE?
THAT'S A LOTTA MILES FOR NOT MUCH PAYOFF, HERR "CHUCKLES."
WE'RE HERE BECAUSE WE NEED A BASE CAMP AND THIS HAMLET IS STILL DESERTED.
WE'LL HAVE PLENTY OF SHELTER, FIREPLACES, EVEN SOME HORSE FEED, I THINK.
BASE CAMP?
SO THIS WHERE I HEAD OUT, EH? WHERE AM I GOING?

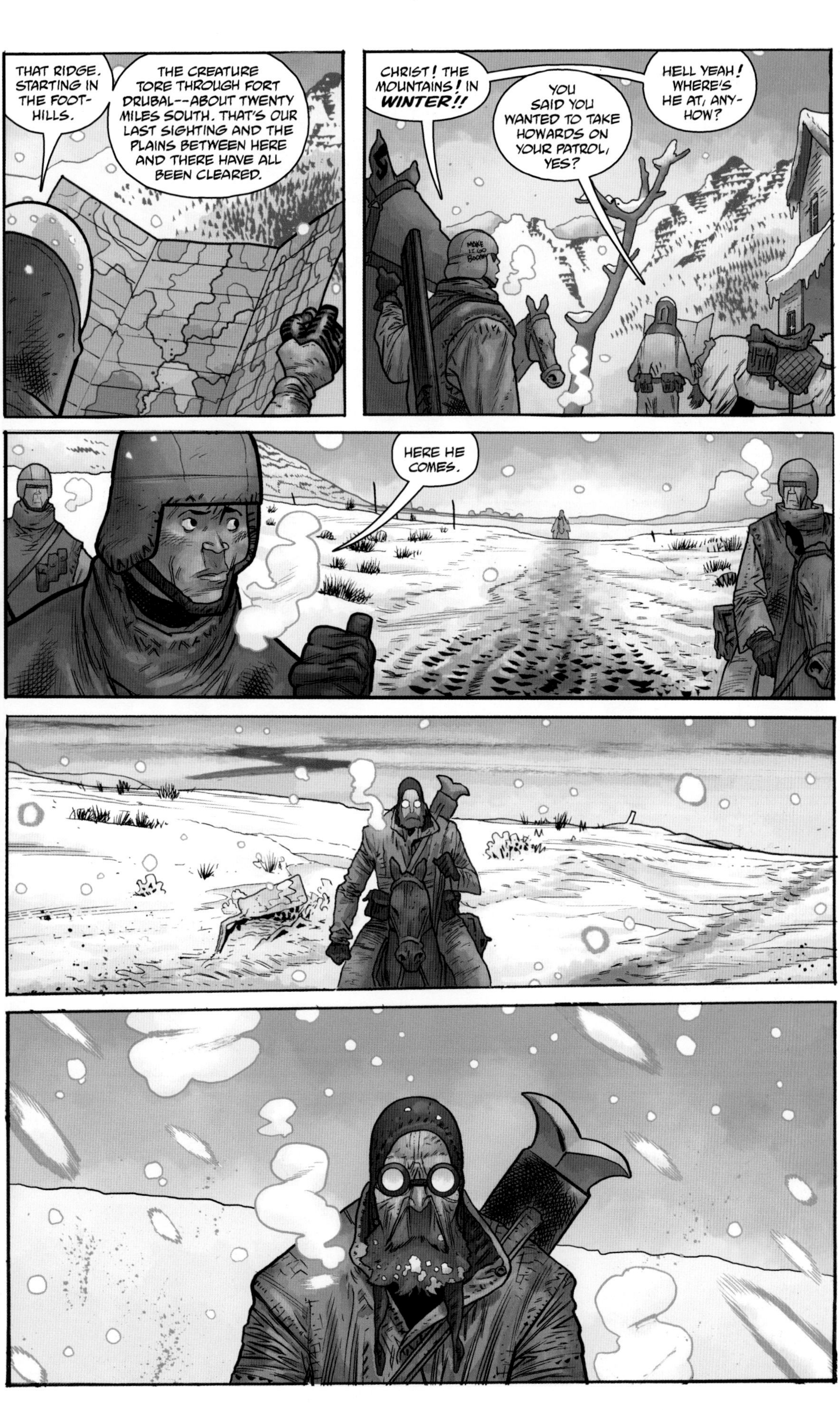
THAT RIDGE. STARTING IN THE FOOT-HILLS.
THE CREATURE TORE THROUGH FORT DRUBAL--ABOUT TWENTY MILES SOUTH. THAT'S OUR LAST SIGHTING AND THE PLAINS BETWEEN HERE AND THERE HAVE ALL BEEN CLEARED.
CHRIST! THE MOUNTAINS! IN WINTER!!
YOU SAID YOU WANTED TO TAKE HOWARDS ON YOUR PATROL, YES?
HELL YEAH! WHERE'S HE AT, ANY-HOW?
MAKE IT GO BOOM
HERE HE COMES.

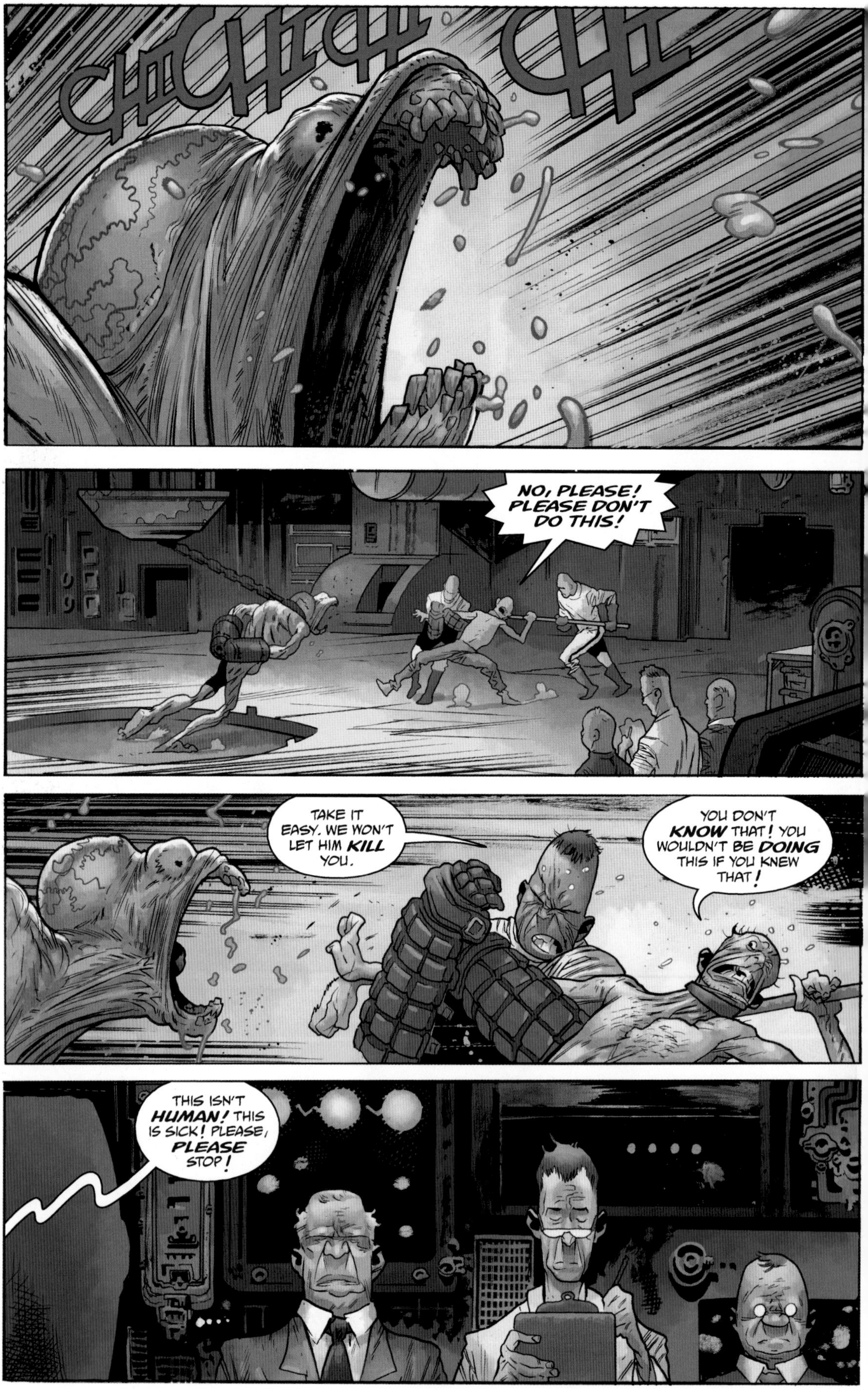
NO, PLEASE! PLEASE DON'T DO THIS!
TAKE IT EASY. WE WON'T LET HIM KILL YOU.
YOU DON'T KNOW THAT! YOU WOULDN'T BE DOING THIS IF YOU KNEW THAT!
THIS ISN'T HUMAN! THIS IS SICK! PLEASE, PLEASE STOP!

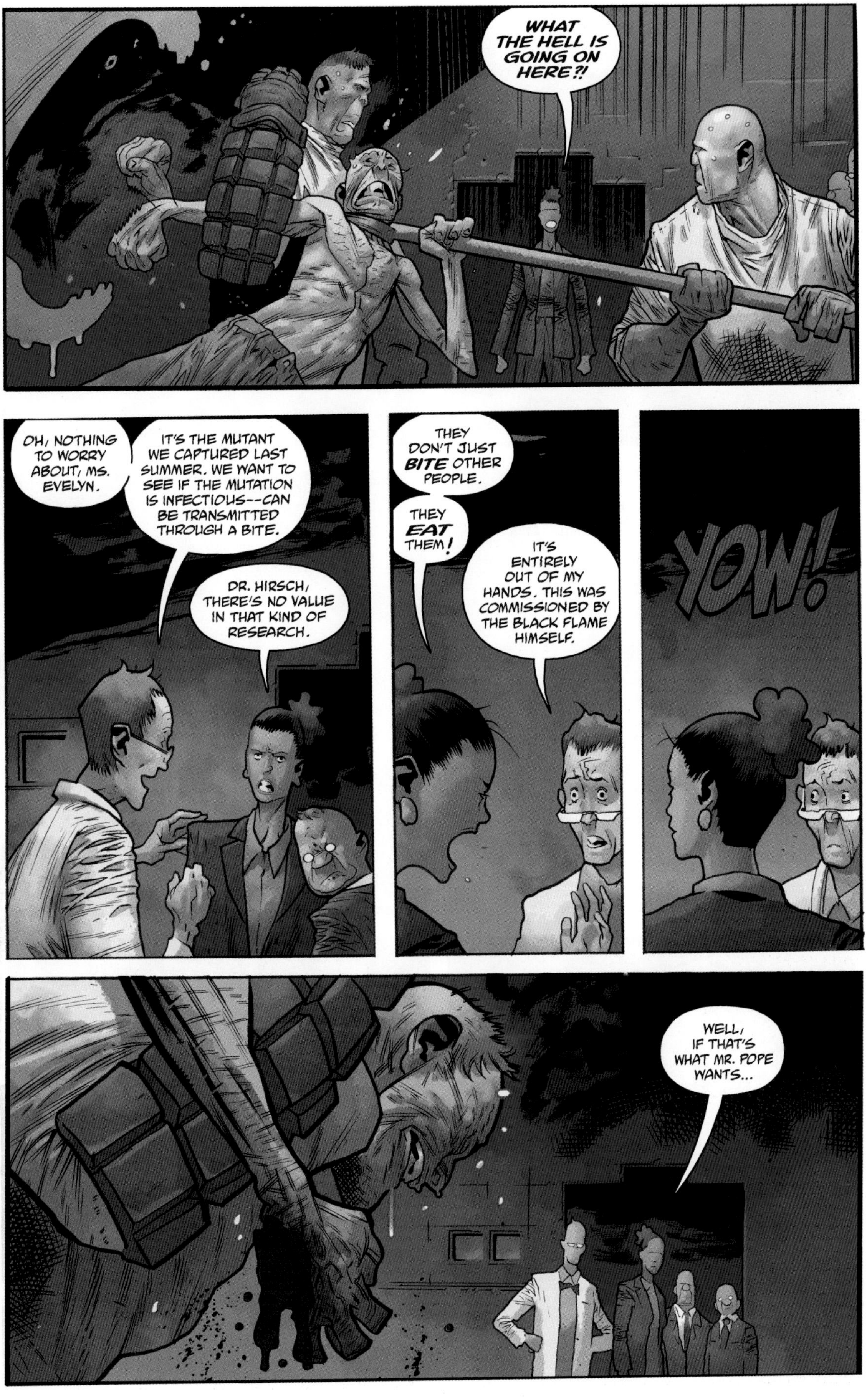
WHAT THE HELL IS GOING ON HERE?!
OH, NOTHING TO WORRY ABOUT, MS. EVELYN.
IT'S THE MUTANT WE CAPTURED LAST SUMMER. WE WANT TO SEE IF THE MUTATION IS INFECTIOUS--CAN BE TRANSMITTED THROUGH A BITE.
DR. HIRSCH, THERE'S NO VALUE IN THAT KIND OF RESEARCH.
THEY DON'T JUST BITE OTHER PEOPLE.
THEY EAT THEM!
IT'S ENTIRELY OUT OF MY HANDS. THIS WAS COMMISSIONED BY THE BLACK FLAME HIMSELF.
YOW!
WELL, IF THAT'S WHAT MR. POPE WANTS...

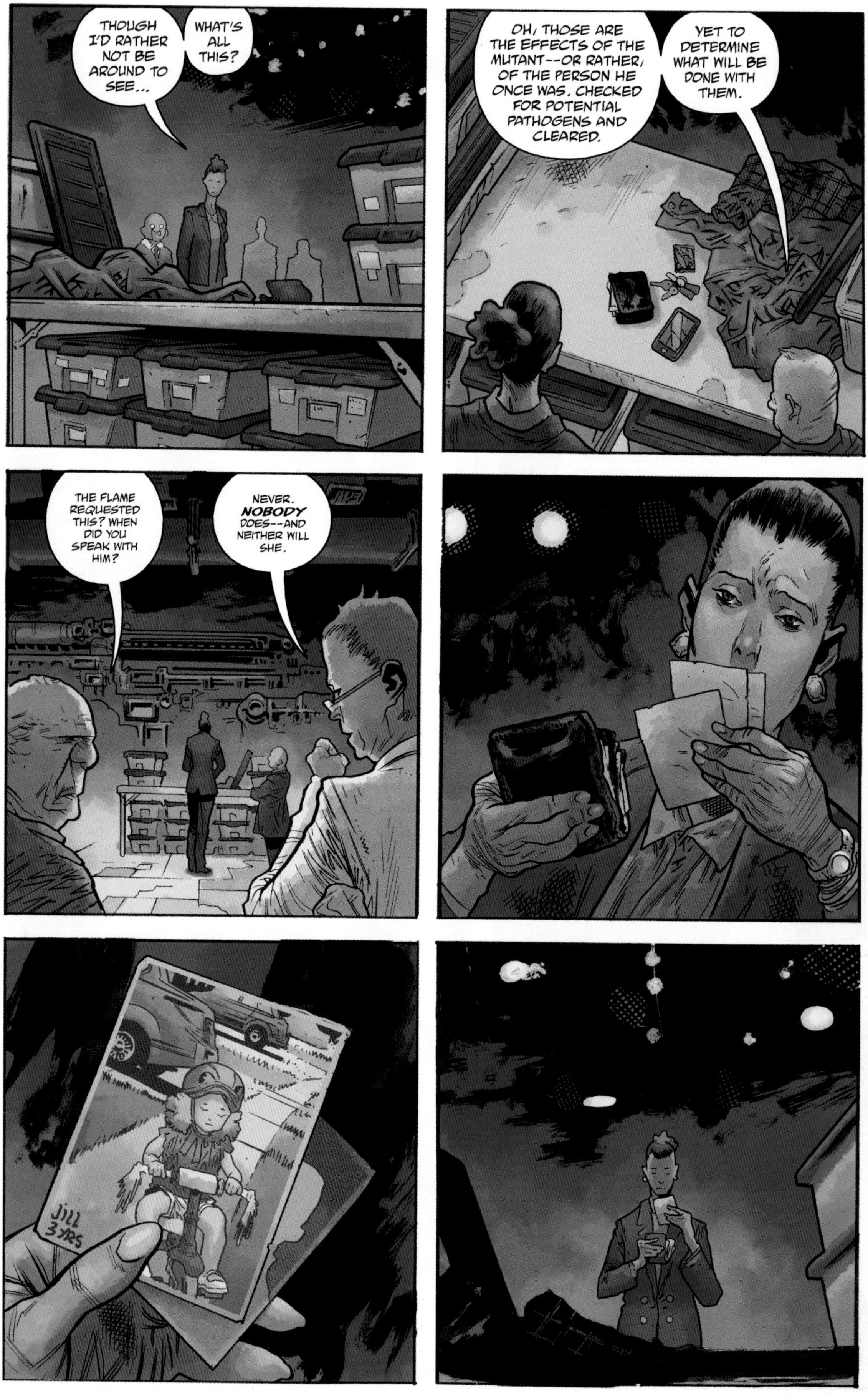
THOUGH I'D RATHER NOT BE AROUND TO SEE...
WHAT'S ALL THIS?
OH, THOSE ARE THE EFFECTS OF THE MUTANT--OR RATHER, OF THE PERSON HE ONCE WAS. CHECKED FOR POTENTIAL PATHOGENS AND CLEARED.
YET TO DETERMINE WHAT WILL BE DONE WITH THEM.
THE FLAME REQUESTED THIS? WHEN DID YOU SPEAK WITH HIM?
NEVER. NOBODY DOES--AND NEITHER WILL SHE.
JILL 3 YRS

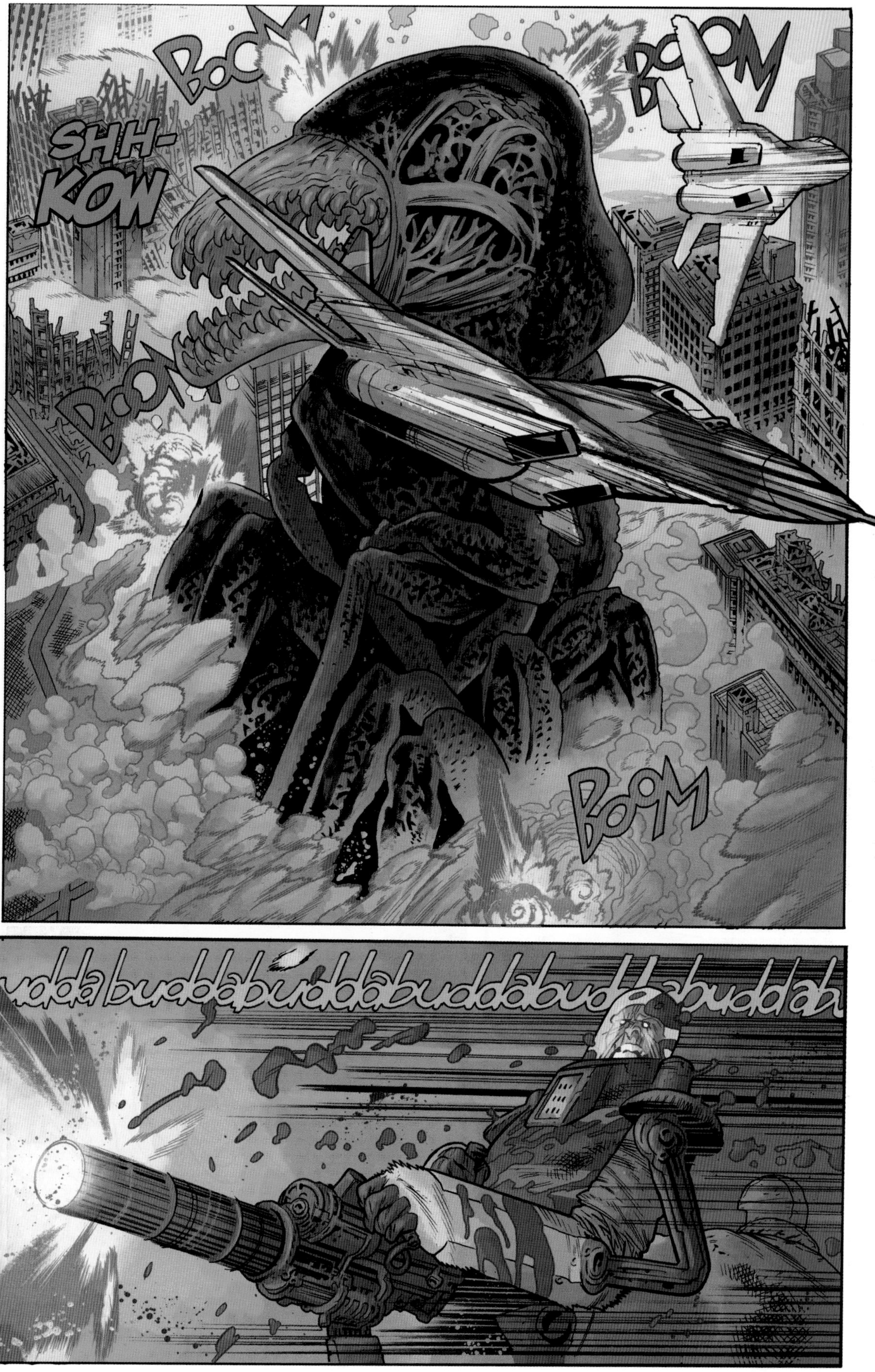
BOOM
SHH-KOW
BOOM
BOOM
BOOM
uddabuddabuddabuddabud
abuddabu

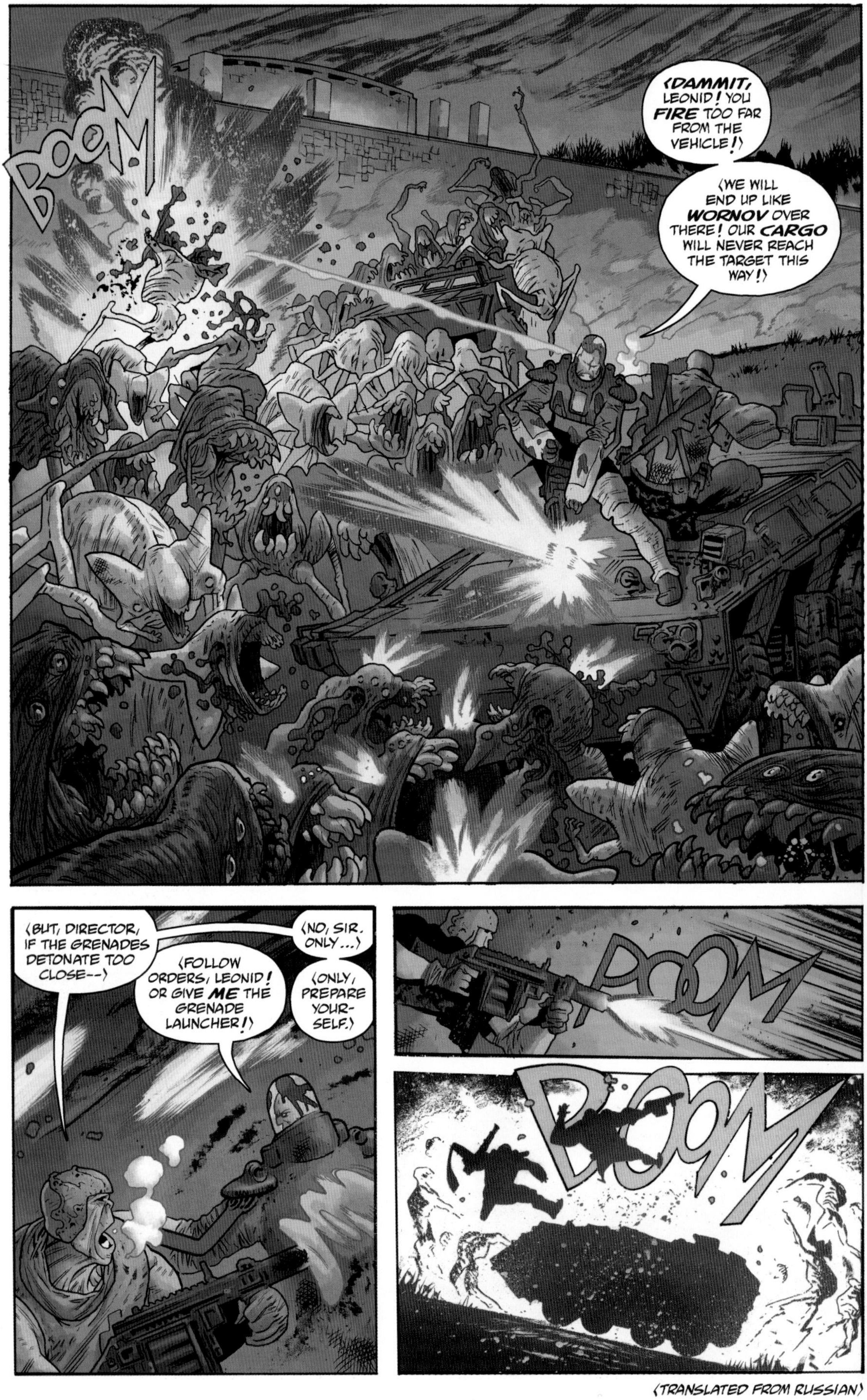
BOOM
⟨DAMMIT, LEONID! YOU FIRE TOO FAR FROM THE VEHICLE!⟩
⟨WE WILL END UP LIKE WORNOV OVER THERE! OUR CARGO WILL NEVER REACH THE TARGET THIS WAY!⟩
⟨BUT, DIRECTOR, IF THE GRENADES DETONATE TOO CLOSE--⟩
⟨FOLLOW ORDERS, LEONID! OR GIVE ME THE GRENADE LAUNCHER!⟩
⟨NO, SIR. ONLY...⟩
⟨ONLY, PREPARE YOURSELF.⟩
BOOM
BOOM

⟨TRANSLATED FROM RUSSIAN⟩

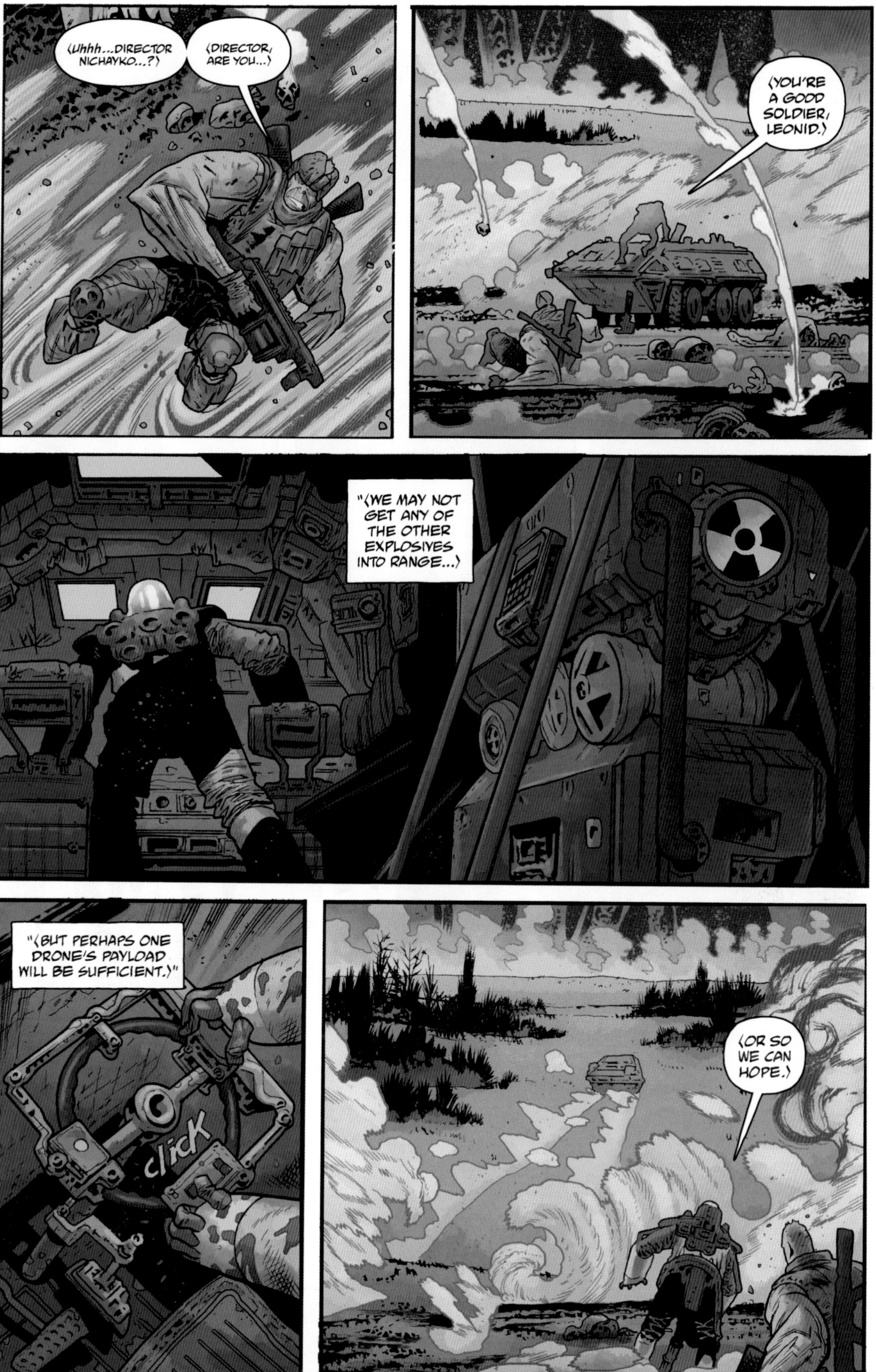
‹Uhhh...DIRECTOR NICHAYKO...?›
‹DIRECTOR, ARE YOU...›
‹YOU'RE A GOOD SOLDIER, LEONID.›
"‹WE MAY NOT GET ANY OF THE OTHER EXPLOSIVES INTO RANGE...›
"‹BUT PERHAPS ONE DRONE'S PAYLOAD WILL BE SUFFICIENT.›"
click
‹OR SO WE CAN HOPE.›

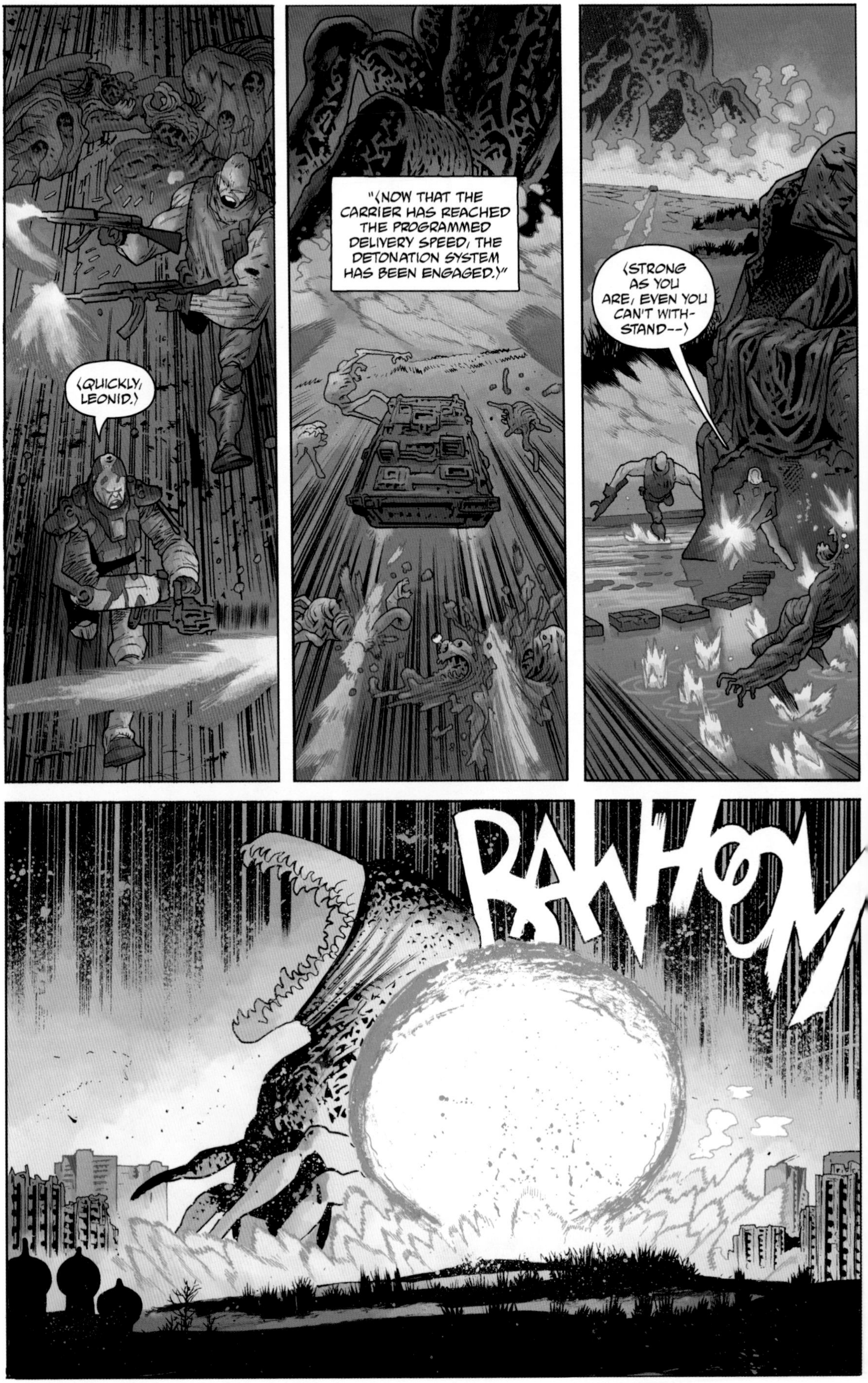
⟨QUICKLY, LEONID.⟩
"⟨NOW THAT THE CARRIER HAS REACHED THE PROGRAMMED DELIVERY SPEED, THE DETONATION SYSTEM HAS BEEN ENGAGED.⟩"
⟨STRONG AS YOU ARE, EVEN YOU CAN'T WITH-STAND--⟩
BAHOOM

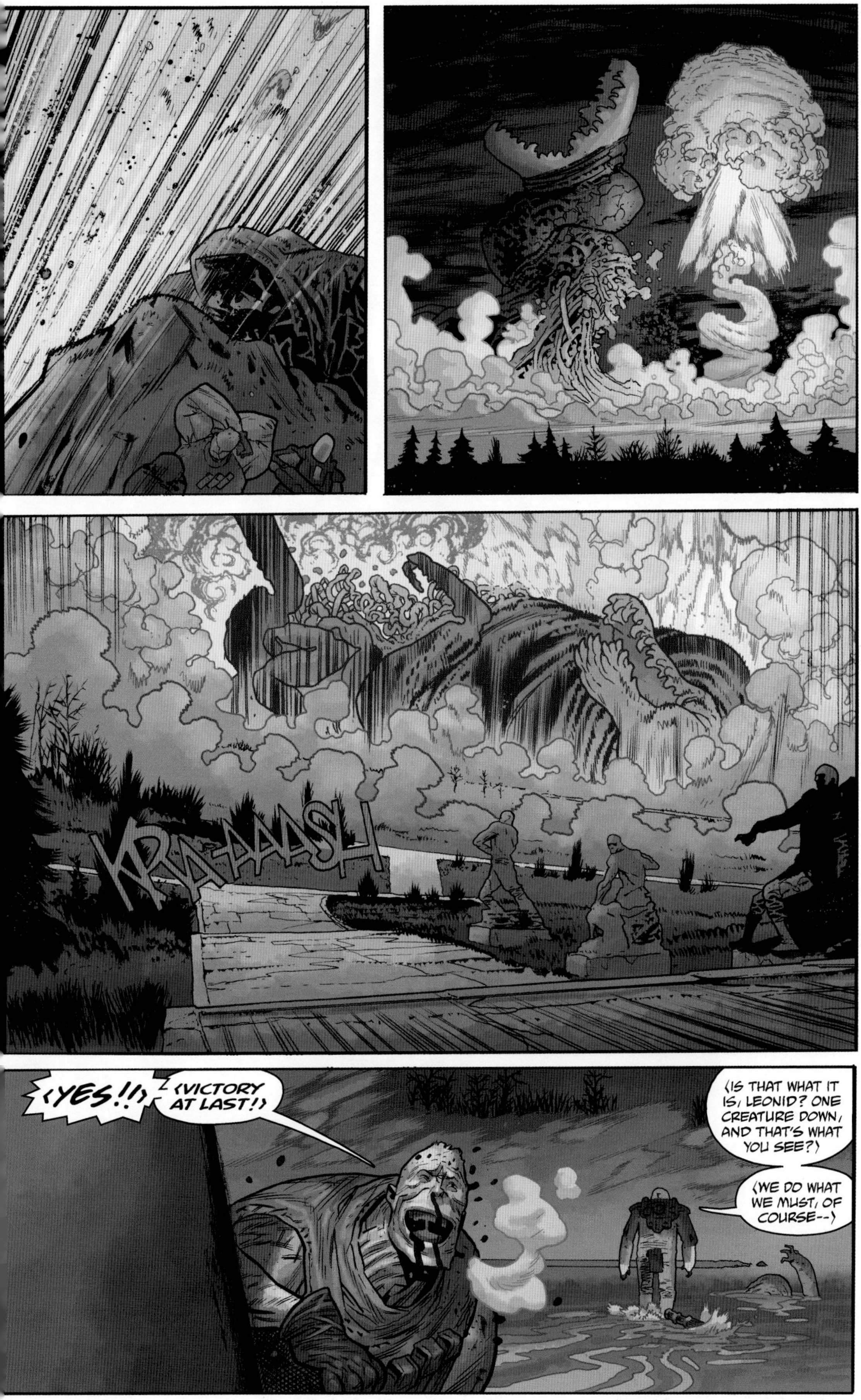

KRAAAASH
‹YES!!›
‹VICTORY AT LAST!›
‹IS THAT WHAT IT IS, LEONID? ONE CREATURE DOWN, AND THAT'S WHAT YOU SEE?›
‹WE DO WHAT WE MUST, OF COURSE--›

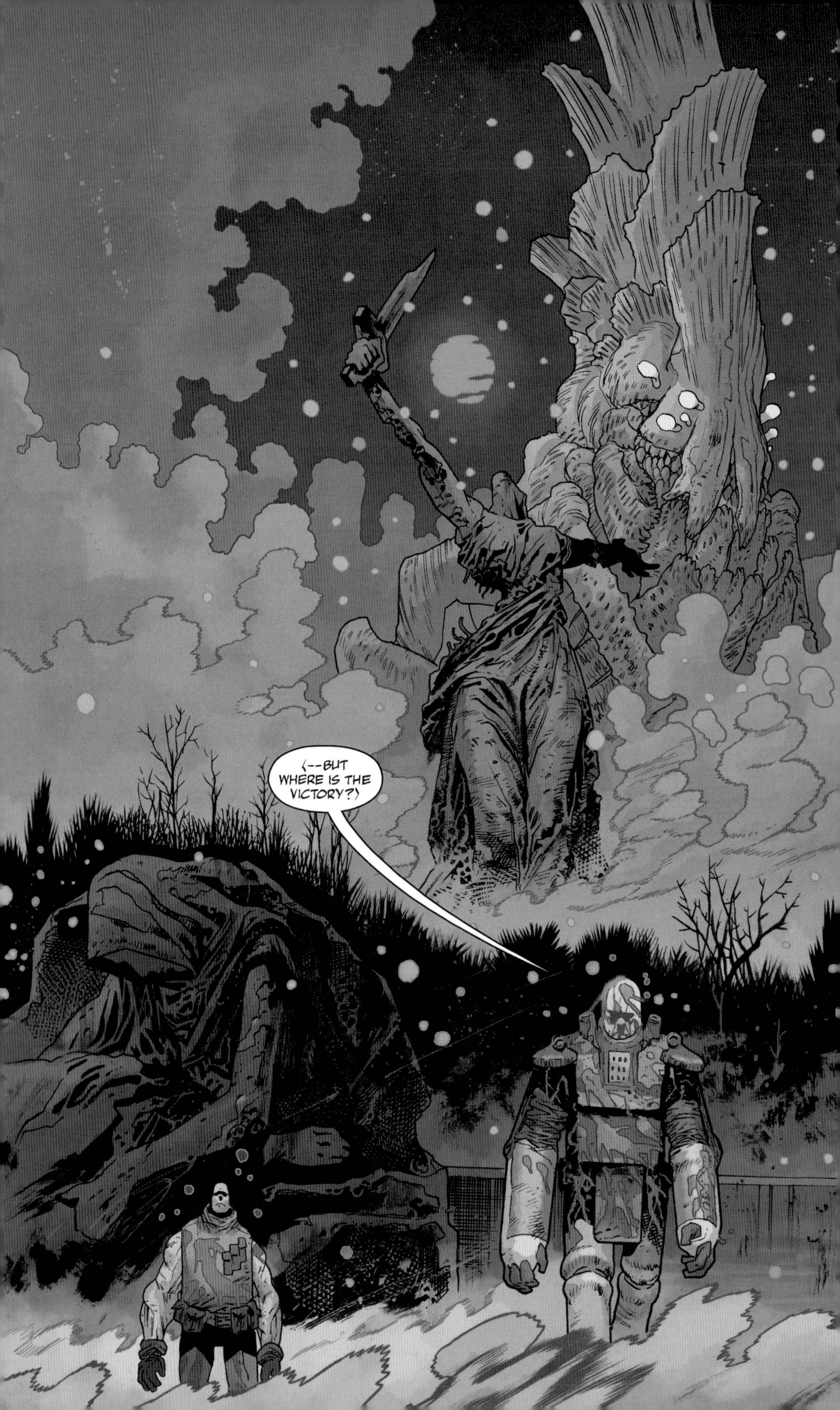
<--BUT WHERE IS THE VICTORY?>

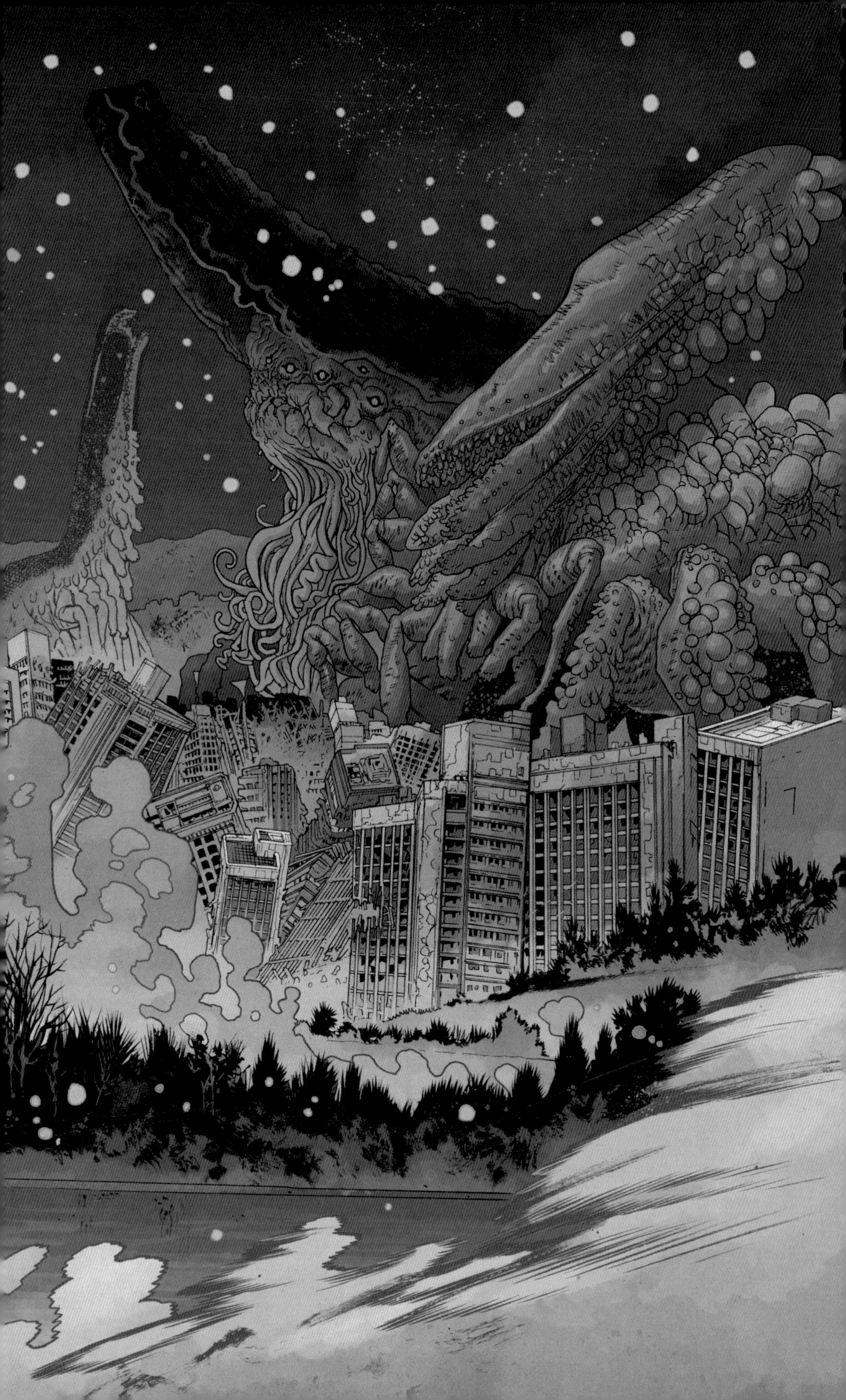

SEEMS WRONG.

I KNOW THEY'RE NEVER COMING BACK, I KNOW THIS HOUSE ISN'T ANYBODY'S "HOME" ANYMORE, BUT I DON'T KNOW...

THAT JUST MAKES IT WORSE.

TO ME IT DOES, ANY- WAY.

I'M STILL SURPRISED YOU SENT ENOS OUT LEADING THE FIRST PATROL. YOU AND HIM, I NEVER SAW YOU AGREE TOO MUCH.

THAT DOESN'T MAKE HIM A BAD LEADER--IT ONLY MEANS I HAVE DIFFICULTY LEADING *HIM*.

SO YOU THINK HE'S A GOOD LEADER?

SOONER OR LATER, TIAN, WE'RE *ALL* GOING TO HAVE TO BE GOOD LEADERS.

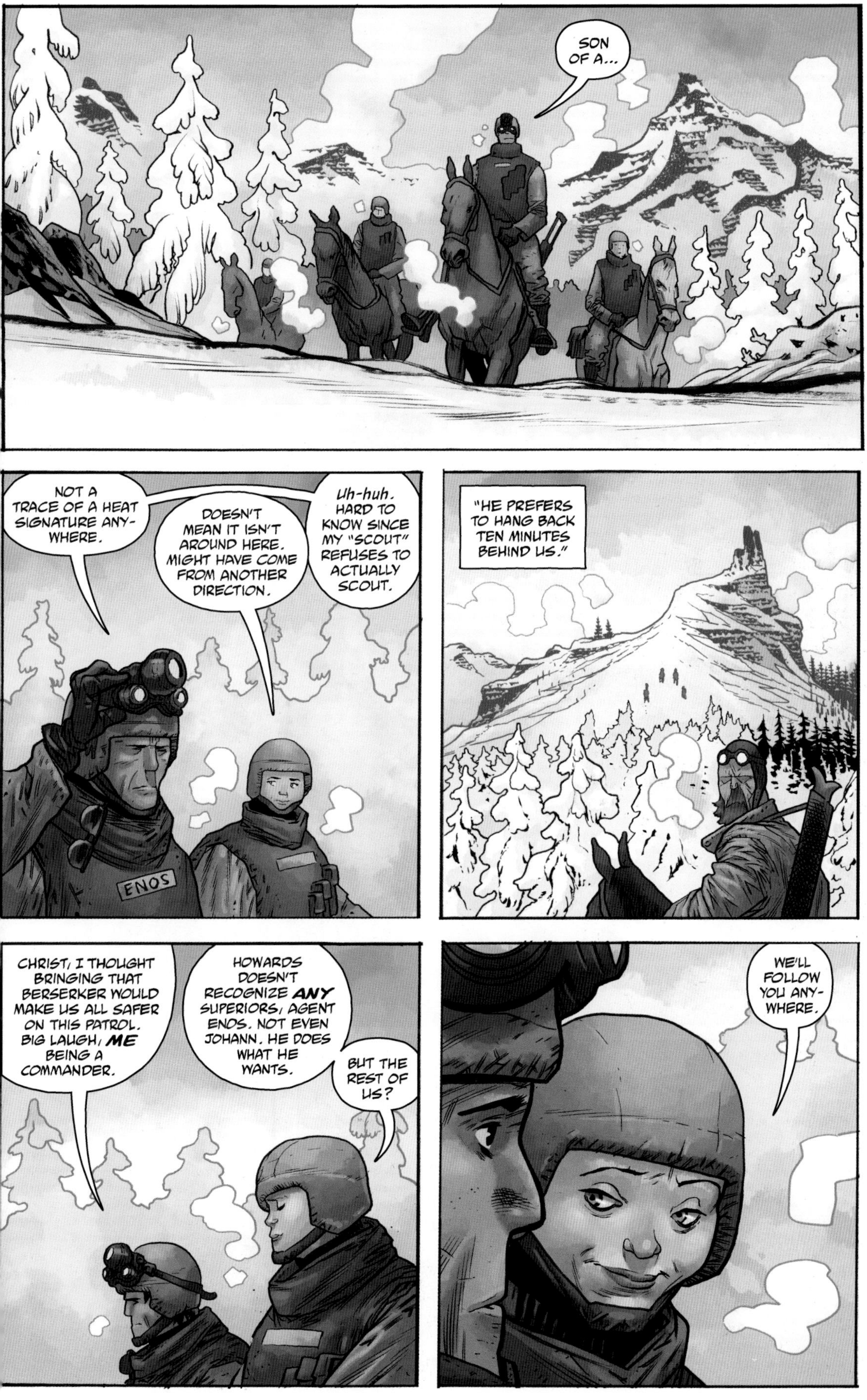
SON OF A...
NOT A TRACE OF A HEAT SIGNATURE ANYWHERE.
DOESN'T MEAN IT ISN'T AROUND HERE. MIGHT HAVE COME FROM ANOTHER DIRECTION.
Uh-huh. HARD TO KNOW SINCE MY "SCOUT" REFUSES TO ACTUALLY SCOUT.
ENOS
"HE PREFERS TO HANG BACK TEN MINUTES BEHIND US."
CHRIST, I THOUGHT BRINGING THAT BERSERKER WOULD MAKE US ALL SAFER ON THIS PATROL. BIG LAUGH, **ME** BEING A COMMANDER.
HOWARDS DOESN'T RECOGNIZE **ANY** SUPERIORS, AGENT ENOS. NOT EVEN JOHANN. HE DOES WHAT HE WANTS.
BUT THE REST OF US?
WE'LL FOLLOW YOU ANYWHERE.

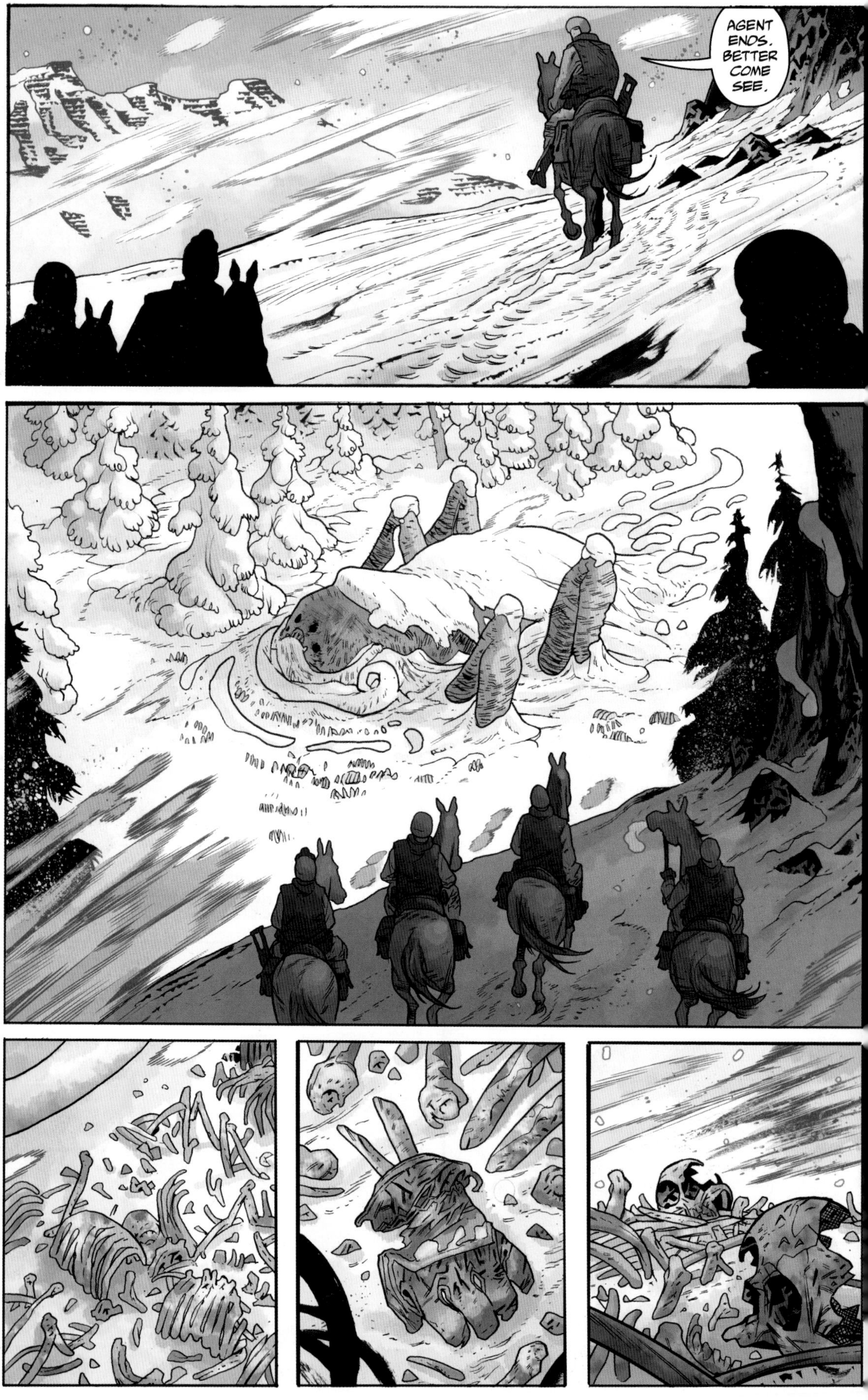
AGENT ENDS. BETTER COME SEE.

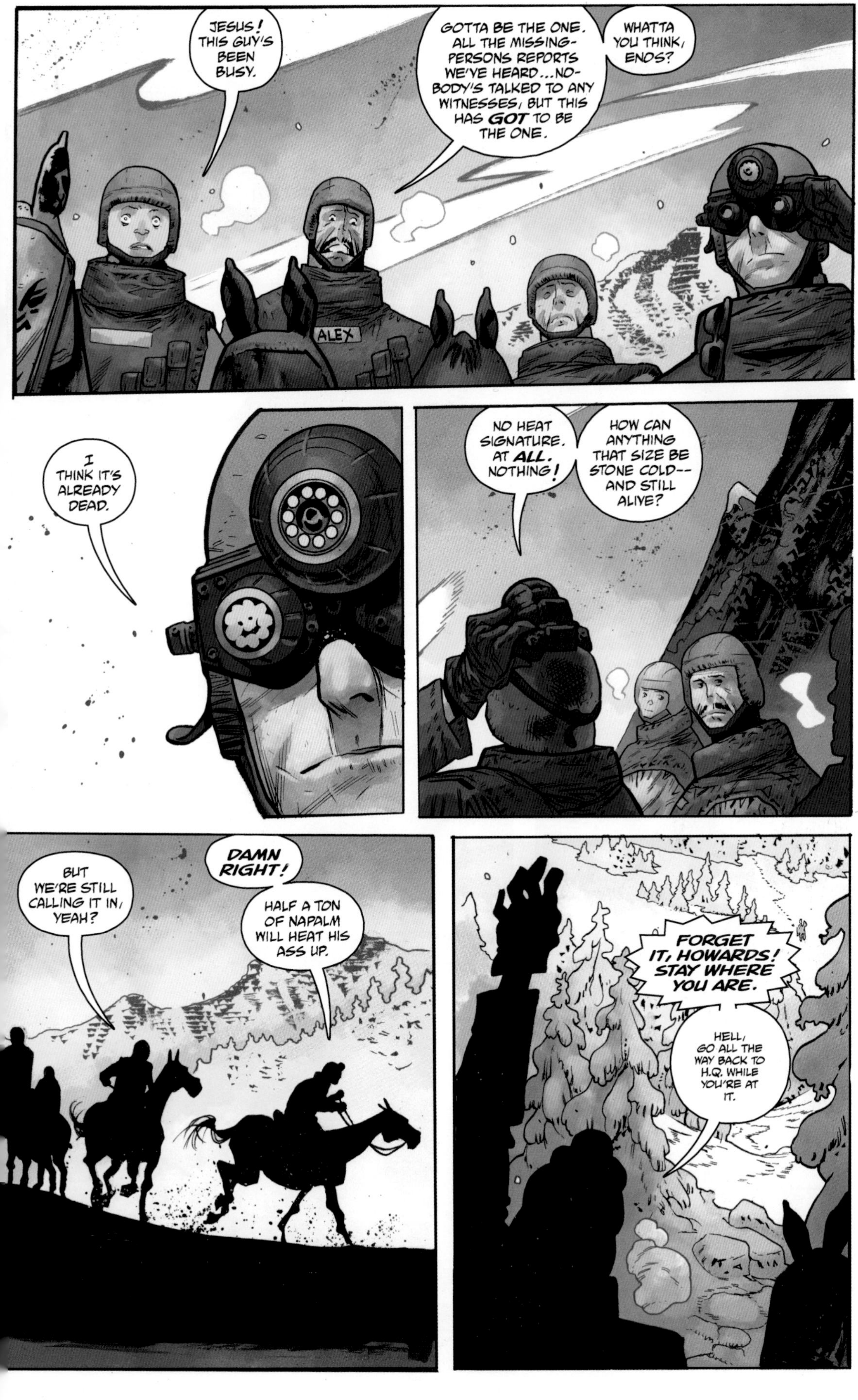
JESUS! THIS GUY'S BEEN BUSY.
GOTTA BE THE ONE. ALL THE MISSING-PERSONS REPORTS WE'VE HEARD...NOBODY'S TALKED TO ANY WITNESSES, BUT THIS HAS GOT TO BE THE ONE.
WHATTA YOU THINK, ENOS?
ALEX
I THINK IT'S ALREADY DEAD.
NO HEAT SIGNATURE. AT ALL. NOTHING!
HOW CAN ANYTHING THAT SIZE BE STONE COLD--AND STILL ALIVE?
BUT WE'RE STILL CALLING IT IN, YEAH?
DAMN RIGHT!
HALF A TON OF NAPALM WILL HEAT HIS ASS UP.
FORGET IT, HOWARDS! STAY WHERE YOU ARE.
HELL, GO ALL THE WAY BACK TO H.Q. WHILE YOU'RE AT IT.

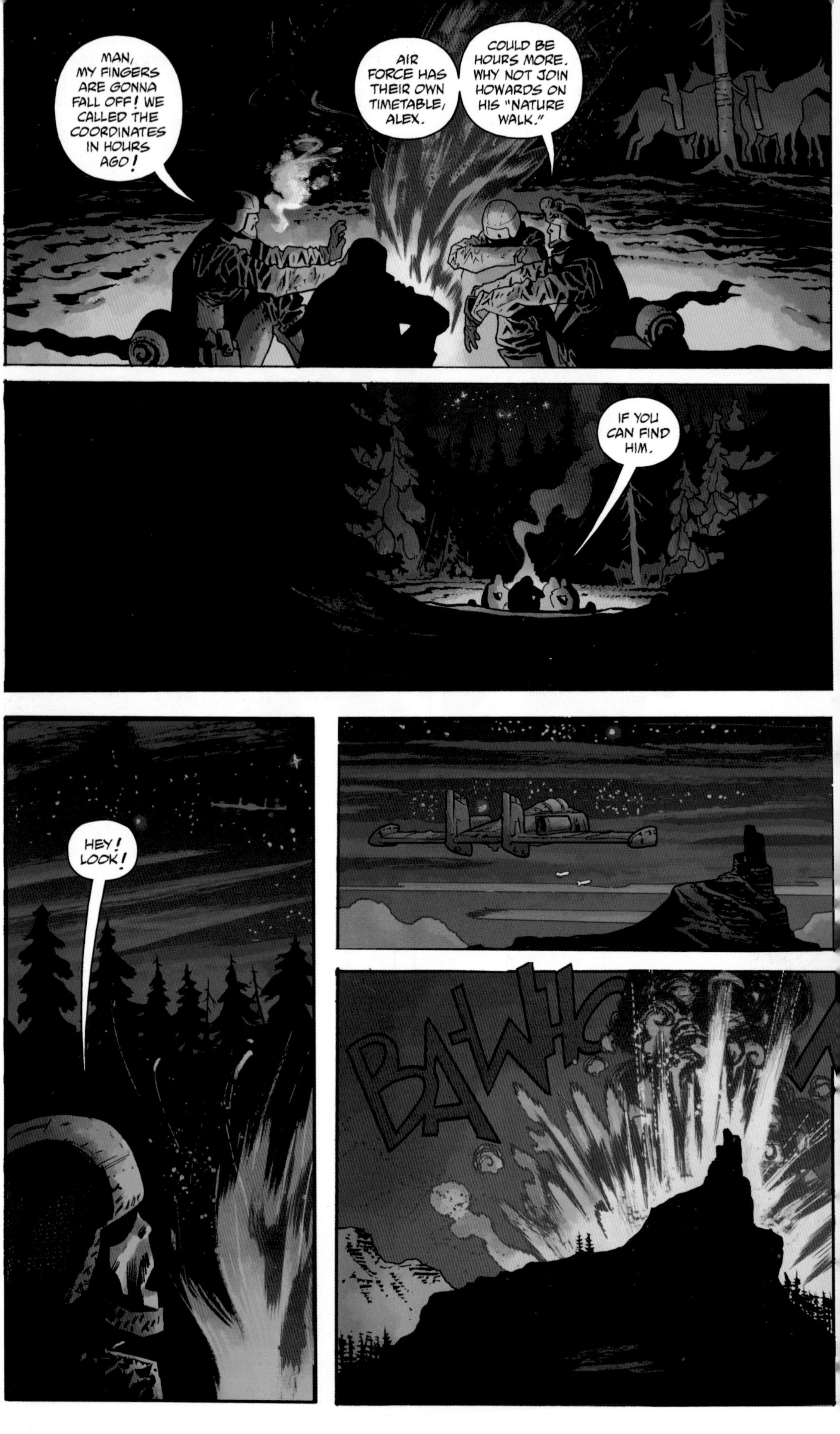
MAN, MY FINGERS ARE GONNA FALL OFF! WE CALLED THE COORDINATES IN HOURS AGO!
AIR FORCE HAS THEIR OWN TIMETABLE, ALEX.
COULD BE HOURS MORE. WHY NOT JOIN HOWARDS ON HIS "NATURE WALK."
IF YOU CAN FIND HIM.
HEY! LOOK!
BA-WHO

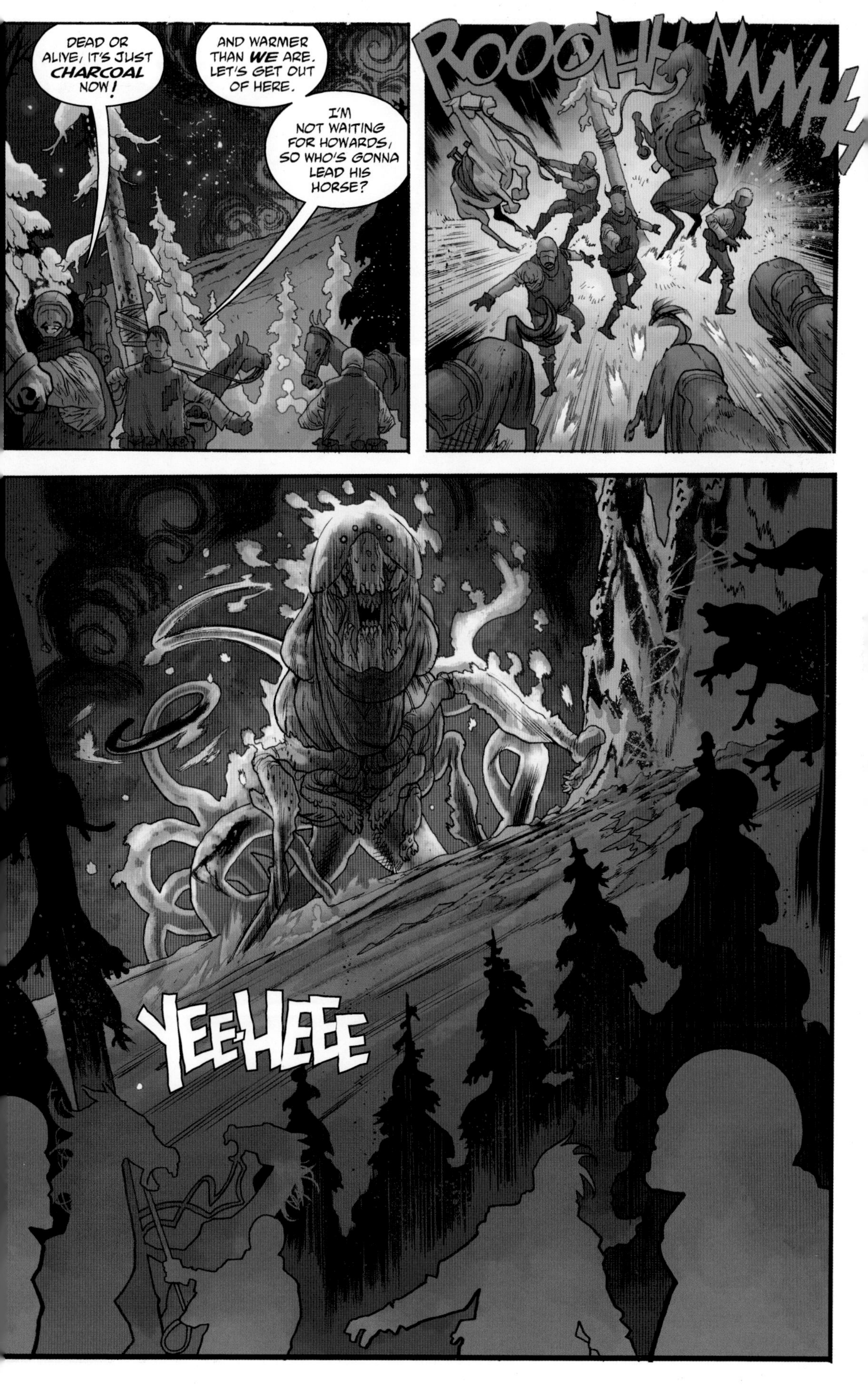

DEAD OR ALIVE, IT'S JUST CHARCOAL NOW!
AND WARMER THAN WE ARE. LET'S GET OUT OF HERE.
I'M NOT WAITING FOR HOWARDS, SO WHO'S GONNA LEAD HIS HORSE?
ROOOHHNWHH
YEE-HEEE

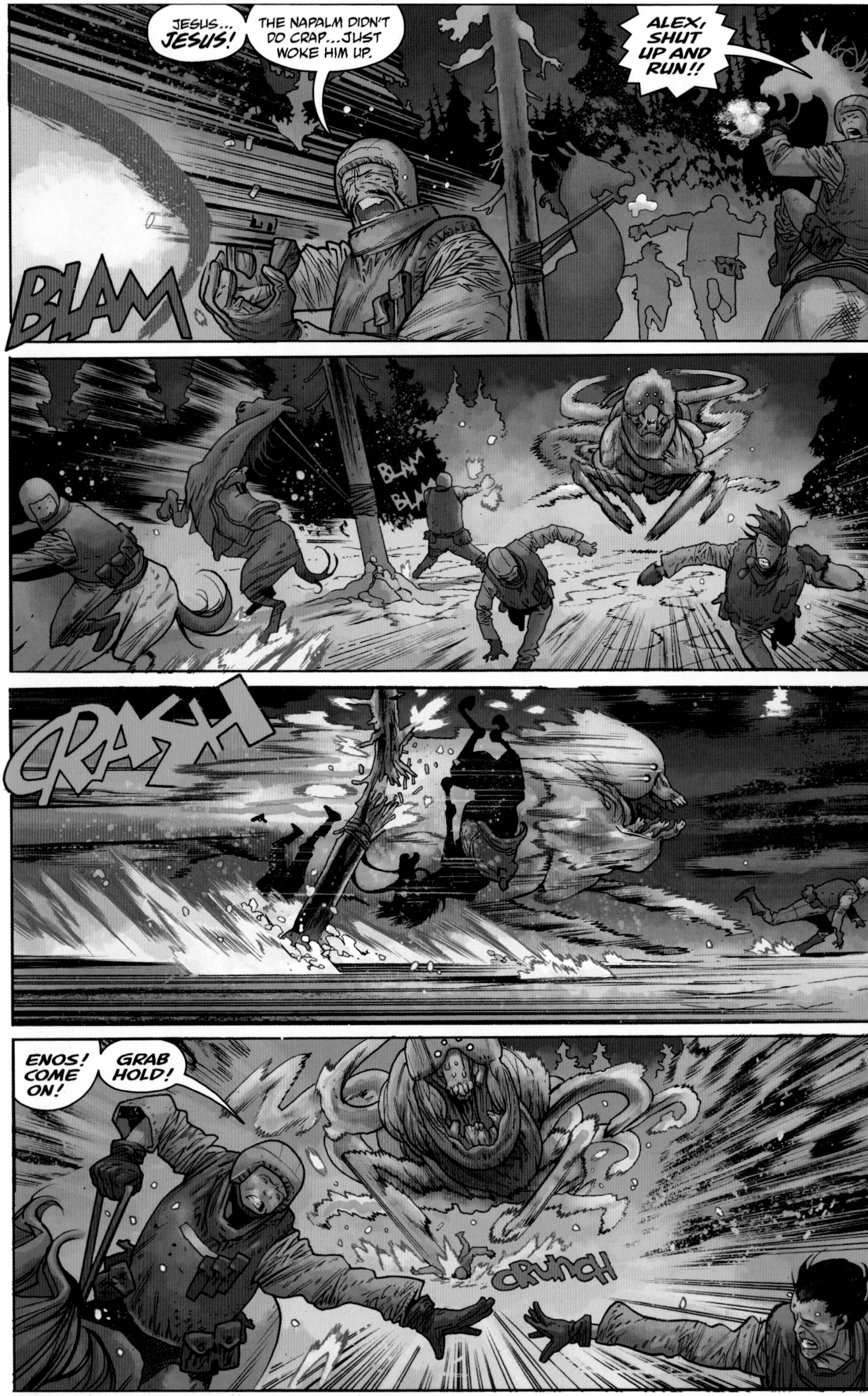
JESUS... JESUS!
THE NAPALM DIDN'T DO CRAP... JUST WOKE HIM UP.
ALEX, SHUT UP AND RUN!!
BLAM
BLAM
BLAM
CRASH
ENOS! COME ON!
GRAB HOLD!
CRUNCH

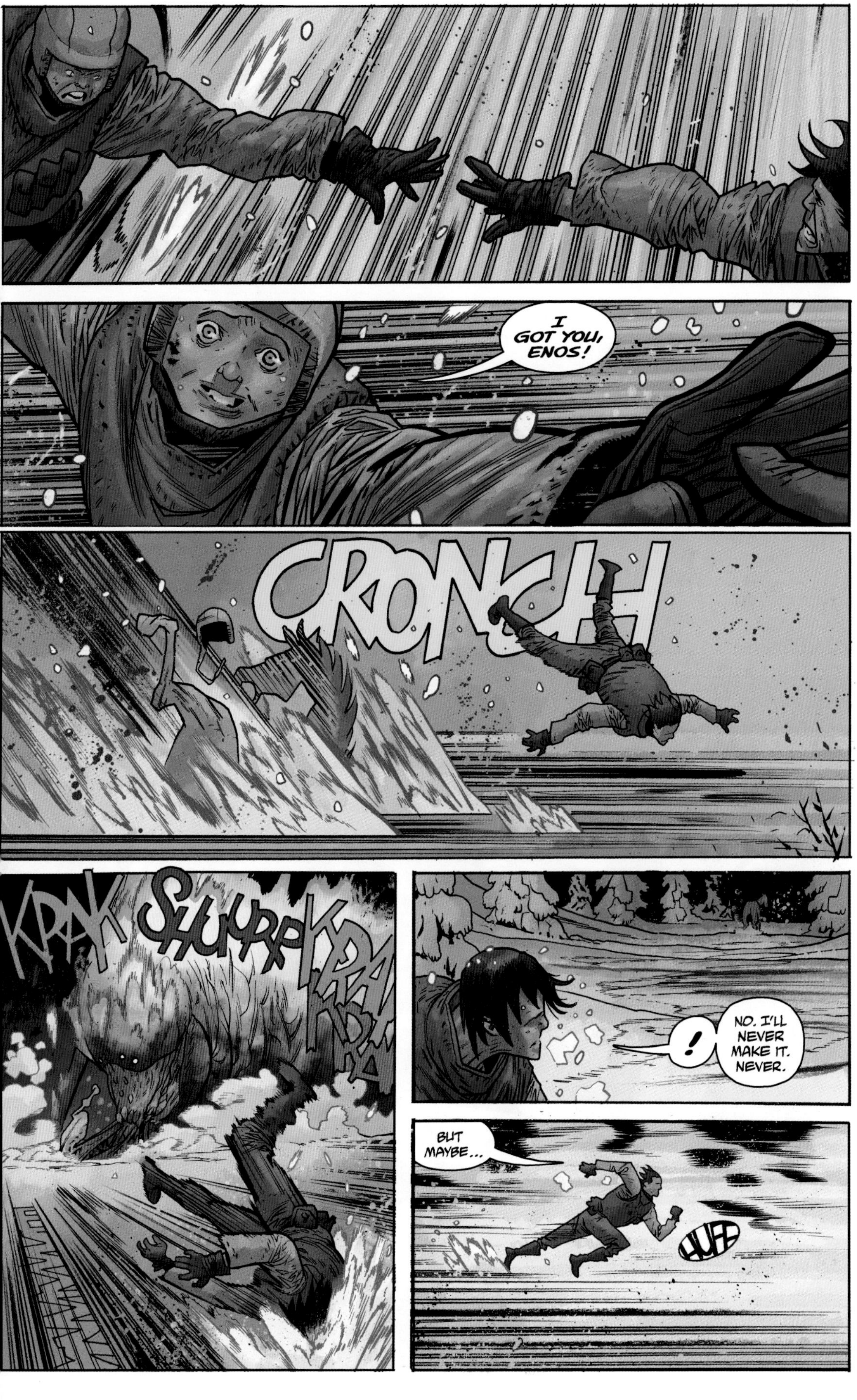
I GOT YOU, ENOS!
CRONCH
KRAK
SHUMP
KRA
KRA
!
NO. I'LL NEVER MAKE IT. NEVER.
BUT MAYBE...
HUFF

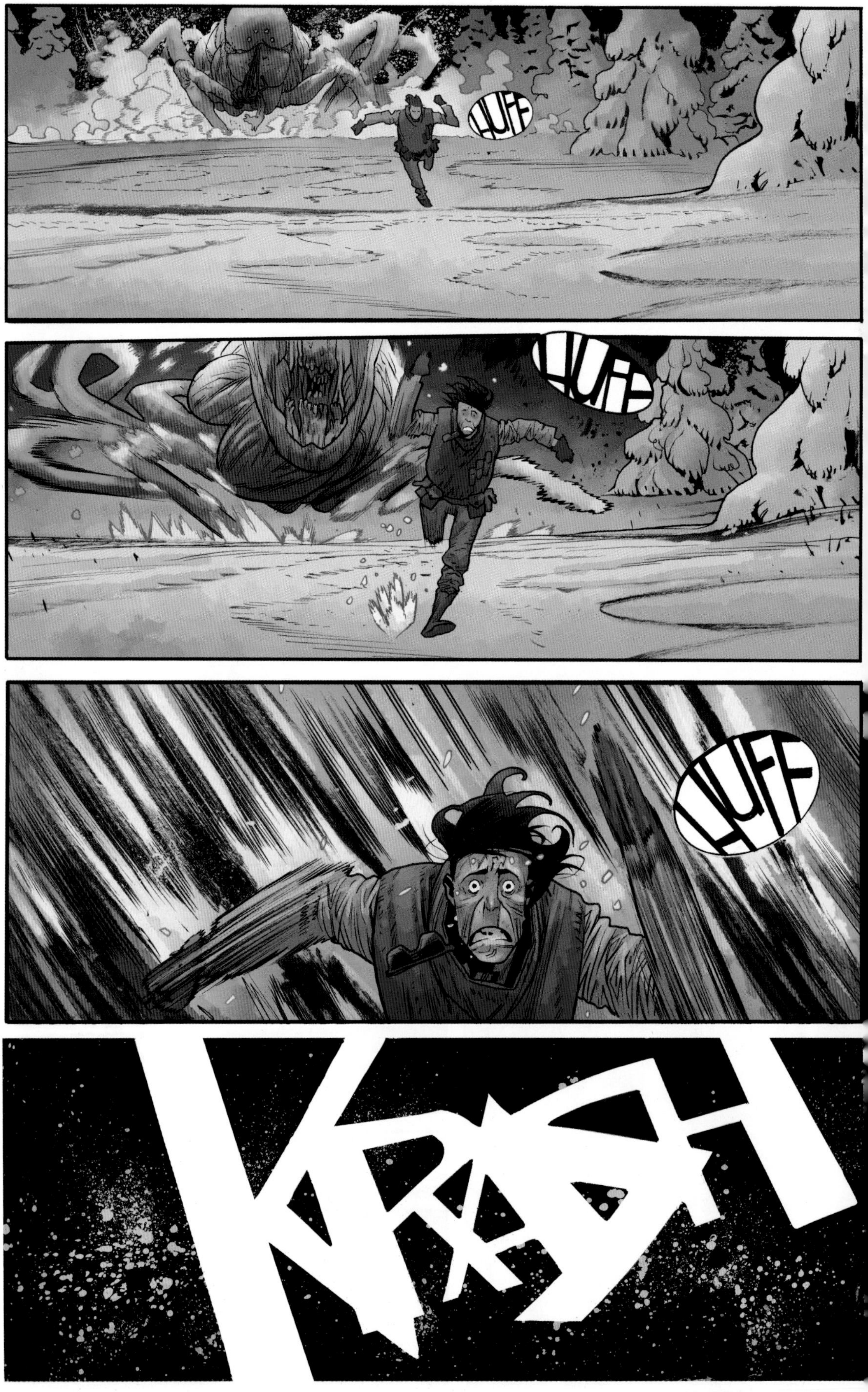
HUFF
HUFF
HUFF
KRASH

CHAPTER THREE

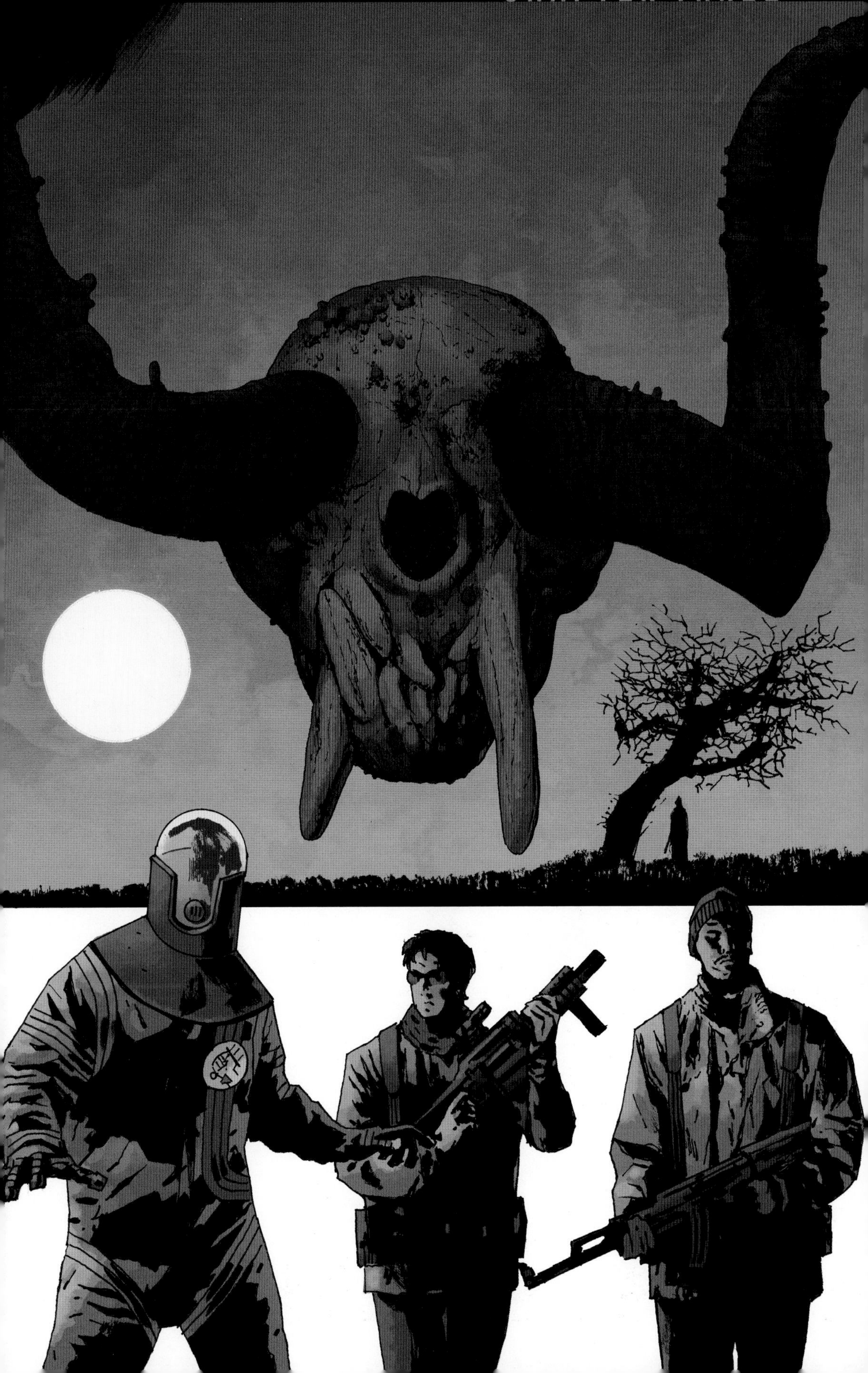

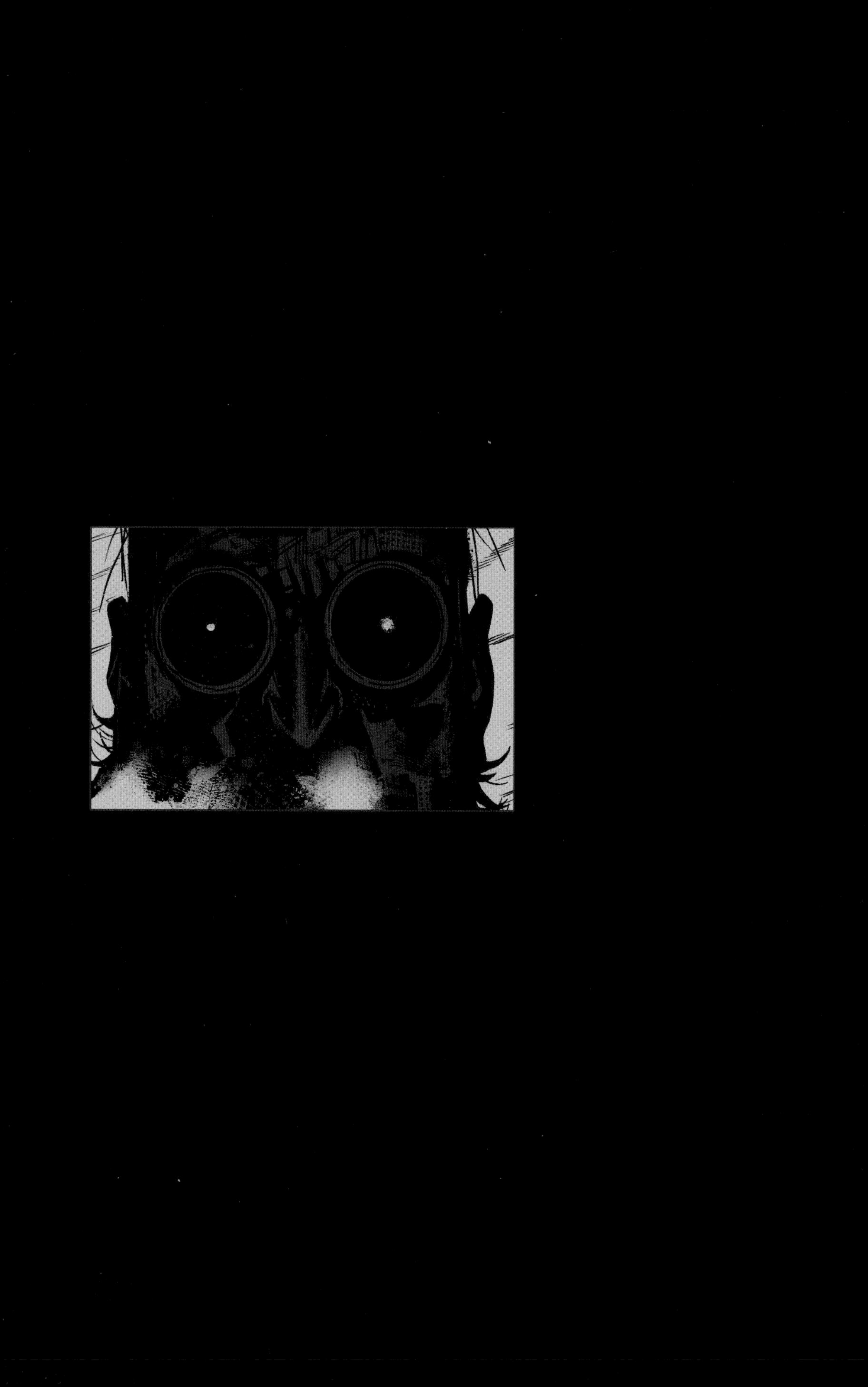

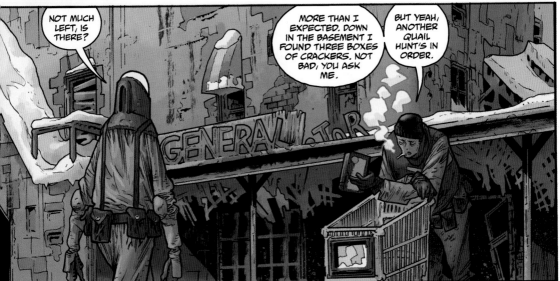

NOT MUCH LEFT, IS THERE?

MORE THAN I EXPECTED. DOWN IN THE BASEMENT I FOUND THREE BOXES OF CRACKERS. NOT BAD, YOU ASK ME.

BUT YEAH, ANOTHER QUAIL HUNT'S IN ORDER.

LISTEN, I'VE BEEN THINKING. WE DON'T **NEED** TO SEND A WHOLE SEARCH PARTY. I'LL DO IT ALONE.

LOOKING AT THE MAP, I SAW THESE VACATION HOMES UP IN THE HILLS--ALL ABANDONED NOW, OF COURSE. THAT'D BE A GOOD PLACE TO START LOOKING.

TIAN, ENOS'S SQUAD WAS TASKED WITH A THREE-DAY MISSION. THIS IS ONLY THE THIRD DAY.

AND I KNOW THE COMPLETE LACK OF RADIO CONTACT SOMEWHAT CHANGES THAT EQUATION. I AM CONCERNED.

BUT THEY ARE NOT YET, TECHNICALLY SPEAKING, MISSING. SO BEFORE I RISK ANY MORE PERSONNEL--

WAIT...

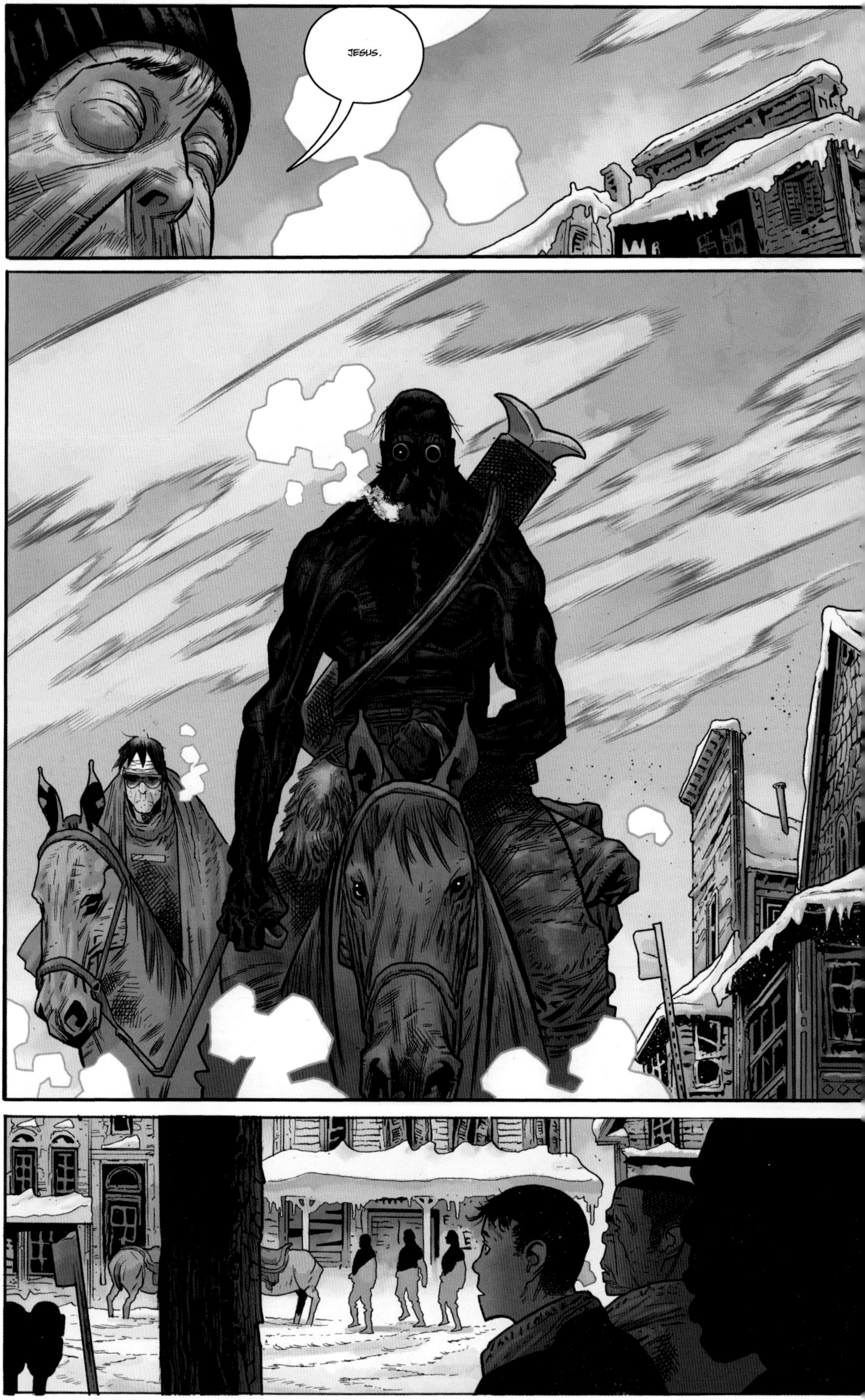
JESUS.

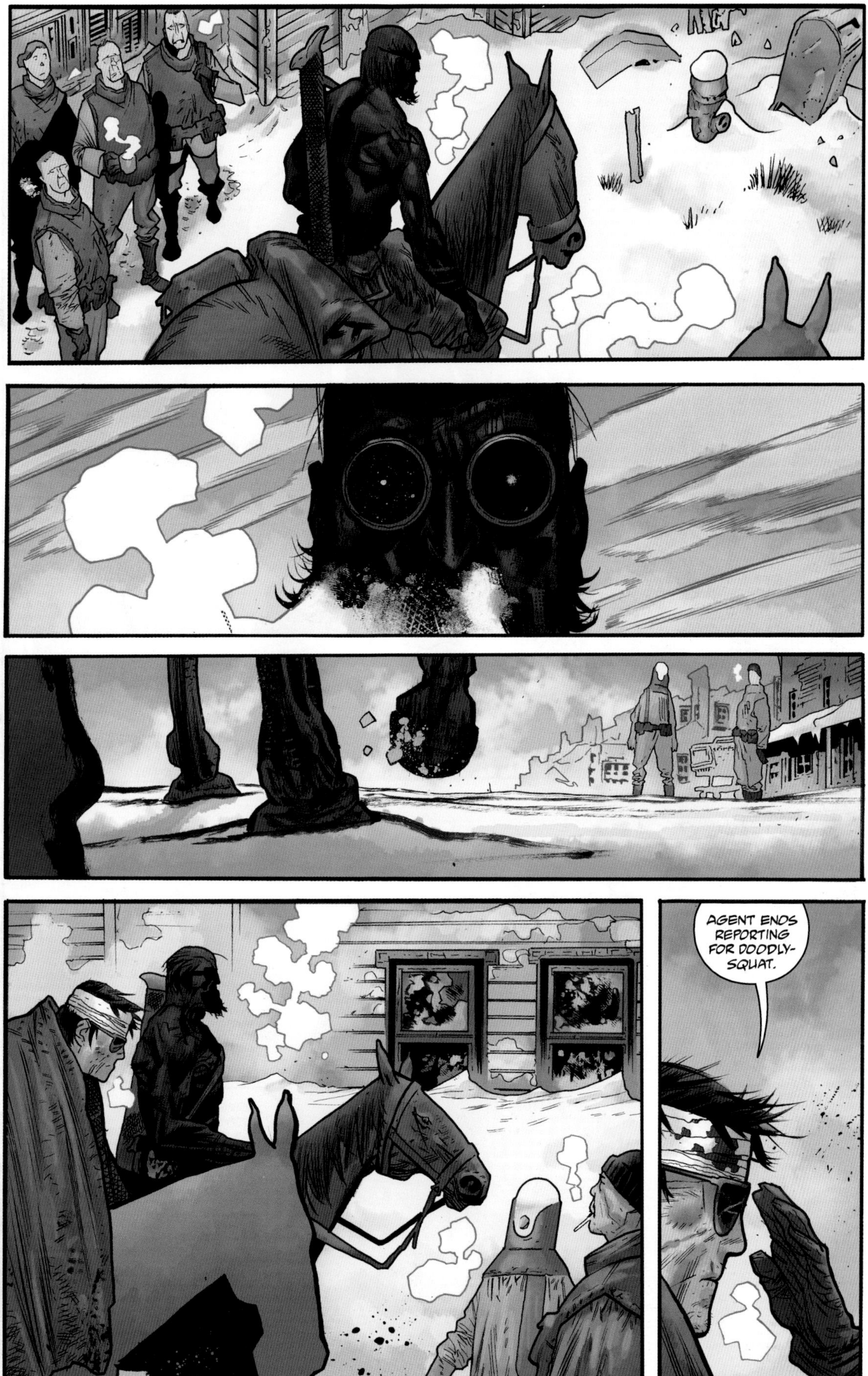
AGENT ENOS REPORTING FOR DOODLY-SQUAT.

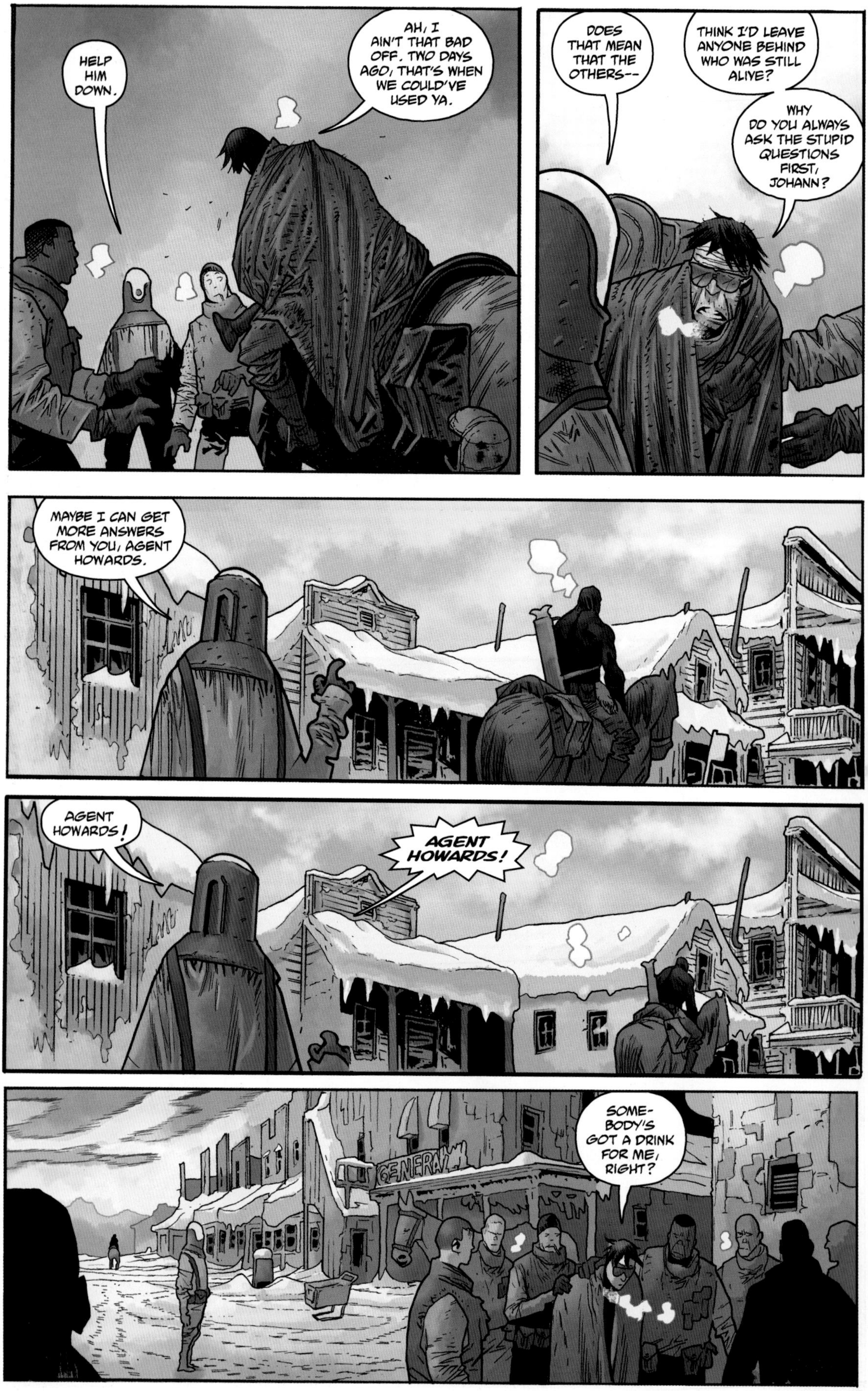
HELP HIM DOWN.
AH, I AIN'T THAT BAD OFF. TWO DAYS AGO, THAT'S WHEN WE COULD'VE USED YA.
DOES THAT MEAN THAT THE OTHERS--
THINK I'D LEAVE ANYONE BEHIND WHO WAS STILL ALIVE?
WHY DO YOU ALWAYS ASK THE STUPID QUESTIONS FIRST, JOHANN?
MAYBE I CAN GET MORE ANSWERS FROM YOU, AGENT HOWARDS.
AGENT HOWARDS!
AGENT HOWARDS!
GENERAL
SOME-BODY'S GOT A DRINK FOR ME, RIGHT?

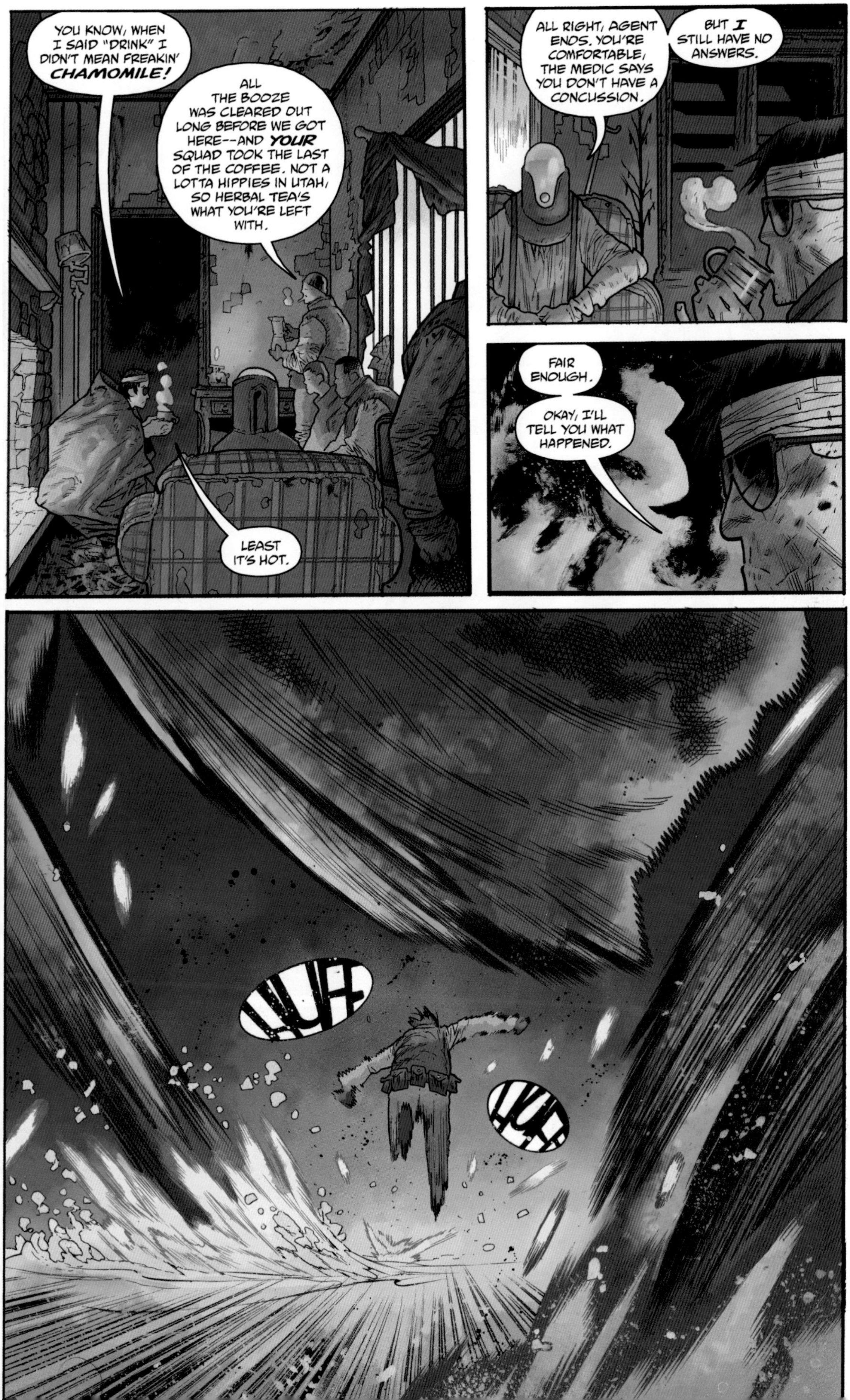
YOU KNOW, WHEN I SAID "DRINK" I DIDN'T MEAN FREAKIN' CHAMOMILE!
ALL THE BOOZE WAS CLEARED OUT LONG BEFORE WE GOT HERE--AND YOUR SQUAD TOOK THE LAST OF THE COFFEE. NOT A LOTTA HIPPIES IN UTAH, SO HERBAL TEA'S WHAT YOU'RE LEFT WITH.
LEAST IT'S HOT.
ALL RIGHT, AGENT ENOS. YOU'RE COMFORTABLE, THE MEDIC SAYS YOU DON'T HAVE A CONCUSSION.
BUT I STILL HAVE NO ANSWERS.
FAIR ENOUGH.
OKAY, I'LL TELL YOU WHAT HAPPENED.

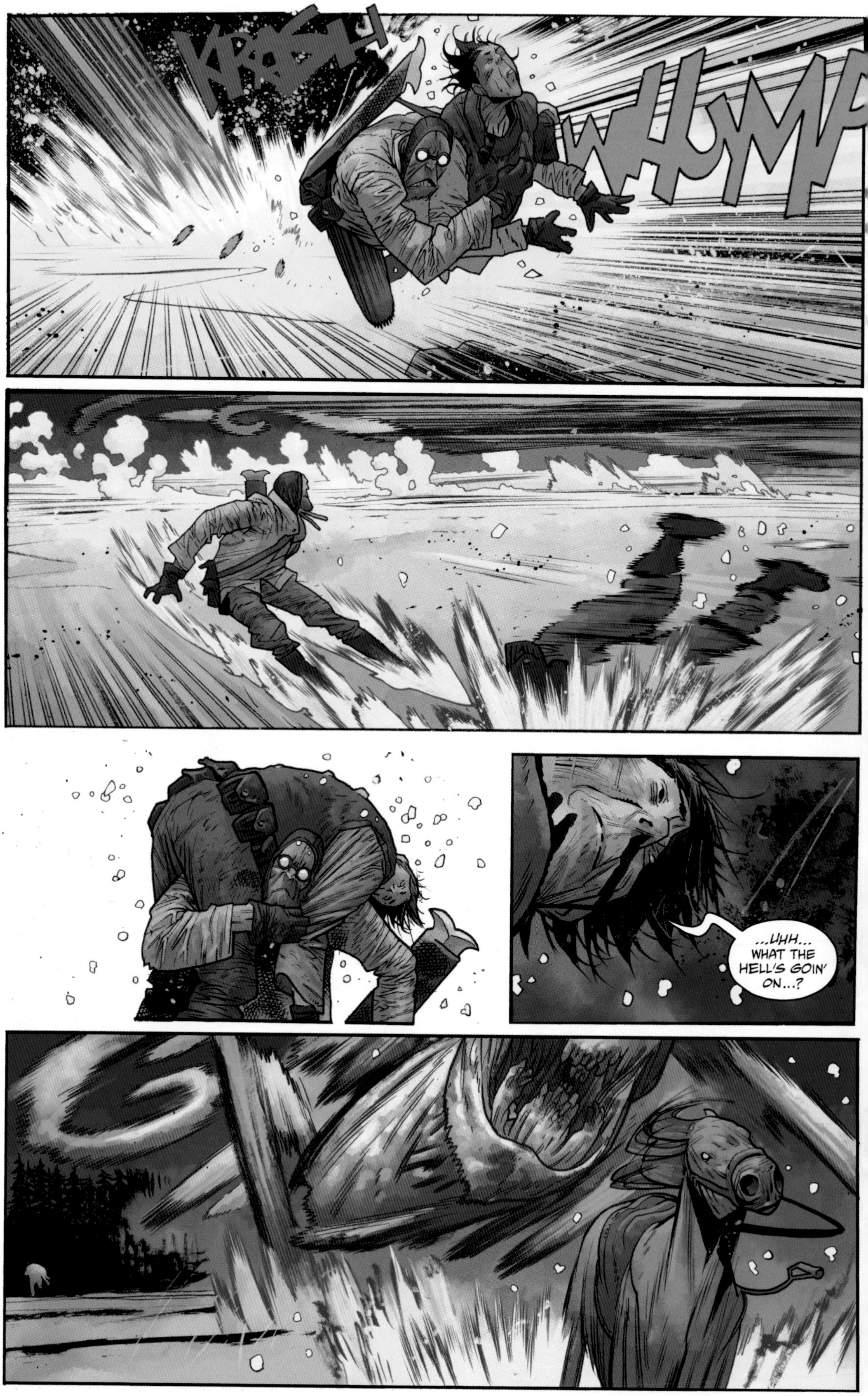
KRASH!
WHUMP
...UHH... WHAT THE HELL'S GOIN' ON...?

"AND I WANT YOU TO KNOW, RIGHT OFF, I TOLD HIM. I SAID--"

YOU NEED TO GO OUT ON YOUR OWN. MAYBE FIND A HORSE, WHATEVER. JUST GET BACK TO CAMP.

I'LL BE OKAY HERE. YOU JUST GET HELP AND BRING 'EM BACK.

"BUT I GUESS YOU KNOW HOW THAT WENT OVER.

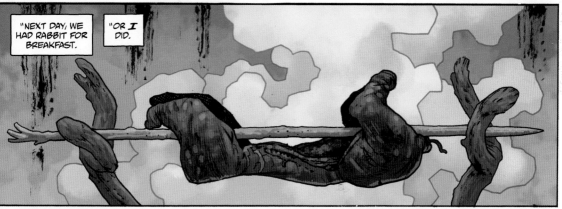

"NEXT DAY, WE HAD RABBIT FOR BREAKFAST.

"OR *I* DID.

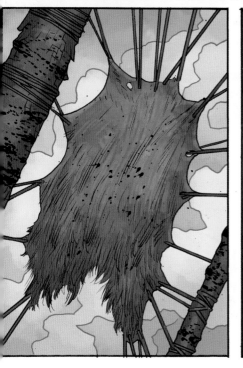

"HOWARDS WAS WORKING ON SOMETHING ELSE.

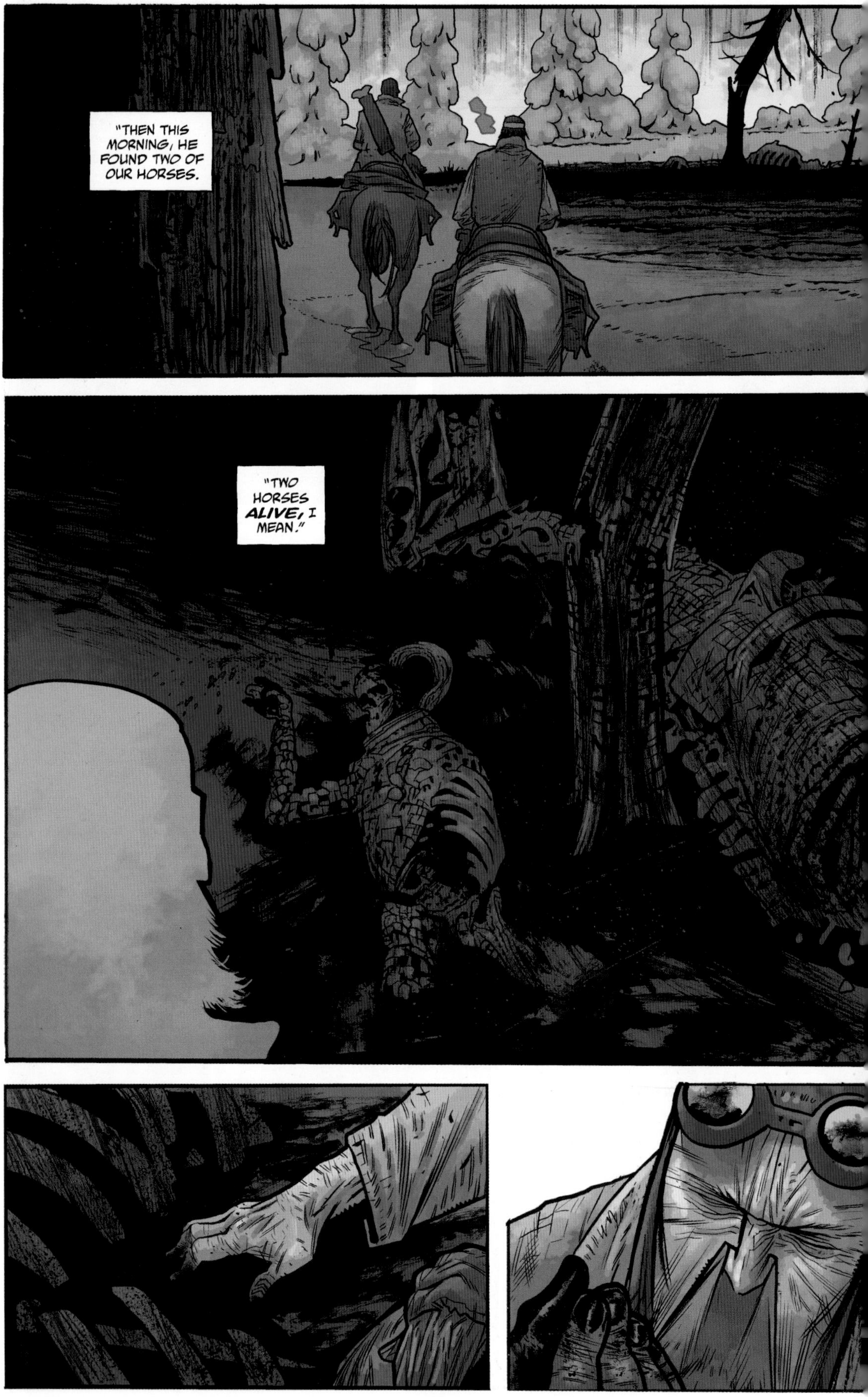
"THEN THIS MORNING, HE FOUND TWO OF OUR HORSES.
"TWO HORSES *ALIVE*, I MEAN."

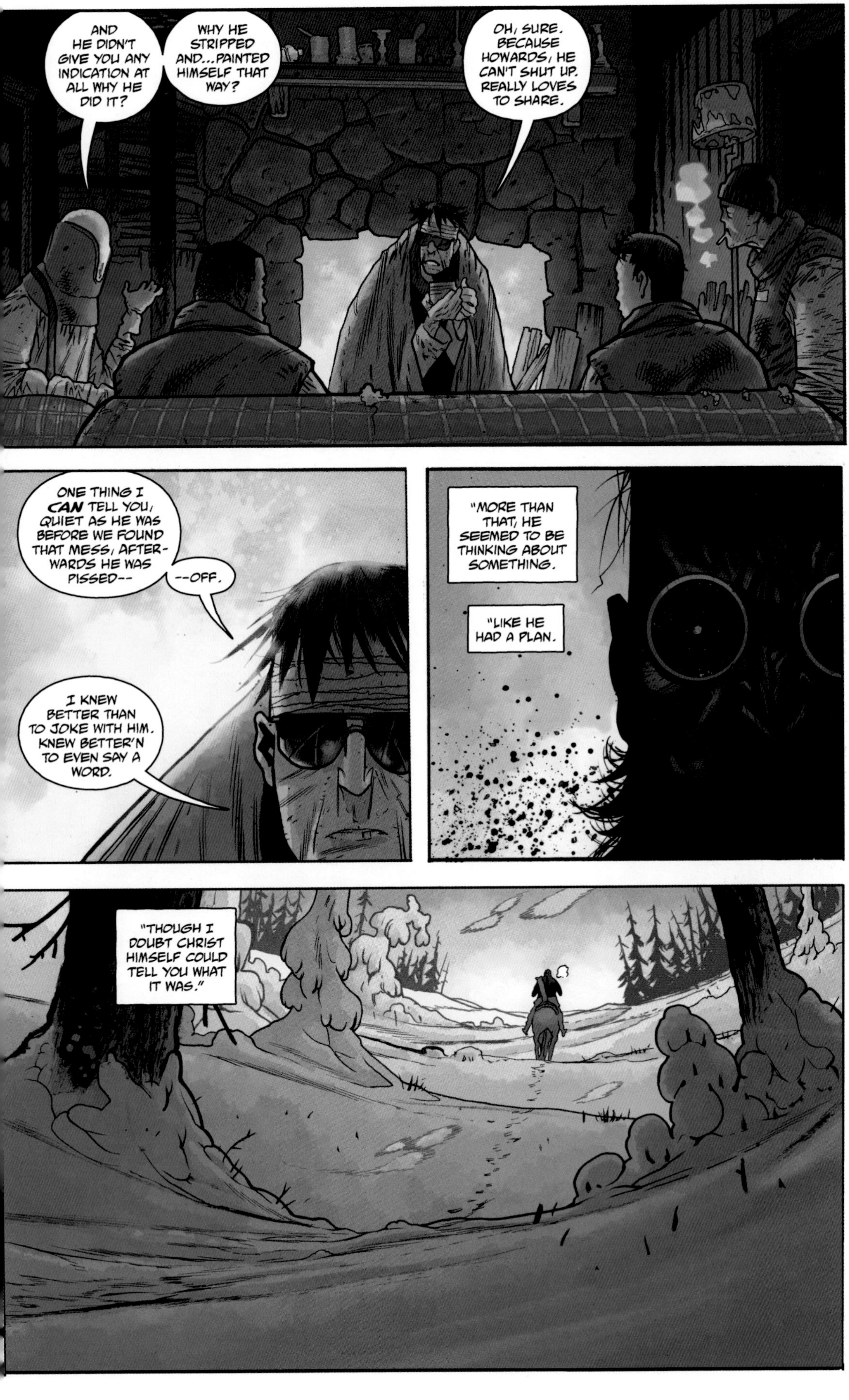
AND HE DIDN'T GIVE YOU ANY INDICATION AT ALL WHY HE DID IT?
WHY HE STRIPPED AND...PAINTED HIMSELF THAT WAY?
OH, SURE. BECAUSE HOWARDS, HE CAN'T SHUT UP. REALLY LOVES TO SHARE.
ONE THING I CAN TELL YOU, QUIET AS HE WAS BEFORE WE FOUND THAT MESS, AFTER-WARDS HE WAS PISSED--
--OFF.
I KNEW BETTER THAN TO JOKE WITH HIM. KNEW BETTER'N TO EVEN SAY A WORD.
"MORE THAN THAT, HE SEEMED TO BE THINKING ABOUT SOMETHING.
"LIKE HE HAD A PLAN.
"THOUGH I DOUBT CHRIST HIMSELF COULD TELL YOU WHAT IT WAS."

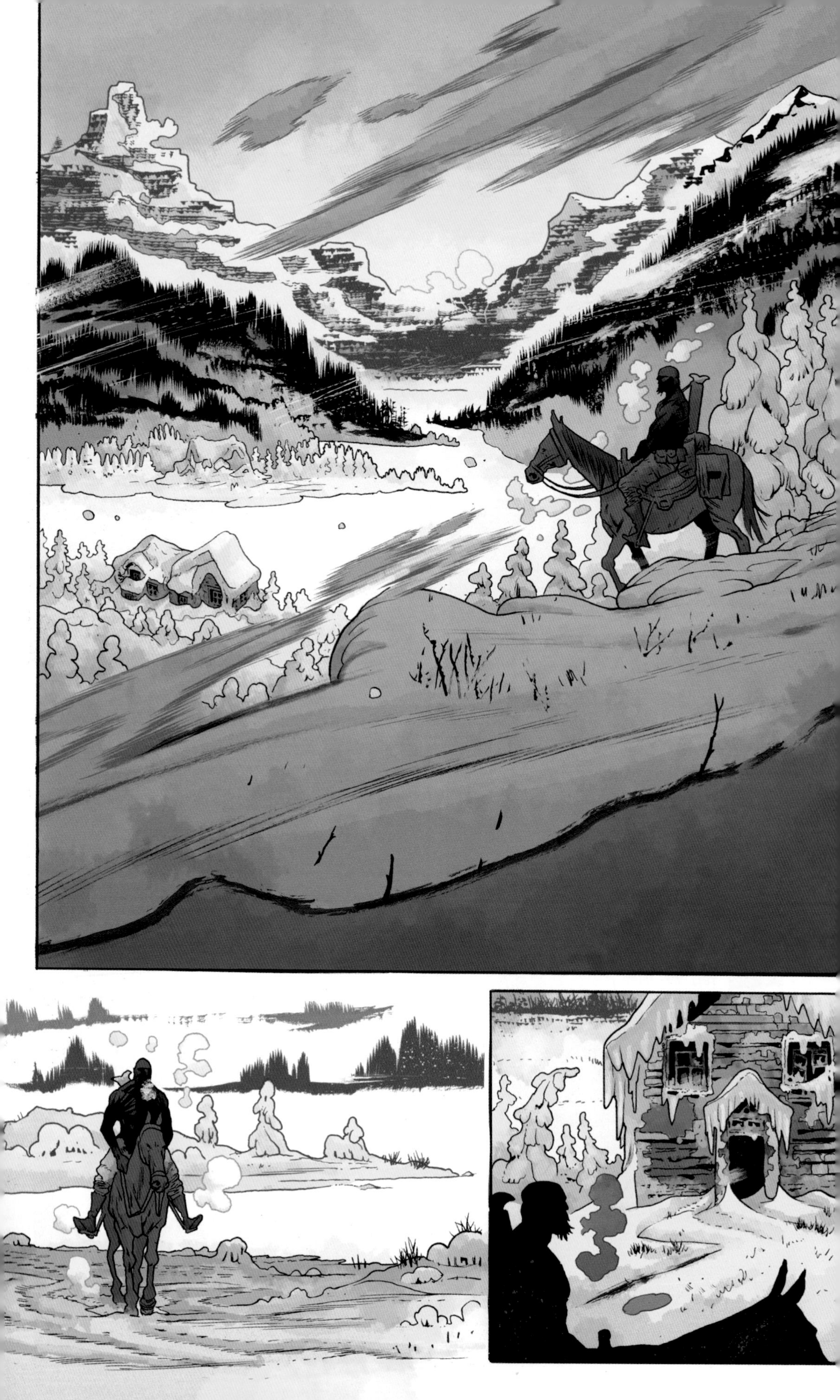

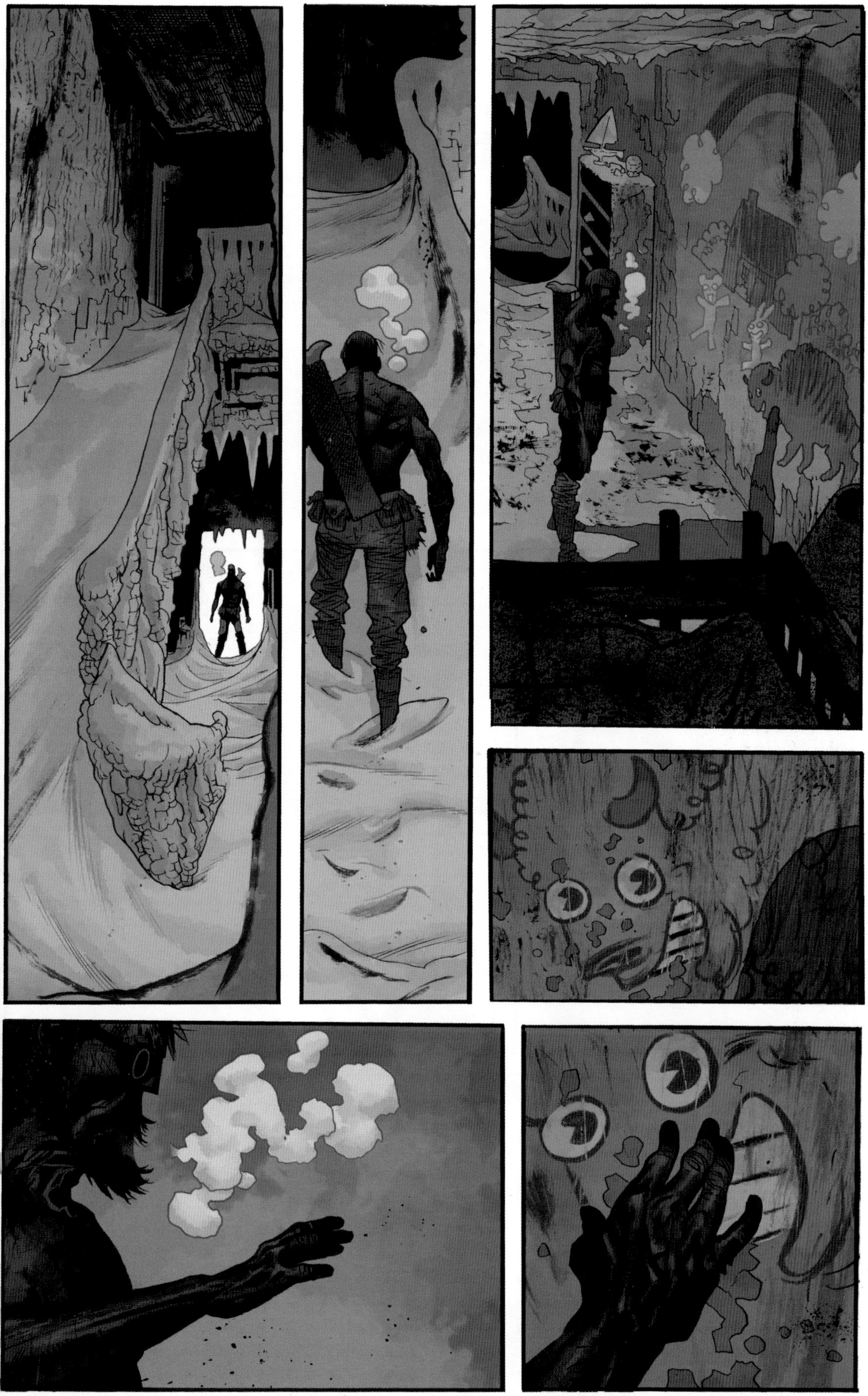

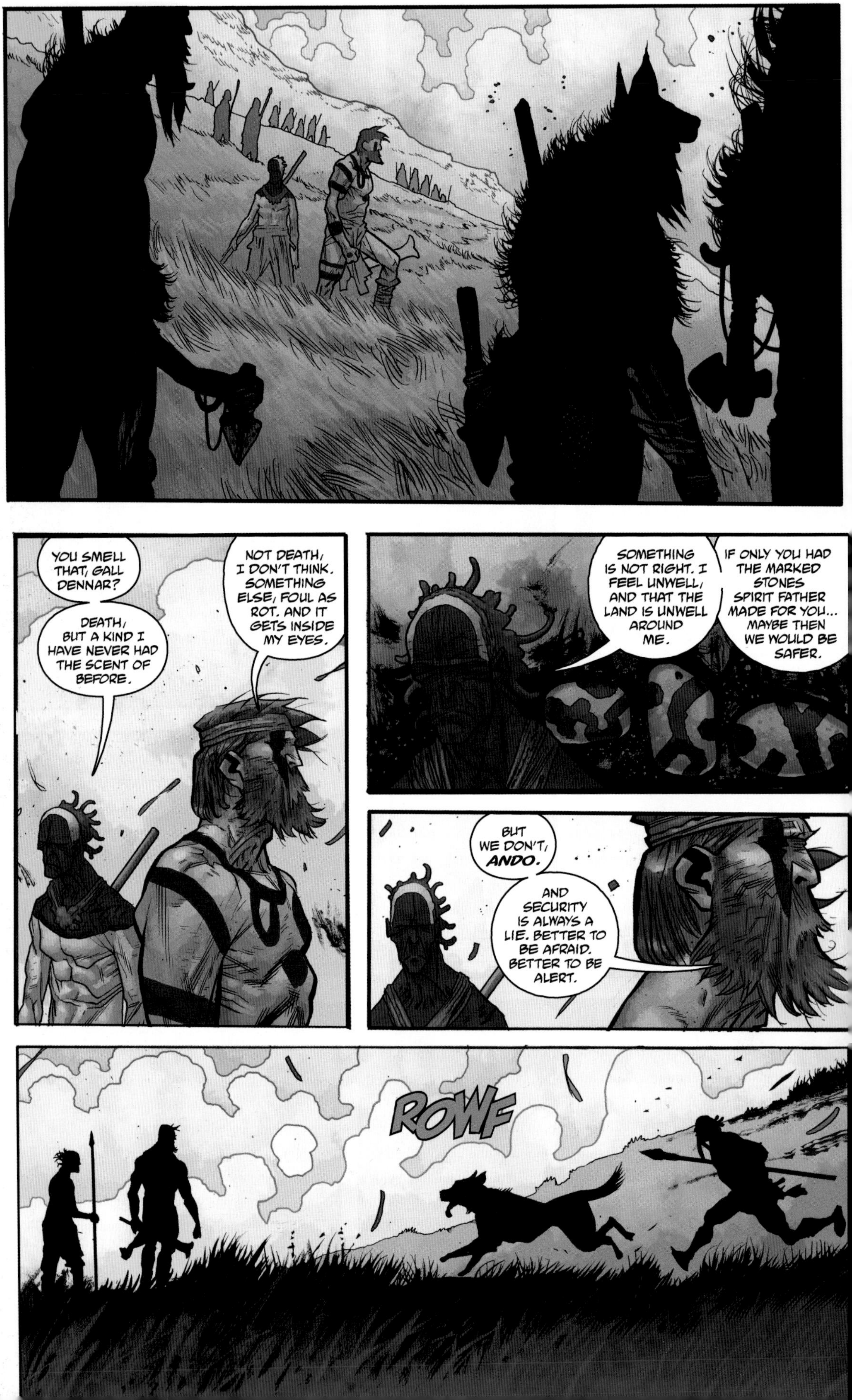
YOU SMELL THAT, GALL DENNAR?
DEATH, BUT A KIND I HAVE NEVER HAD THE SCENT OF BEFORE.
NOT DEATH, I DON'T THINK. SOMETHING ELSE, FOUL AS ROT. AND IT GETS INSIDE MY EYES.
SOMETHING IS NOT RIGHT. I FEEL UNWELL, AND THAT THE LAND IS UNWELL AROUND ME.
IF ONLY YOU HAD THE MARKED STONES SPIRIT FATHER MADE FOR YOU... MAYBE THEN WE WOULD BE SAFER.
BUT WE DON'T, ANDO.
AND SECURITY IS ALWAYS A LIE. BETTER TO BE AFRAID. BETTER TO BE ALERT.
ROWF

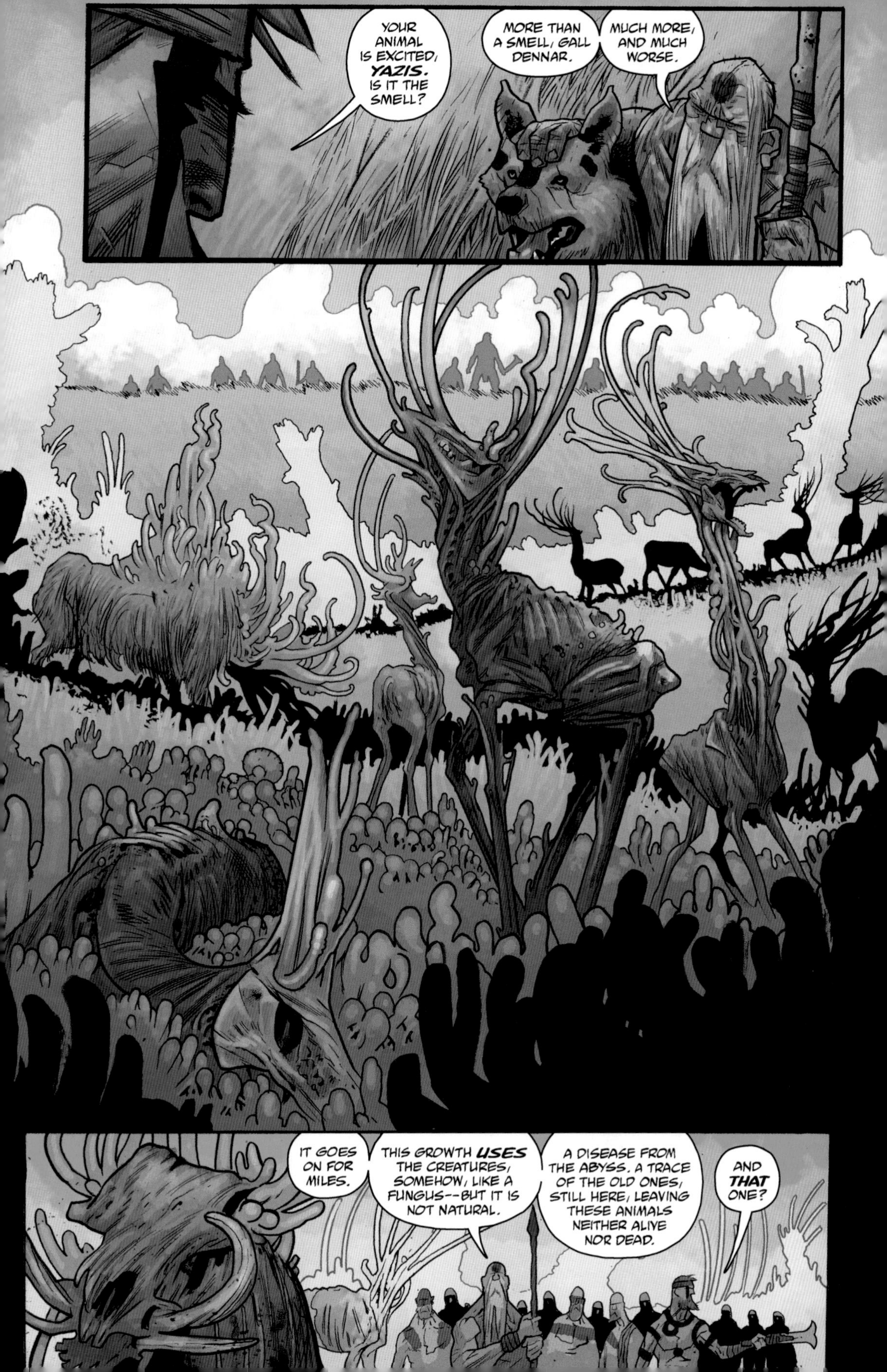
YOUR ANIMAL IS EXCITED, YAZIS. IS IT THE SMELL?
MORE THAN A SMELL, GALL DENNAR.
MUCH MORE, AND MUCH WORSE.
IT GOES ON FOR MILES.
THIS GROWTH USES THE CREATURES, SOMEHOW, LIKE A FUNGUS--BUT IT IS NOT NATURAL.
A DISEASE FROM THE ABYSS. A TRACE OF THE OLD ONES, STILL HERE, LEAVING THESE ANIMALS NEITHER ALIVE NOR DEAD.
AND THAT ONE?

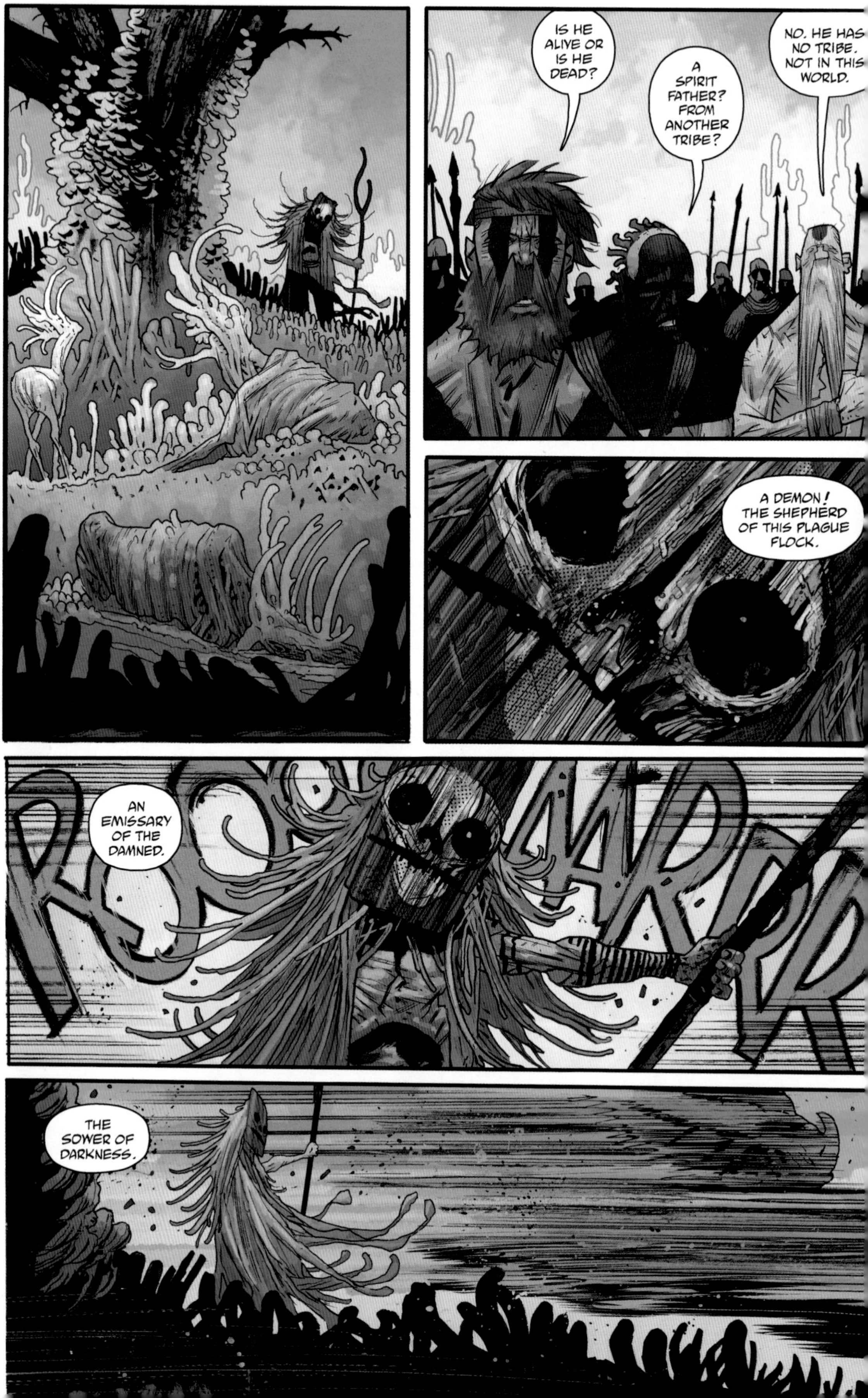
IS HE ALIVE OR IS HE DEAD?
A SPIRIT FATHER? FROM ANOTHER TRIBE?
NO. HE HAS NO TRIBE. NOT IN THIS WORLD.
A DEMON! THE SHEPHERD OF THIS PLAGUE FLOCK.
AN EMISSARY OF THE DAMNED.
THE SOWER OF DARKNESS.

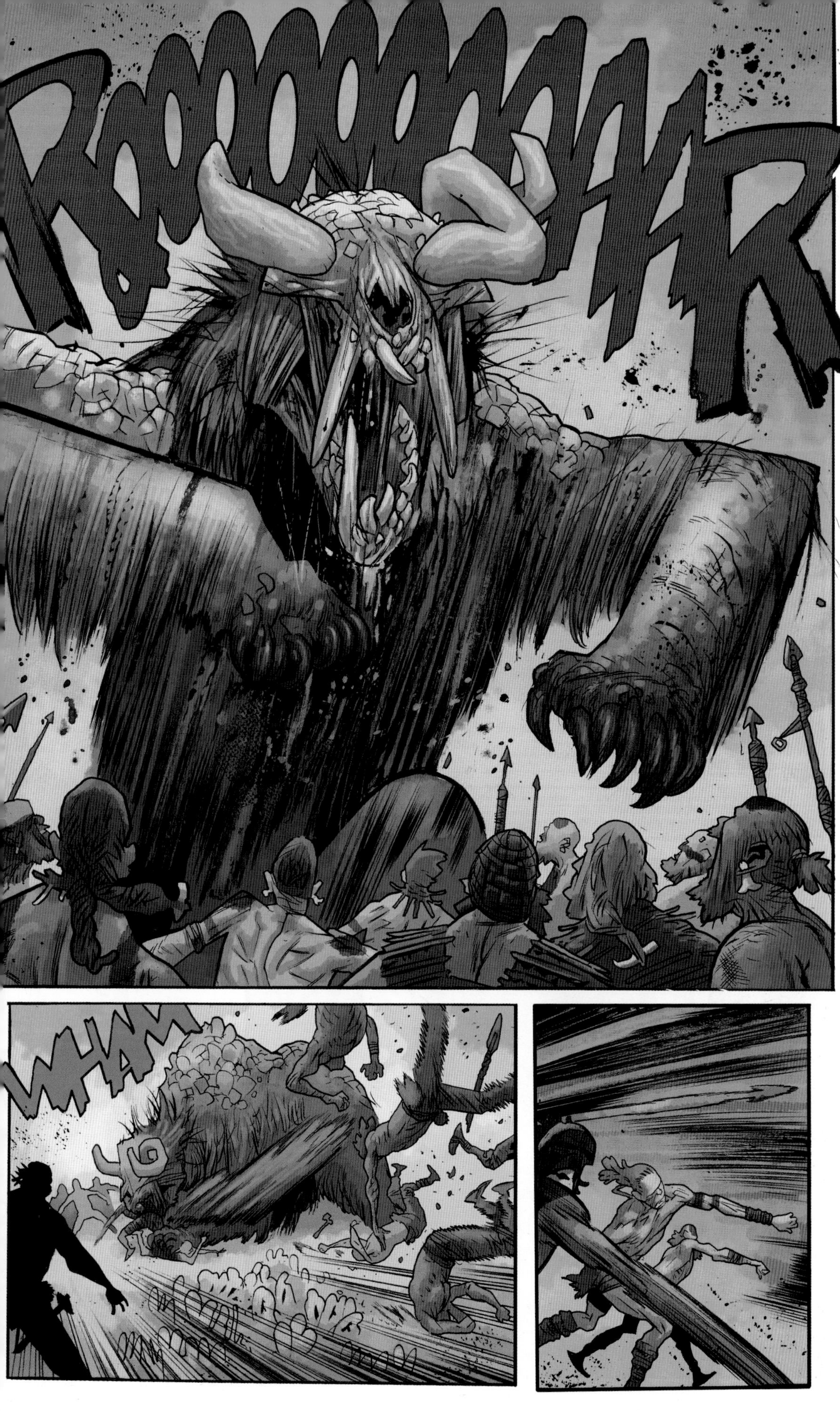
ROOOOOOOOAAR
WHAM

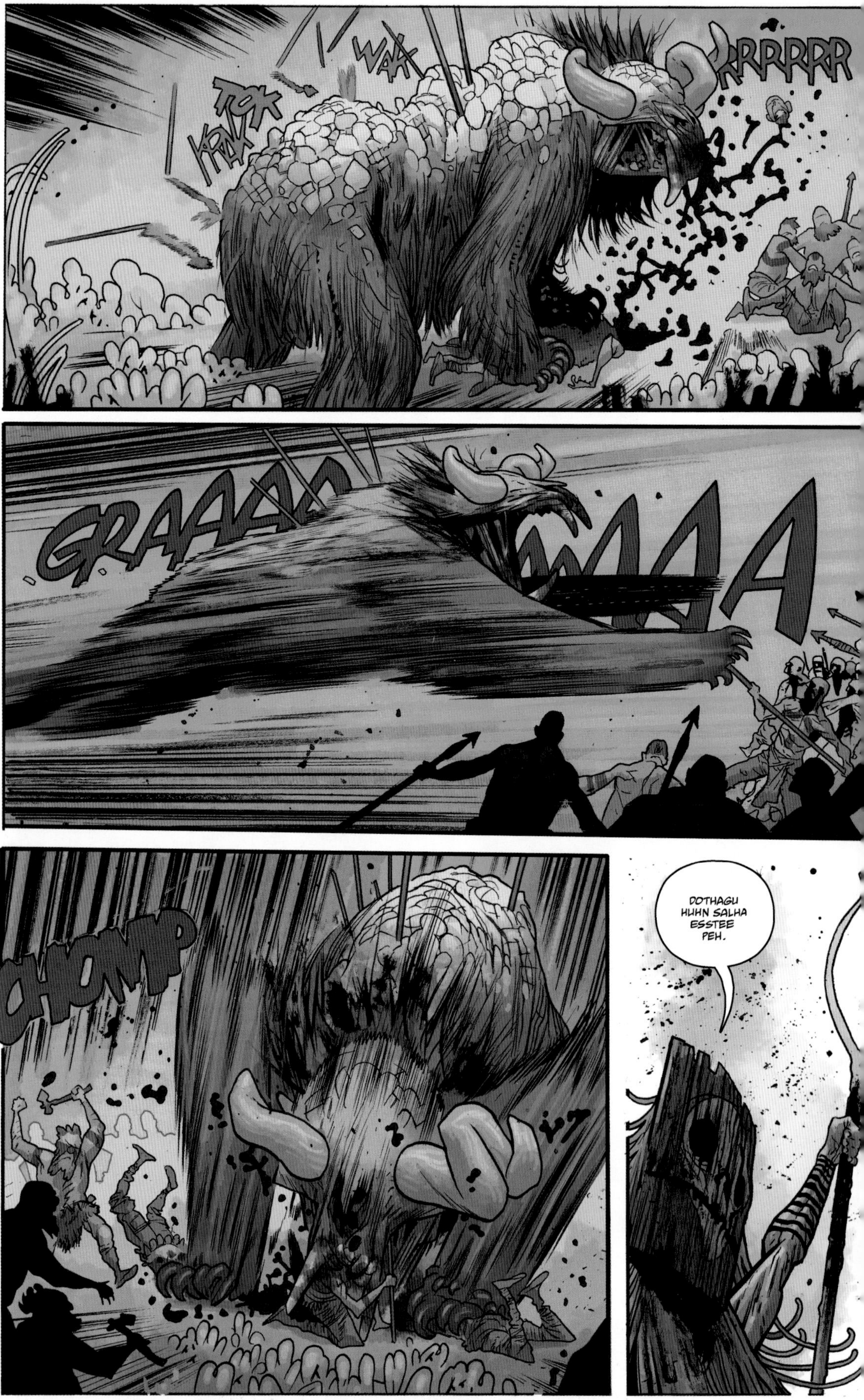

TOK
KRAK
WAK
RRRRRR
GRAAAAAAAAA
CHOMP
DOTHAGU HUHN SALHA ESSTEE PEH.

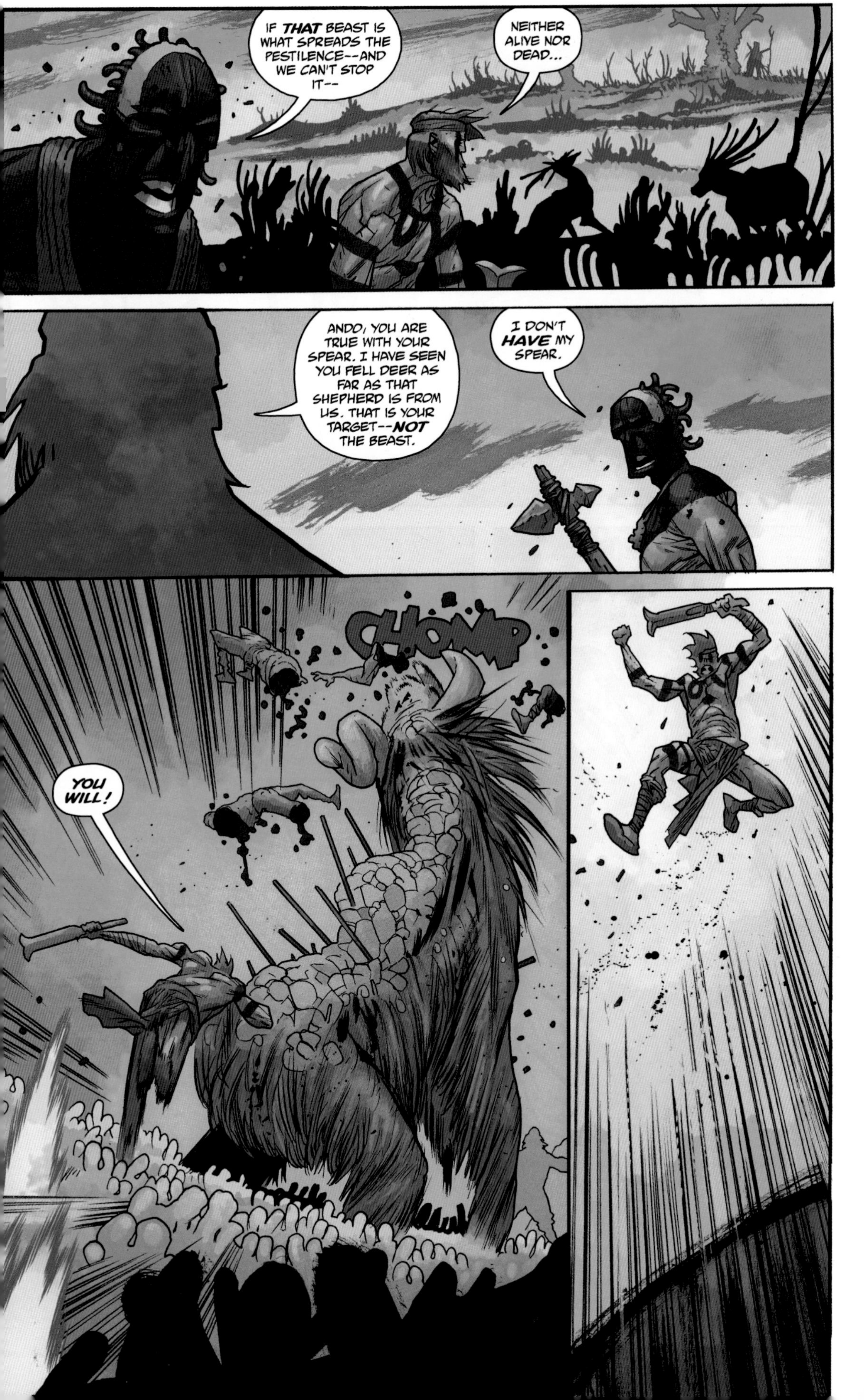

IF THAT BEAST IS WHAT SPREADS THE PESTILENCE--AND WE CAN'T STOP IT--
NEITHER ALIVE NOR DEAD...
ANDO, YOU ARE TRUE WITH YOUR SPEAR. I HAVE SEEN YOU FELL DEER AS FAR AS THAT SHEPHERD IS FROM US. THAT IS YOUR TARGET--NOT THE BEAST.
I DON'T HAVE MY SPEAR.
CHOMP
YOU WILL!

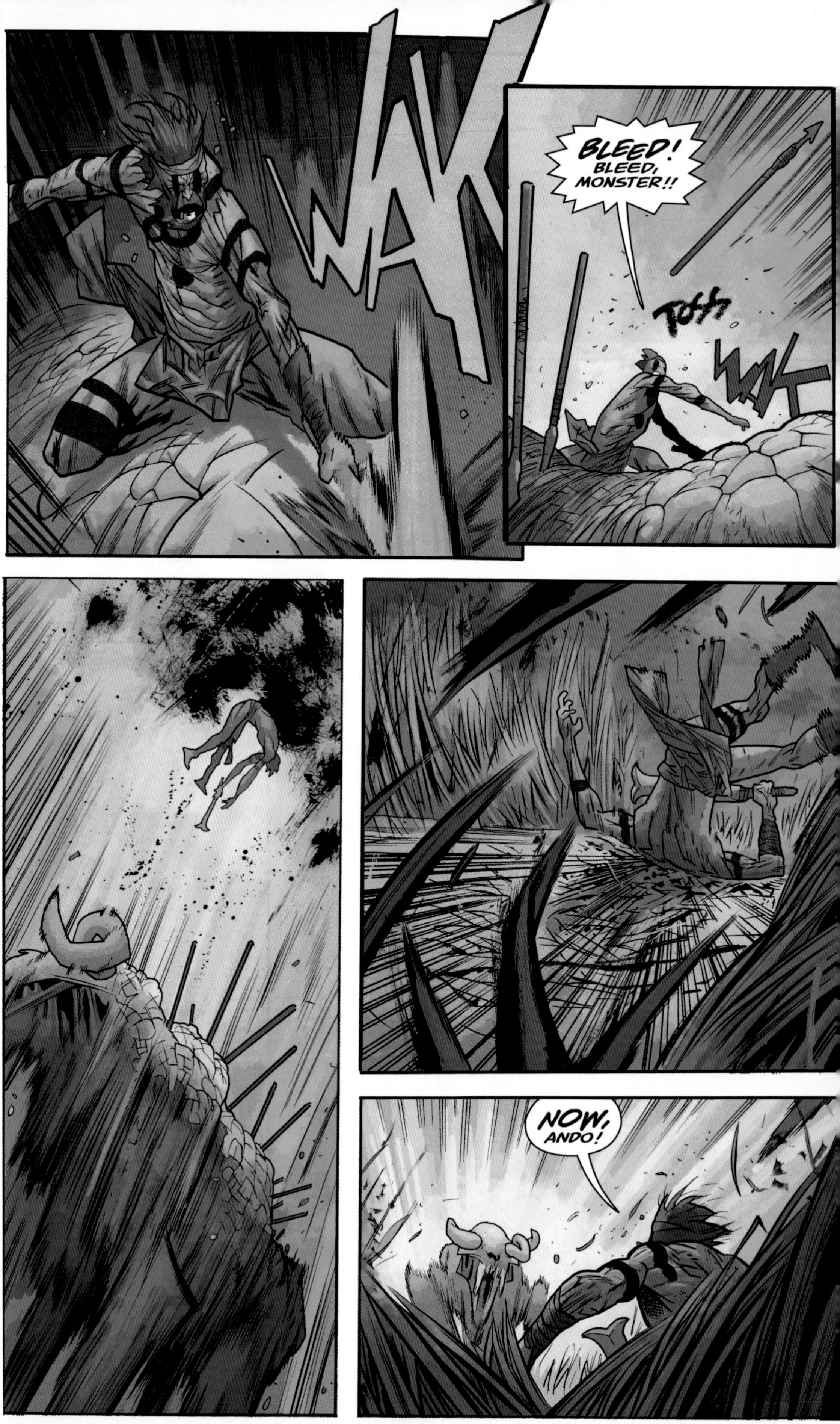
WAK
BLEED! BLEED, MONSTER!!
TOSS
WAK
NOW, ANDO!

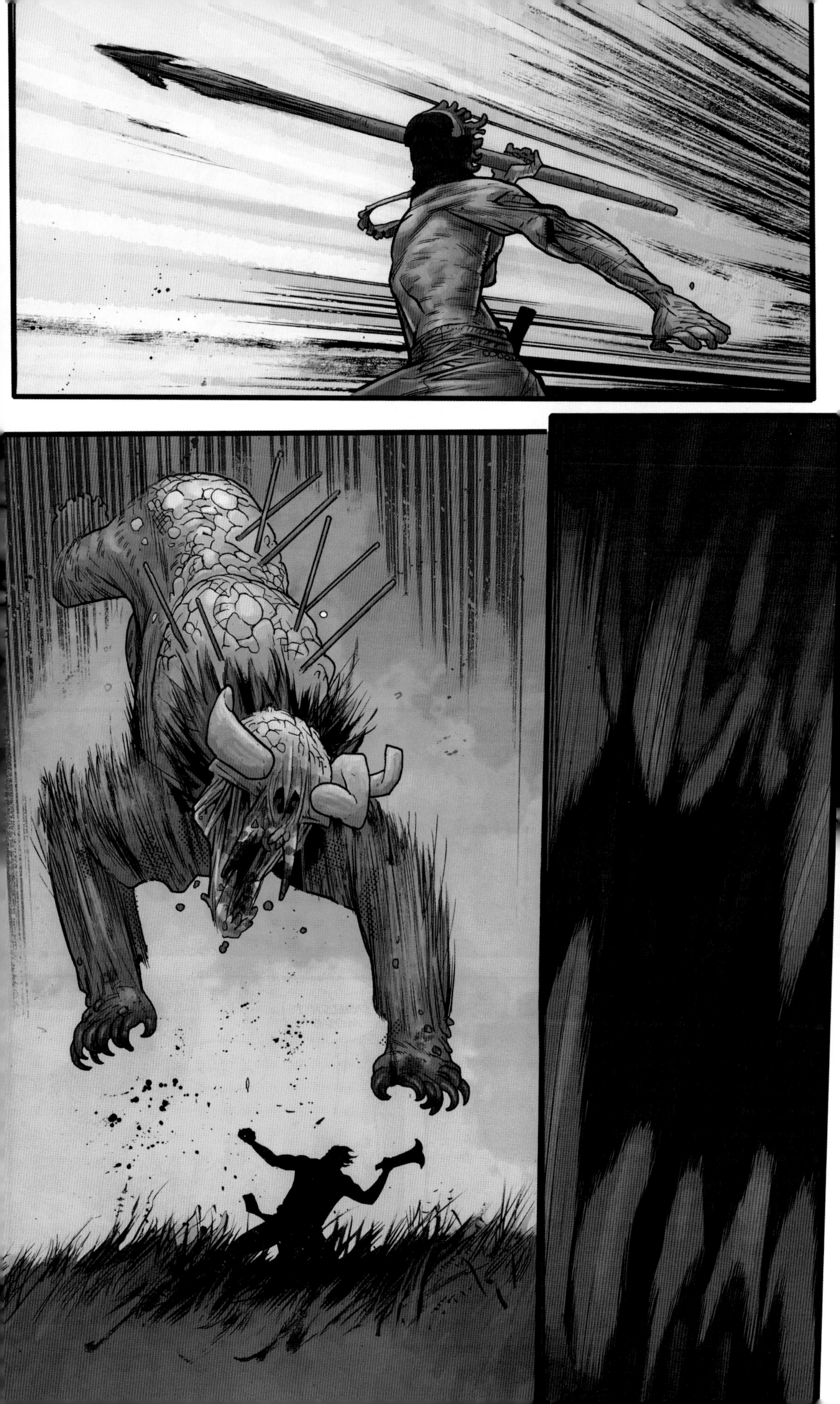

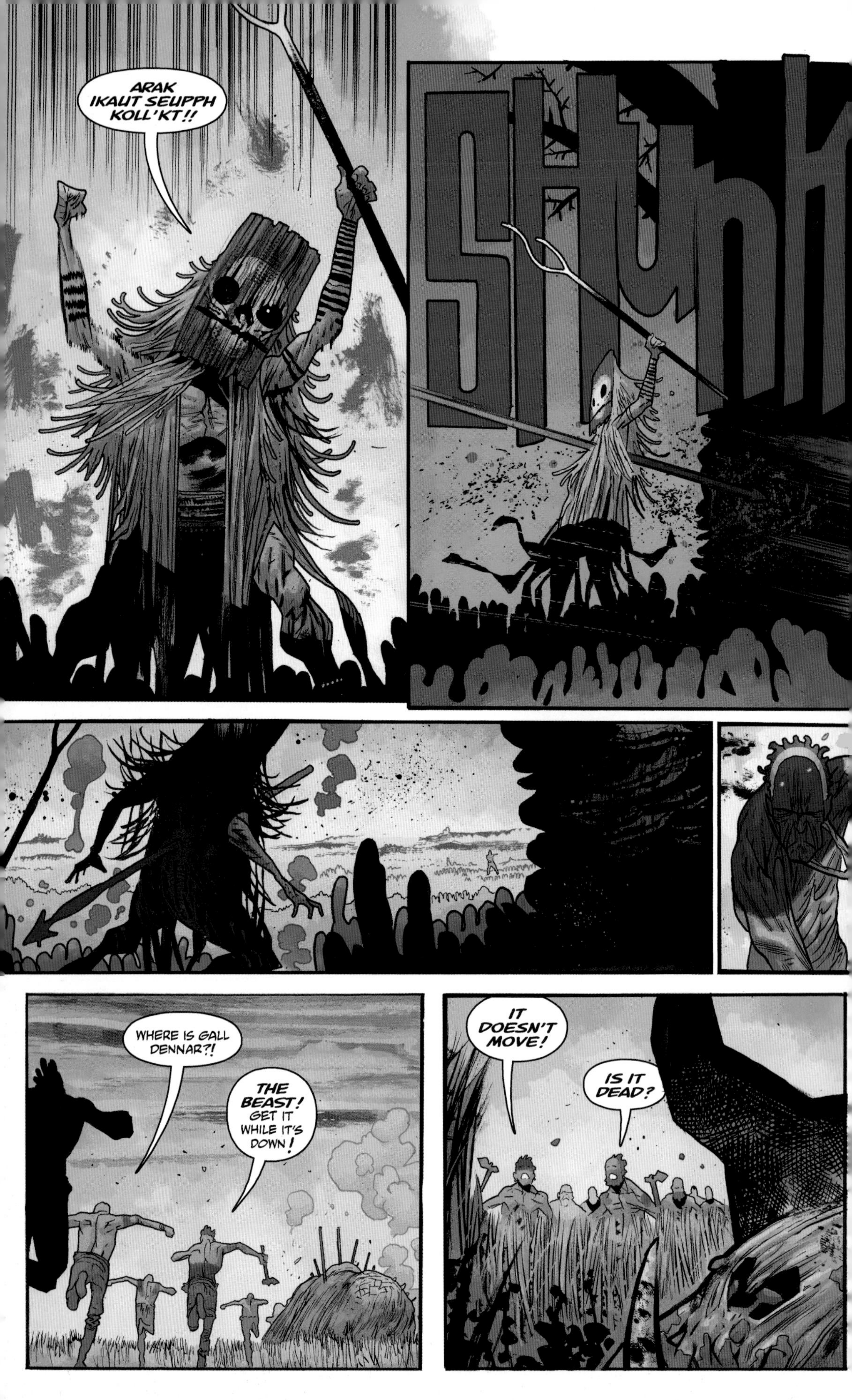

ARAK IKAUT SEUPPH KOLL'KT!!
WHERE IS GALL DENNAR?!
THE BEAST! GET IT WHILE IT'S DOWN!
IT DOESN'T MOVE!
IS IT DEAD?

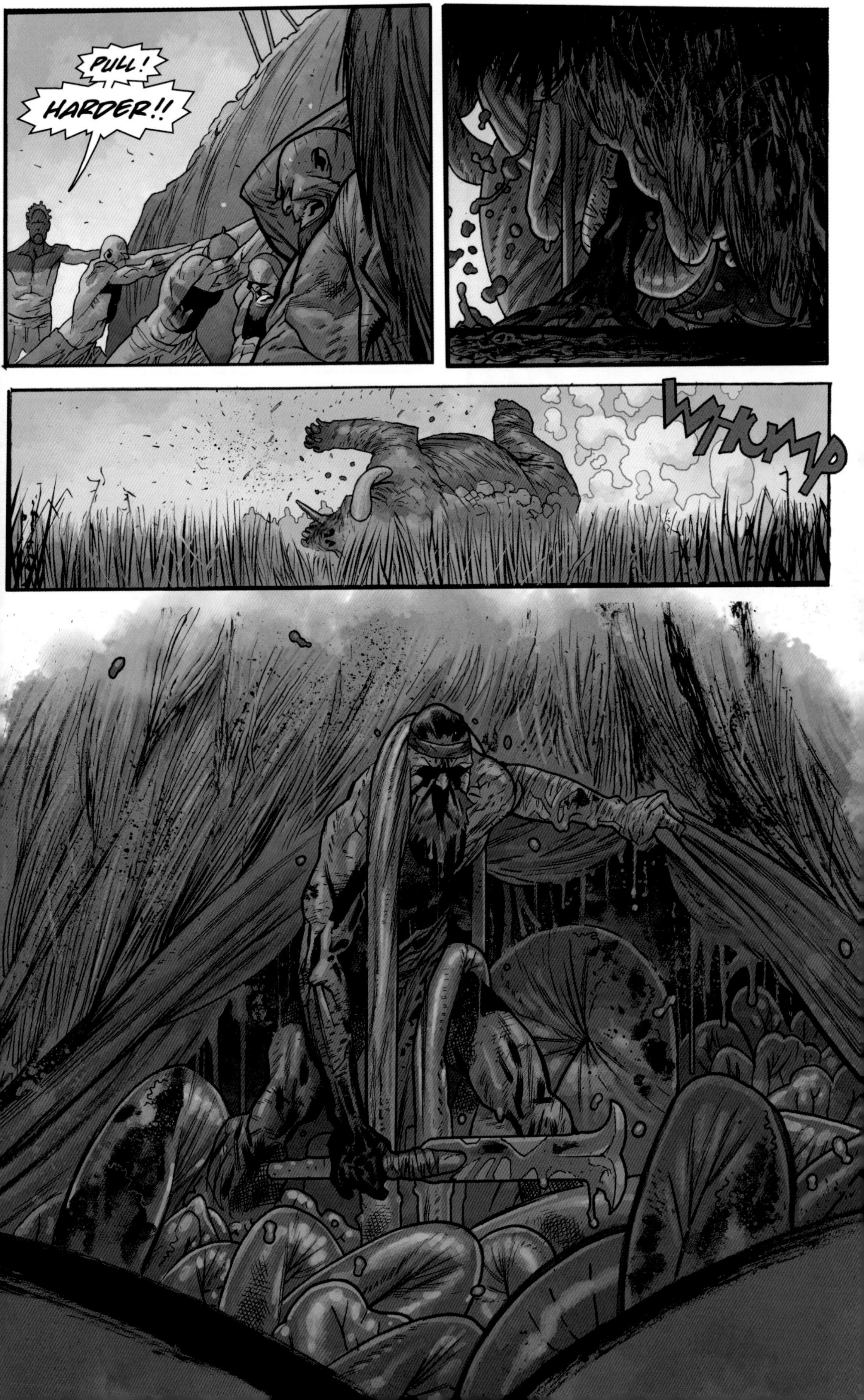
PULL!
HARDER!!
WHUMP

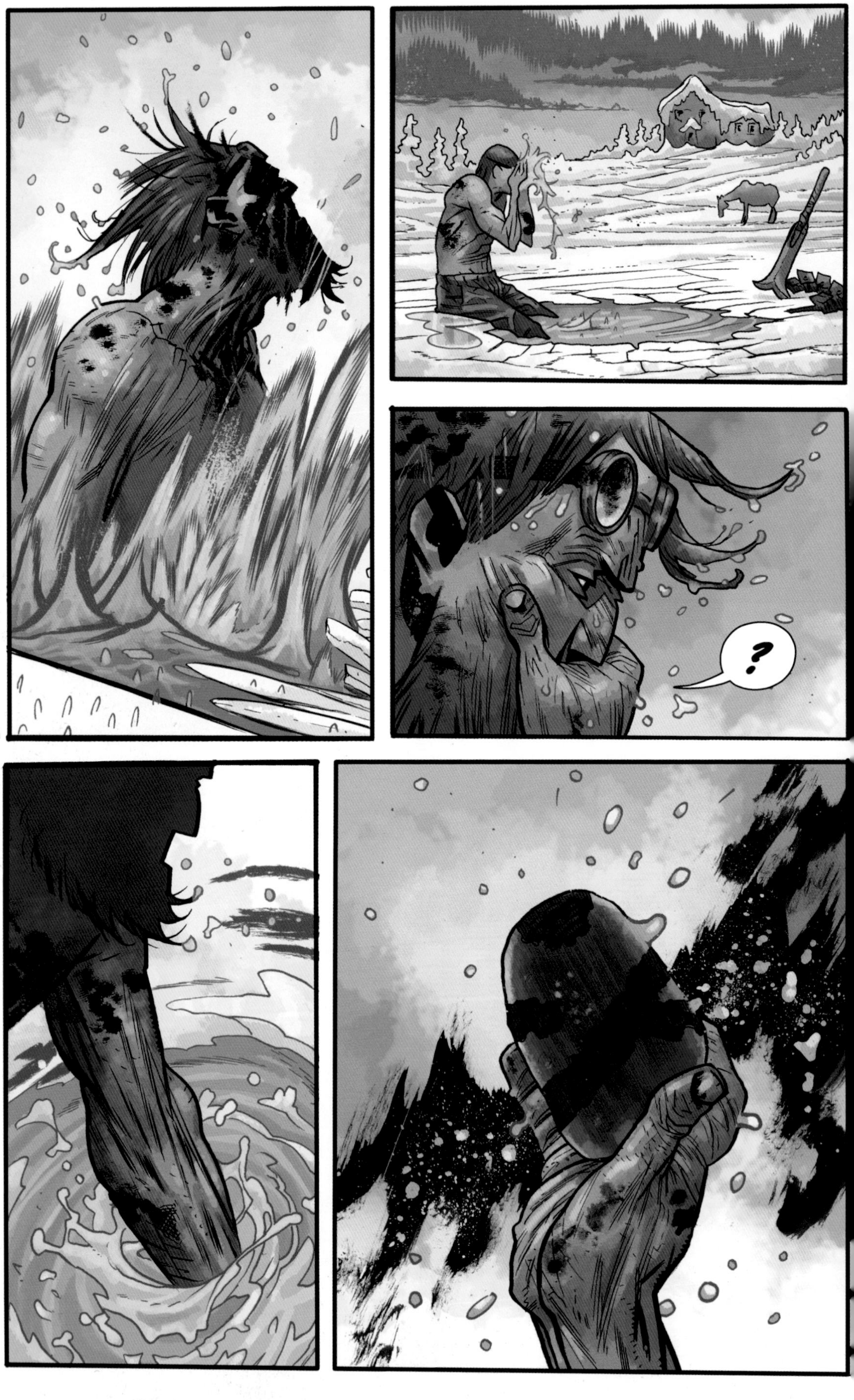
?

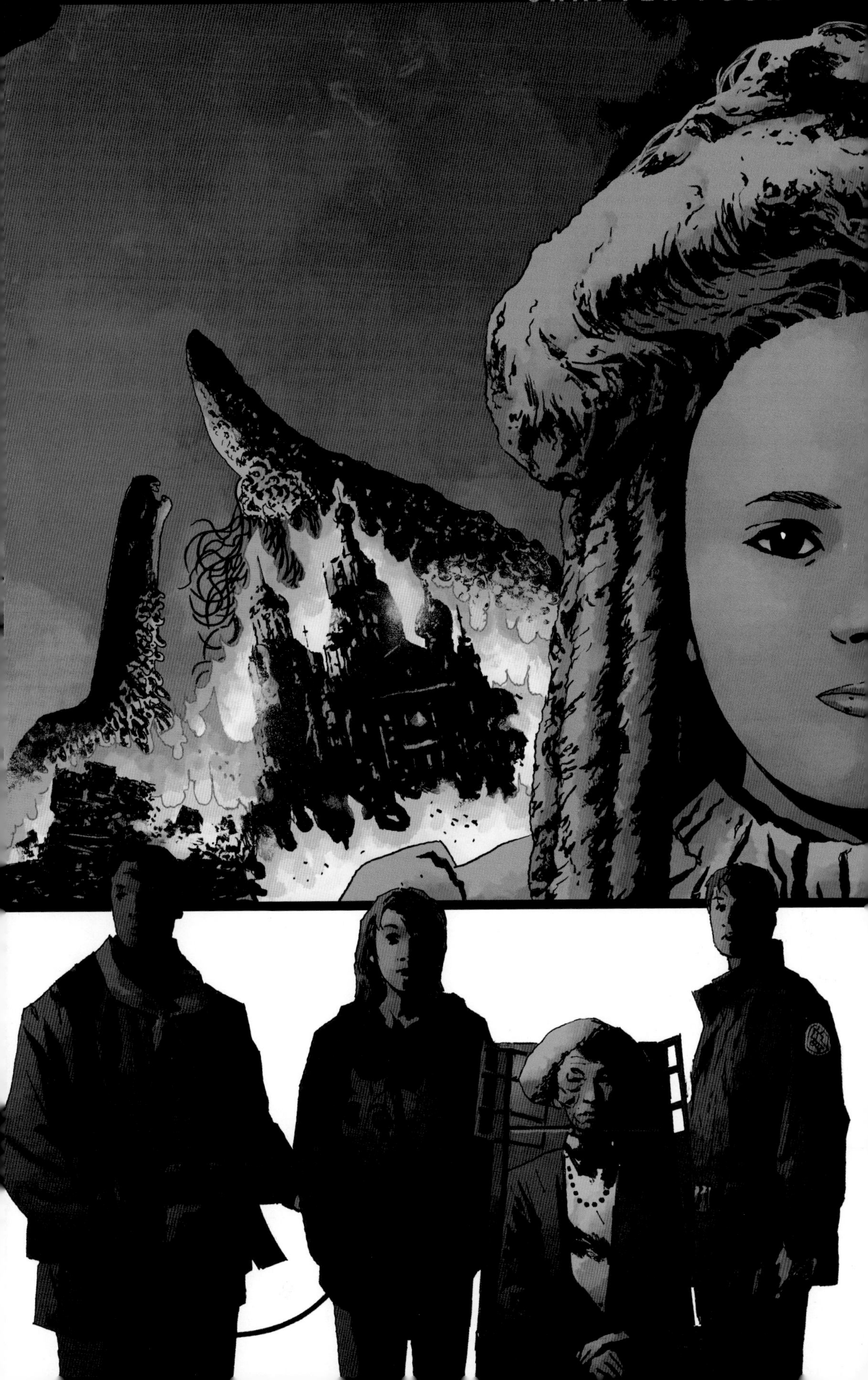

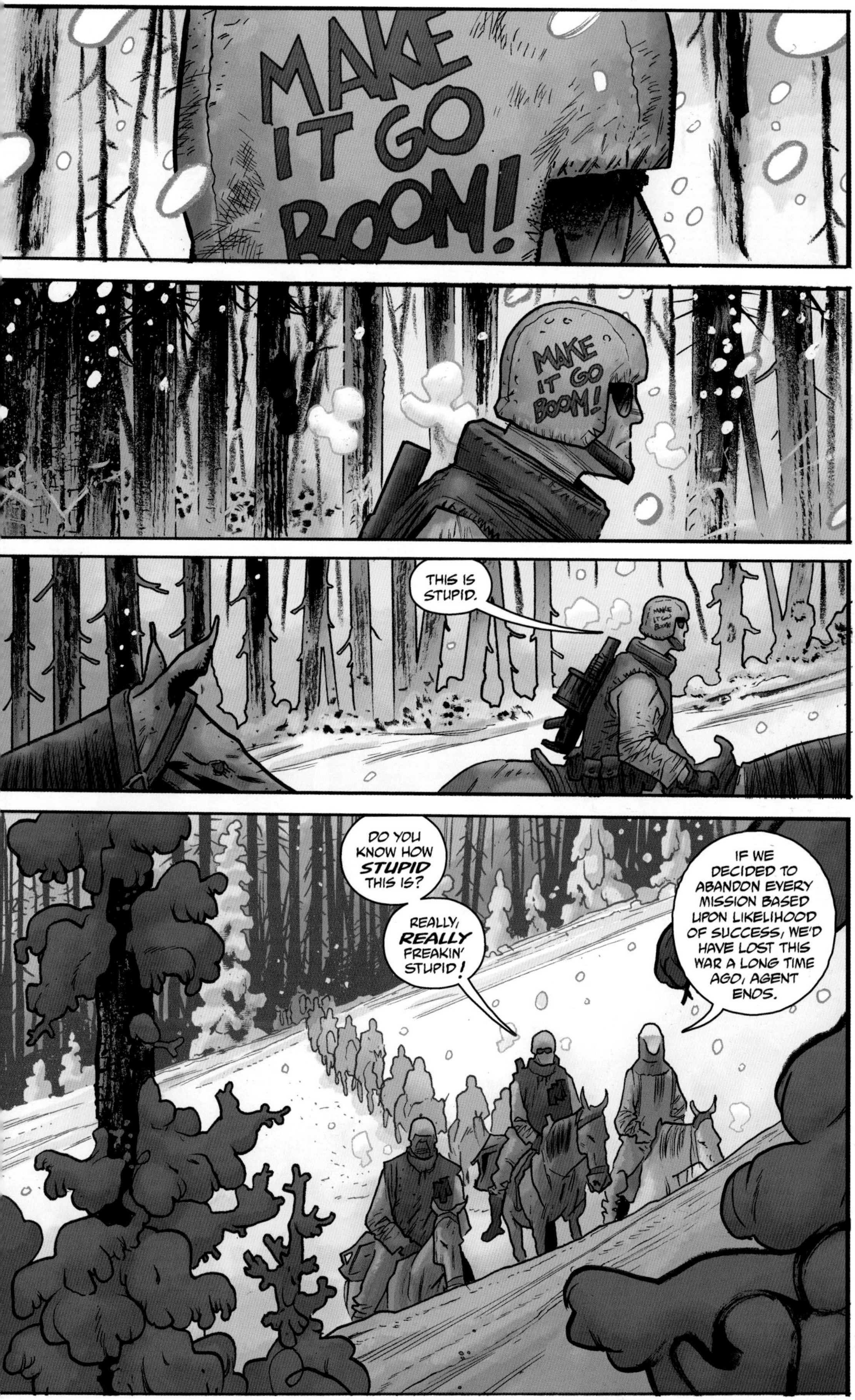
MAKE IT GO BOOM!
MAKE IT GO BOOM!
THIS IS STUPID.
DO YOU KNOW HOW STUPID THIS IS?
REALLY, REALLY FREAKIN' STUPID!
IF WE DECIDED TO ABANDON EVERY MISSION BASED UPON LIKELIHOOD OF SUCCESS, WE'D HAVE LOST THIS WAR A LONG TIME AGO, AGENT ENOS.

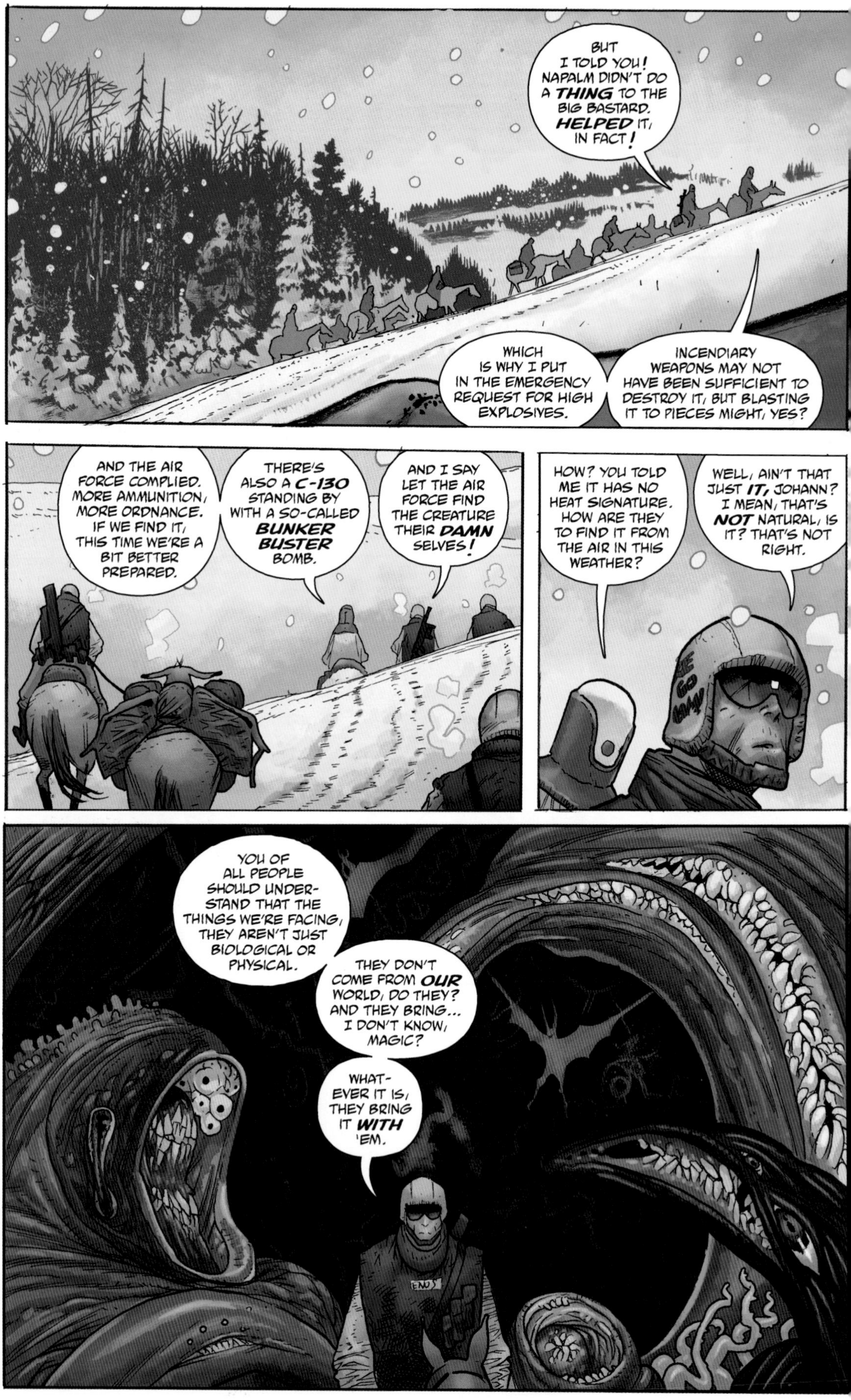
BUT I TOLD YOU! NAPALM DIDN'T DO A **THING** TO THE BIG BASTARD. **HELPED** IT, IN FACT!
WHICH IS WHY I PUT IN THE EMERGENCY REQUEST FOR HIGH EXPLOSIVES.
INCENDIARY WEAPONS MAY NOT HAVE BEEN SUFFICIENT TO DESTROY IT, BUT BLASTING IT TO PIECES MIGHT, YES?
AND THE AIR FORCE COMPLIED. MORE AMMUNITION, MORE ORDNANCE. IF WE FIND IT, THIS TIME WE'RE A BIT BETTER PREPARED.
THERE'S ALSO A **C-130** STANDING BY WITH A SO-CALLED **BUNKER BUSTER** BOMB.
AND I SAY LET THE AIR FORCE FIND THE CREATURE THEIR **DAMN** SELVES!
HOW? YOU TOLD ME IT HAS NO HEAT SIGNATURE. HOW ARE THEY TO FIND IT FROM THE AIR IN THIS WEATHER?
WELL, AIN'T THAT JUST **IT,** JOHANN? I MEAN, THAT'S **NOT** NATURAL, IS IT? THAT'S NOT RIGHT.
YOU OF ALL PEOPLE SHOULD UNDER-STAND THAT THE THINGS WE'RE FACING, THEY AREN'T JUST BIOLOGICAL OR PHYSICAL.
THEY DON'T COME FROM **OUR** WORLD, DO THEY? AND THEY BRING... I DON'T KNOW, MAGIC?
WHAT-EVER IT IS, THEY BRING IT **WITH** 'EM.

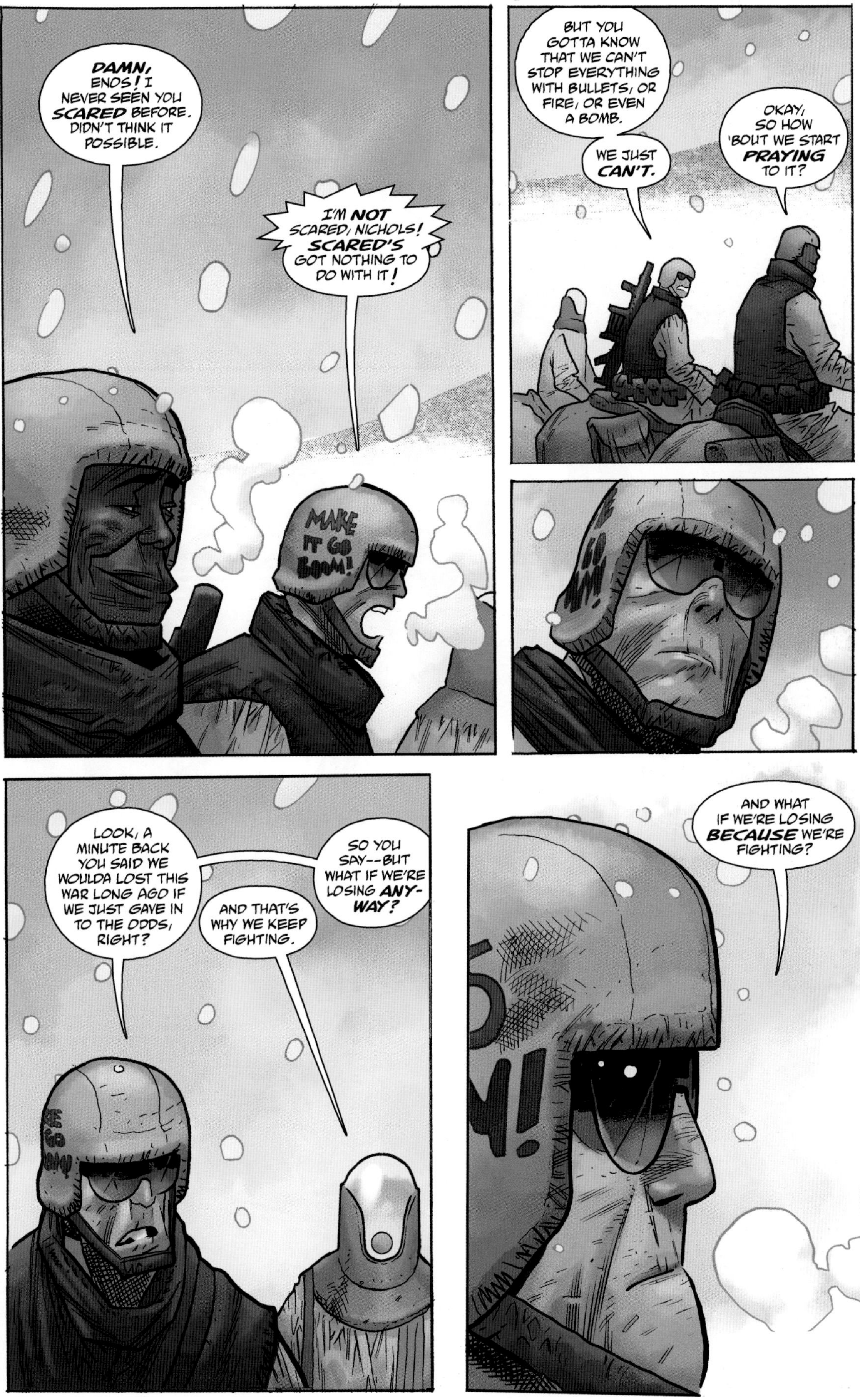
DAMN, ENOS! I NEVER SEEN YOU SCARED BEFORE. DIDN'T THINK IT POSSIBLE.
I'M NOT SCARED, NICHOLS! SCARED'S GOT NOTHING TO DO WITH IT!
MAKE IT GO BOOM!
BUT YOU GOTTA KNOW THAT WE CAN'T STOP EVERYTHING WITH BULLETS, OR FIRE, OR EVEN A BOMB.
WE JUST CAN'T.
OKAY, SO HOW 'BOUT WE START PRAYING TO IT?
LOOK, A MINUTE BACK YOU SAID WE WOULDA LOST THIS WAR LONG AGO IF WE JUST GAVE IN TO THE ODDS, RIGHT?
AND THAT'S WHY WE KEEP FIGHTING.
SO YOU SAY--BUT WHAT IF WE'RE LOSING ANYWAY?
AND WHAT IF WE'RE LOSING BECAUSE WE'RE FIGHTING?

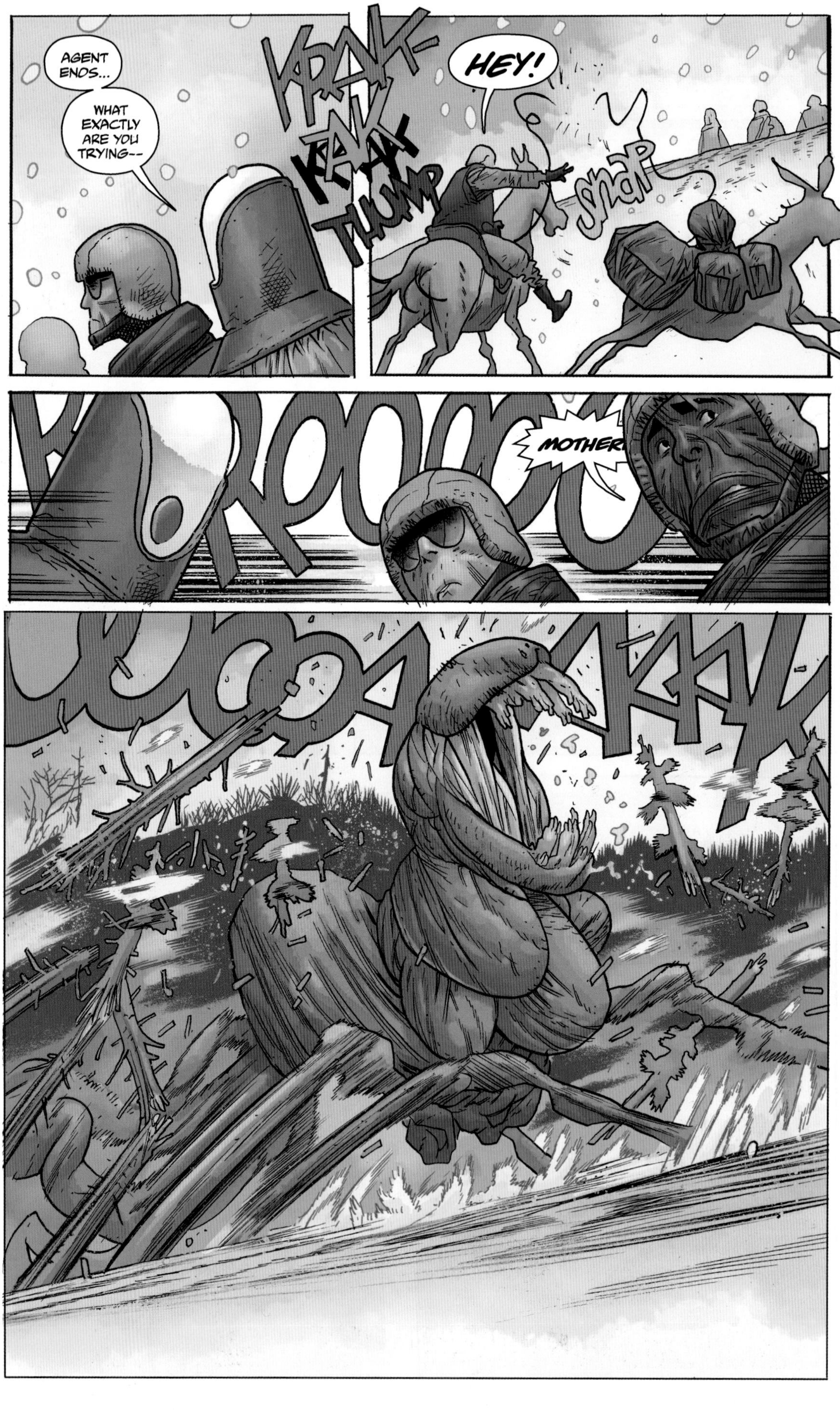
AGENT ENOS...
WHAT EXACTLY ARE YOU TRYING--
KRAK-KAK
KRAK
THUMP
HEY!
SNAP
MOTHER!
KAK

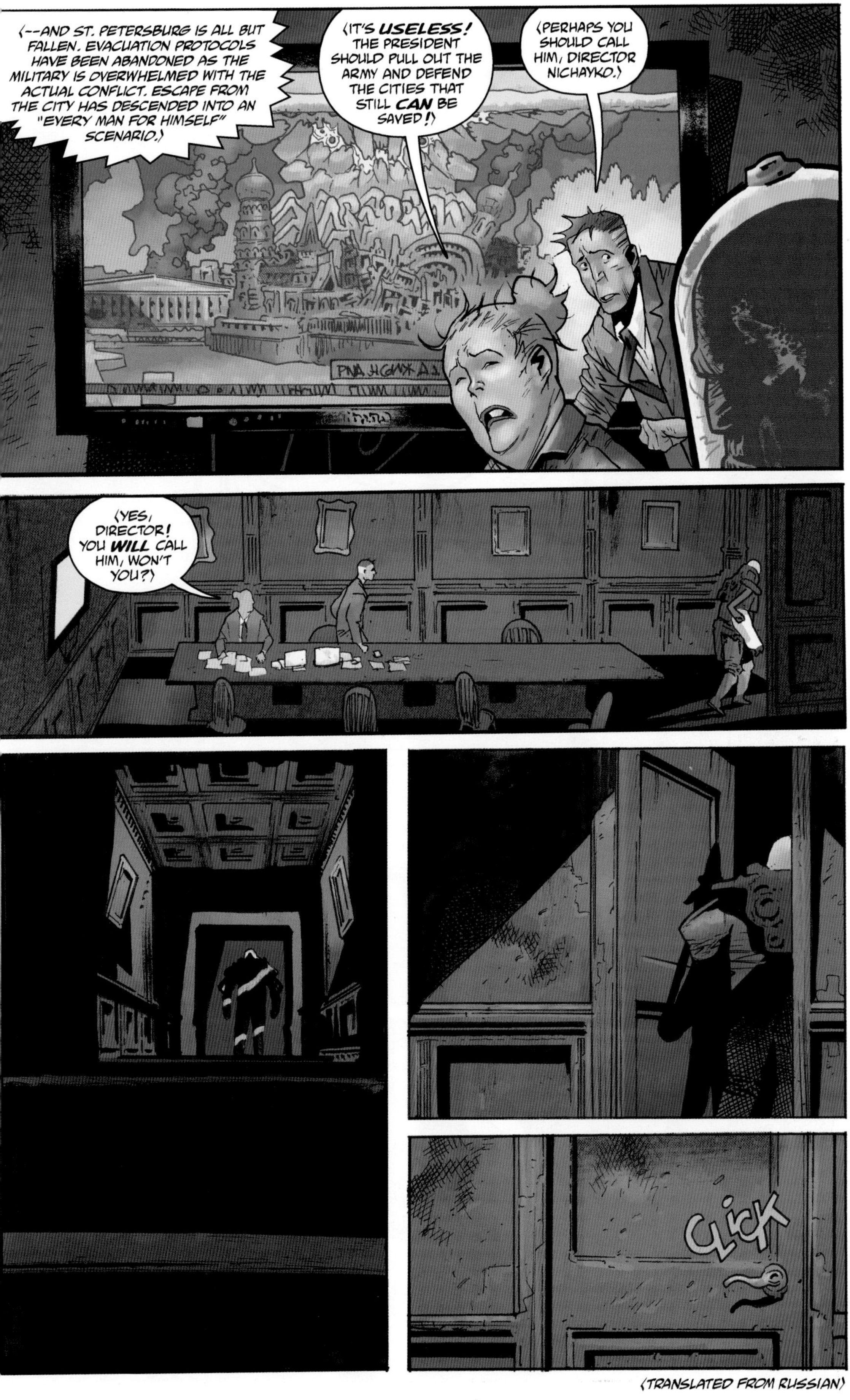

⟨--AND ST. PETERSBURG IS ALL BUT FALLEN. EVACUATION PROTOCOLS HAVE BEEN ABANDONED AS THE MILITARY IS OVERWHELMED WITH THE ACTUAL CONFLICT. ESCAPE FROM THE CITY HAS DESCENDED INTO AN "EVERY MAN FOR HIMSELF" SCENARIO.⟩
⟨IT'S **USELESS!** THE PRESIDENT SHOULD PULL OUT THE ARMY AND DEFEND THE CITIES THAT STILL **CAN** BE SAVED!⟩
⟨PERHAPS YOU SHOULD CALL HIM, DIRECTOR NICHAYKO.⟩
⟨YES, DIRECTOR! YOU **WILL** CALL HIM, WON'T YOU?⟩
CLICK

⟨TRANSLATED FROM RUSSIAN⟩

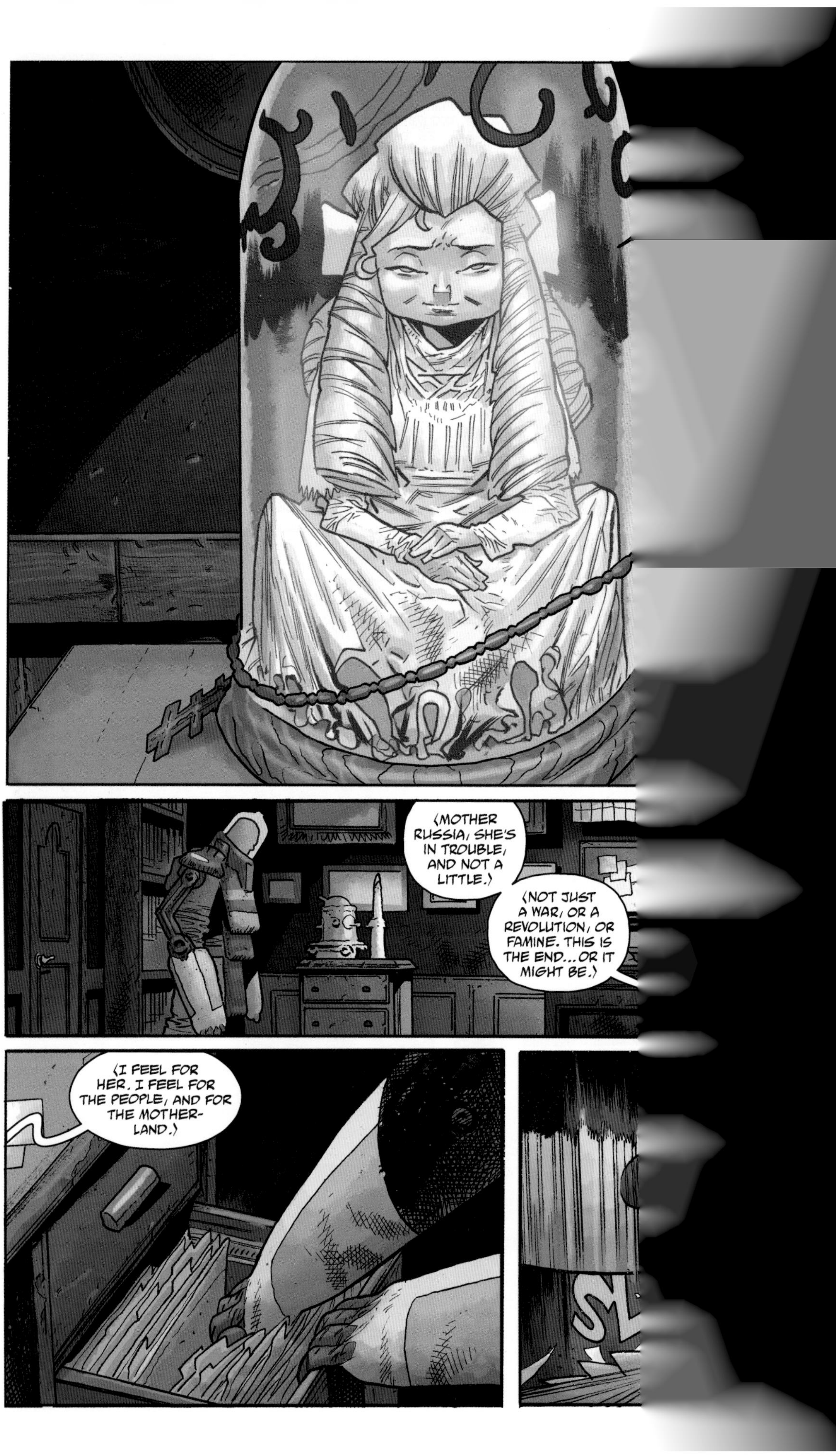
‹MOTHER RUSSIA, SHE'S IN TROUBLE, AND NOT A LITTLE.›
‹NOT JUST A WAR, OR A REVOLUTION, OR FAMINE. THIS IS THE END... OR IT MIGHT BE.›
‹I FEEL FOR HER. I FEEL FOR THE PEOPLE, AND FOR THE MOTHER-LAND.›

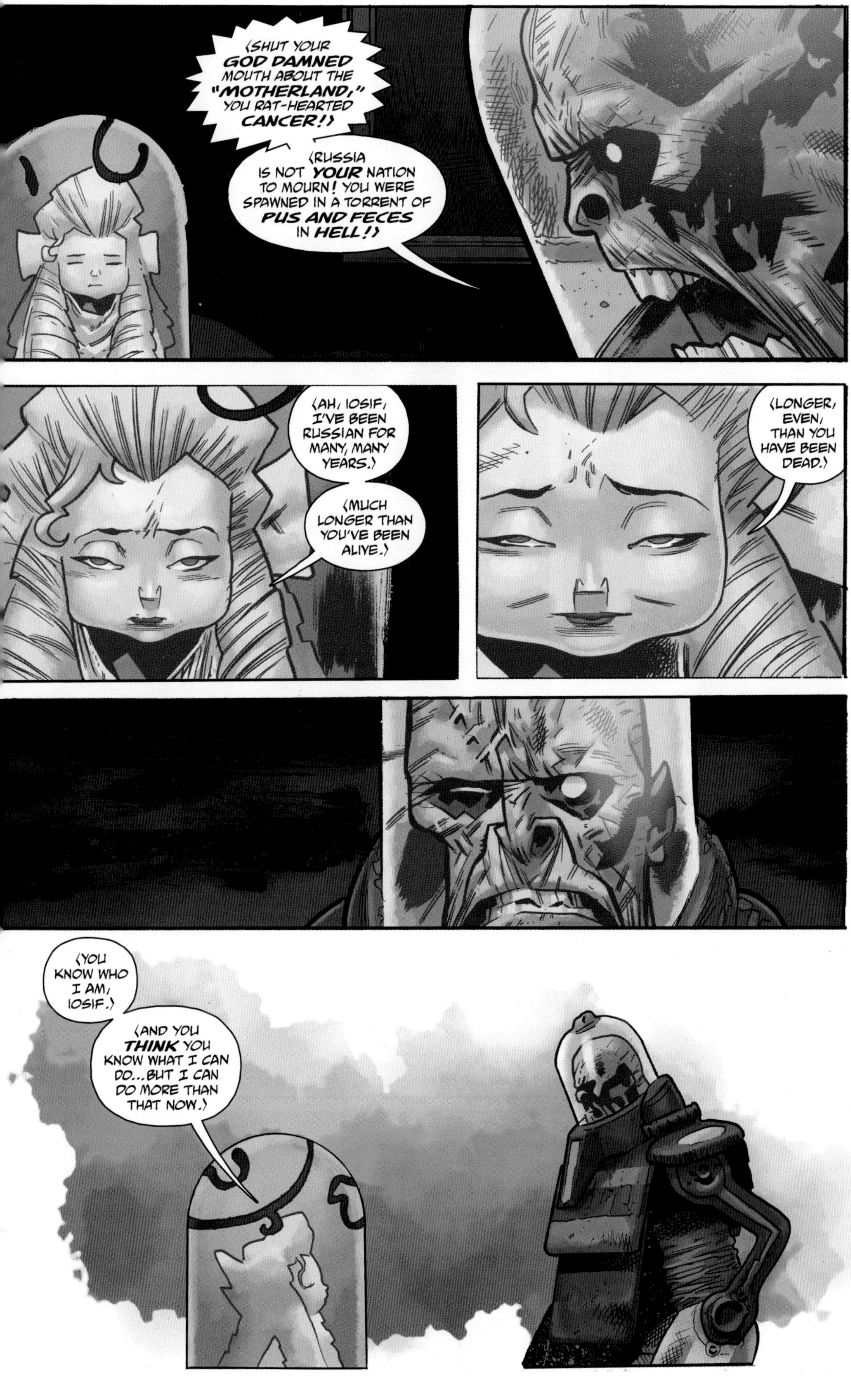
⟨SHUT YOUR GOD DAMNED MOUTH ABOUT THE "MOTHERLAND," YOU RAT-HEARTED CANCER!⟩
⟨RUSSIA IS NOT YOUR NATION TO MOURN! YOU WERE SPAWNED IN A TORRENT OF PUS AND FECES IN HELL!⟩
⟨AH, IOSIF, I'VE BEEN RUSSIAN FOR MANY, MANY YEARS.⟩
⟨MUCH LONGER THAN YOU'VE BEEN ALIVE.⟩
⟨LONGER, EVEN, THAN YOU HAVE BEEN DEAD.⟩
⟨YOU KNOW WHO I AM, IOSIF.⟩
⟨AND YOU THINK YOU KNOW WHAT I CAN DO...BUT I CAN DO MORE THAN THAT NOW.⟩

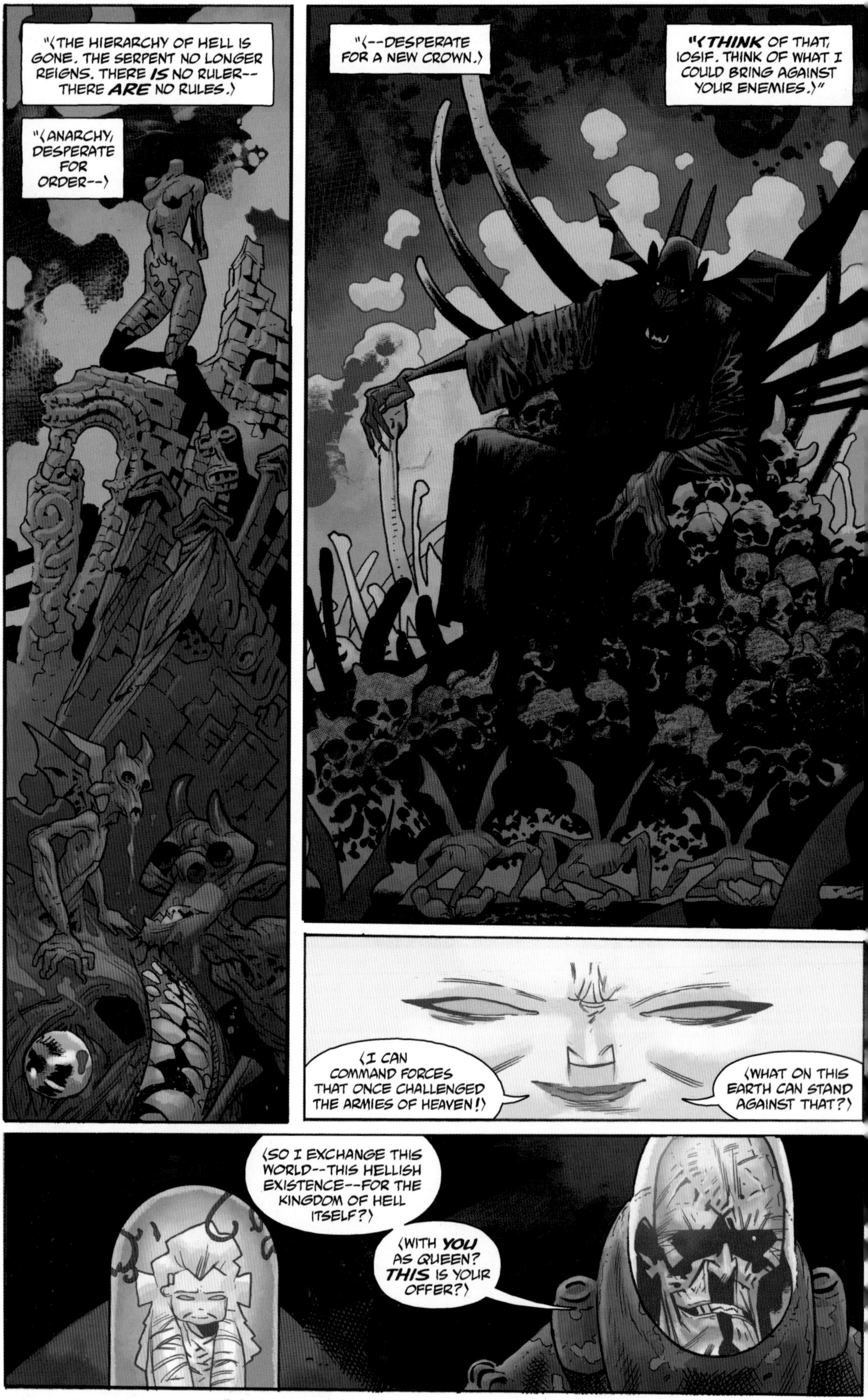
"⟨THE HIERARCHY OF HELL IS GONE. THE SERPENT NO LONGER REIGNS. THERE IS NO RULER-- THERE ARE NO RULES.⟩
"⟨ANARCHY, DESPERATE FOR ORDER--⟩
"⟨--DESPERATE FOR A NEW CROWN.⟩
"⟨THINK OF THAT, IOSIF. THINK OF WHAT I COULD BRING AGAINST YOUR ENEMIES.⟩"
⟨I CAN COMMAND FORCES THAT ONCE CHALLENGED THE ARMIES OF HEAVEN!⟩
⟨WHAT ON THIS EARTH CAN STAND AGAINST THAT?⟩
⟨SO I EXCHANGE THIS WORLD--THIS HELLISH EXISTENCE--FOR THE KINGDOM OF HELL ITSELF?⟩
⟨WITH YOU AS QUEEN? THIS IS YOUR OFFER?⟩

⟨YOU THINK I WOULD HURT THE HUMANS, IS THAT IT? I *LIKE* THEM! THEY'RE FUNNY.⟩

⟨*ALIVE* THEY ARE FUNNY. DEAD, SO DREARY, SO SERIOUS. I WANT NO MORE OF HELL, OF LOST SOULS MOURNING THEM-SELVES.⟩

⟨THIS IS *FOOLISH!* YOU TALK OF YOUR "POWER"?⟩

⟨ALL WHILE YOU ARE STUCK UNDER A JAR LIKE A HEAP OF PICKLE SALAD?⟩

ting ting

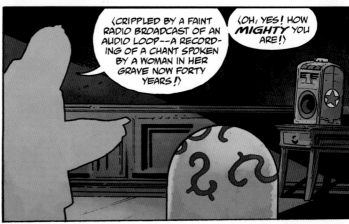

⟨CRIPPLED BY A FAINT RADIO BROADCAST OF AN AUDIO LOOP--A RECORD-ING OF A CHANT SPOKEN BY A WOMAN IN HER GRAVE NOW FORTY YEARS!⟩

⟨OH, YES! HOW *MIGHTY* YOU ARE!⟩

⟨WHATEVER THIS NEW HELL IS, *YOU'LL* BE NO *ROYALTY* IN IT.⟩

⟨YOU WILL VANISH IN THE INFERNO! YOU WILL MELT AWAY IN AN INSTANT, LITTLE SNOWBALL!⟩

⟨I RELEASE YOU...THERE IS ONLY *ONE* THING I CAN TRUST YOU TO DO.⟩

⟨ONLY *ONE* CHILD OF GOD FOR WHOM ALL THIS SUFFERING WILL END.⟩

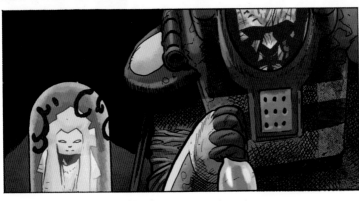

‹LORD *JESUS!* IF I COULD JUST HAVE A *DRINK!*›

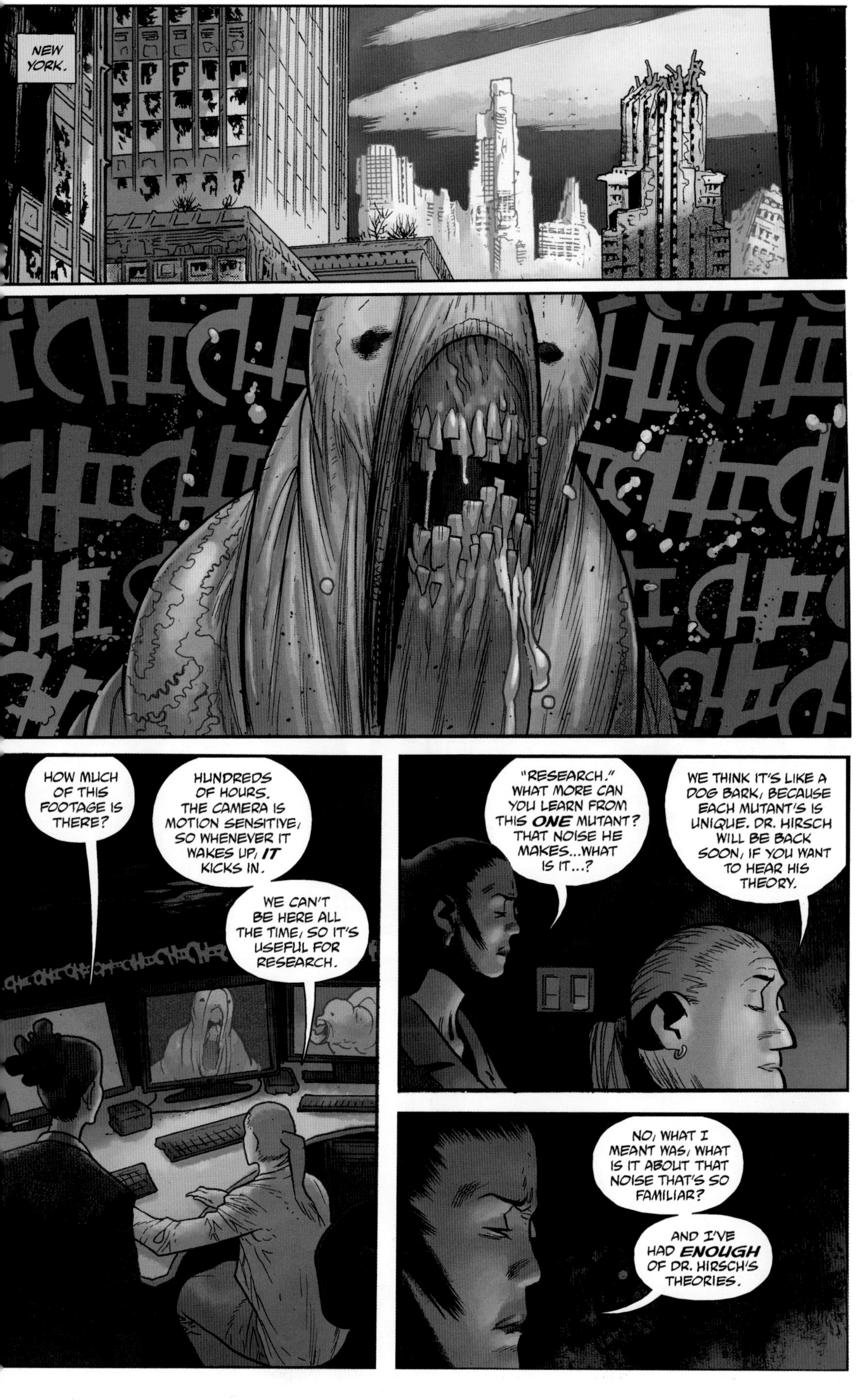
NEW YORK.
HOW MUCH OF THIS FOOTAGE IS THERE?
HUNDREDS OF HOURS. THE CAMERA IS MOTION SENSITIVE, SO WHENEVER IT WAKES UP, *IT* KICKS IN.
WE CAN'T BE HERE ALL THE TIME, SO IT'S USEFUL FOR RESEARCH.
"RESEARCH." WHAT MORE CAN YOU LEARN FROM THIS *ONE* MUTANT? THAT NOISE HE MAKES...WHAT IS IT...?
WE THINK IT'S LIKE A DOG BARK, BECAUSE EACH MUTANT'S IS UNIQUE. DR. HIRSCH WILL BE BACK SOON, IF YOU WANT TO HEAR HIS THEORY.
NO, WHAT I MEANT WAS, WHAT IS IT ABOUT THAT NOISE THAT'S SO FAMILIAR?
AND I'VE HAD *ENOUGH* OF DR. HIRSCH'S THEORIES.

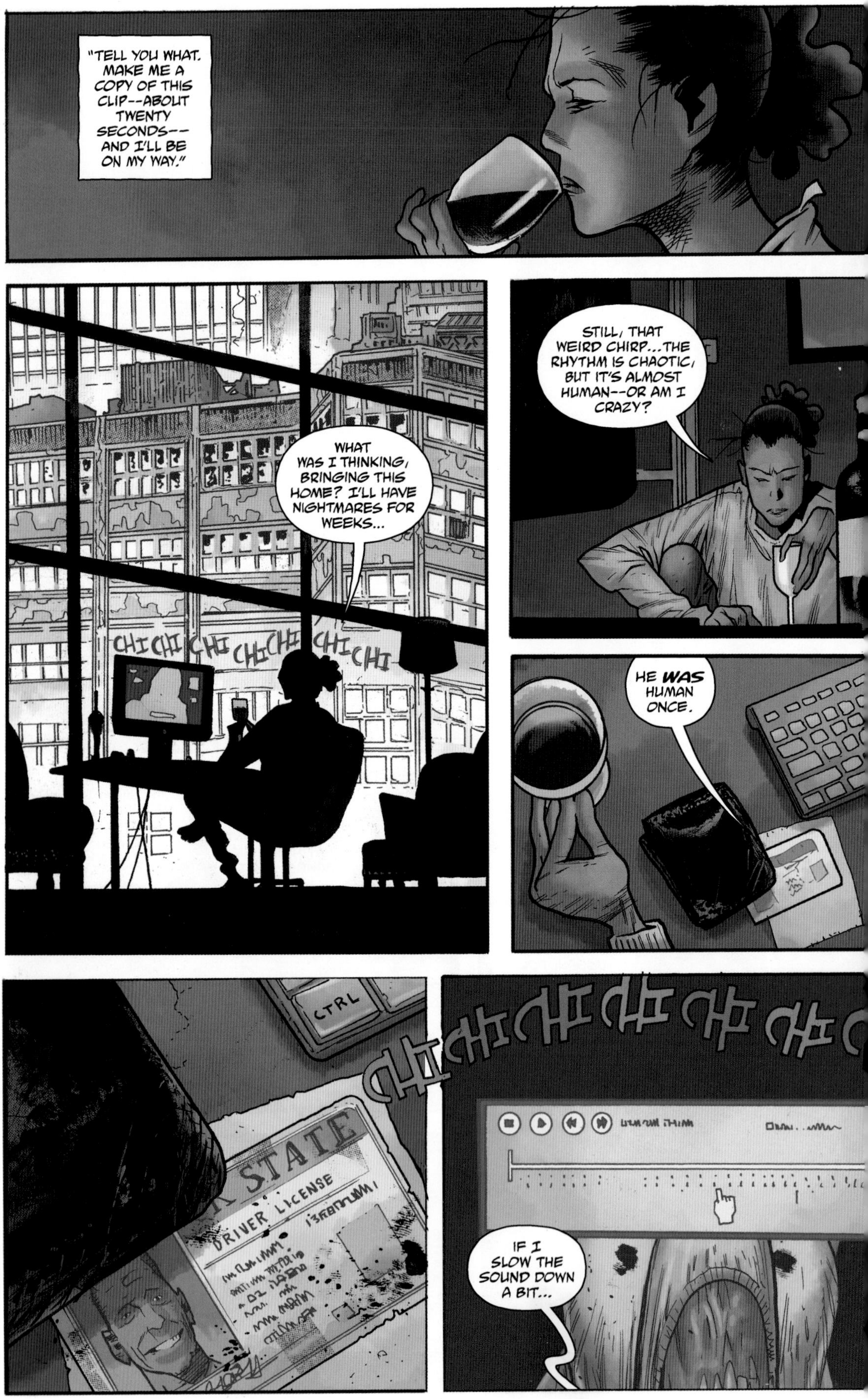
"TELL YOU WHAT. MAKE ME A COPY OF THIS CLIP--ABOUT TWENTY SECONDS--AND I'LL BE ON MY WAY."
WHAT WAS I THINKING, BRINGING THIS HOME? I'LL HAVE NIGHTMARES FOR WEEKS...
CHICHI CHICHI CHICHI CHICHI
STILL, THAT WEIRD CHIRP...THE RHYTHM IS CHAOTIC, BUT IT'S ALMOST HUMAN--OR AM I CRAZY?
HE *WAS* HUMAN ONCE.
CTRL
STATE
DRIVER LICENSE
CHICHICHICHICHICHICHICHICHI
IF I SLOW THE SOUND DOWN A BIT...

CHI CHI CHI CHI CHI CHI

Uh-uh. STILL GIBBERISH.

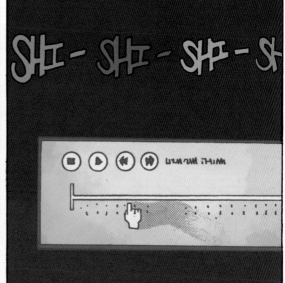

SHI – SHI – SHI – S

SHILL... SHILL SHILL...

JI... JILL...

JILL...

JILL...

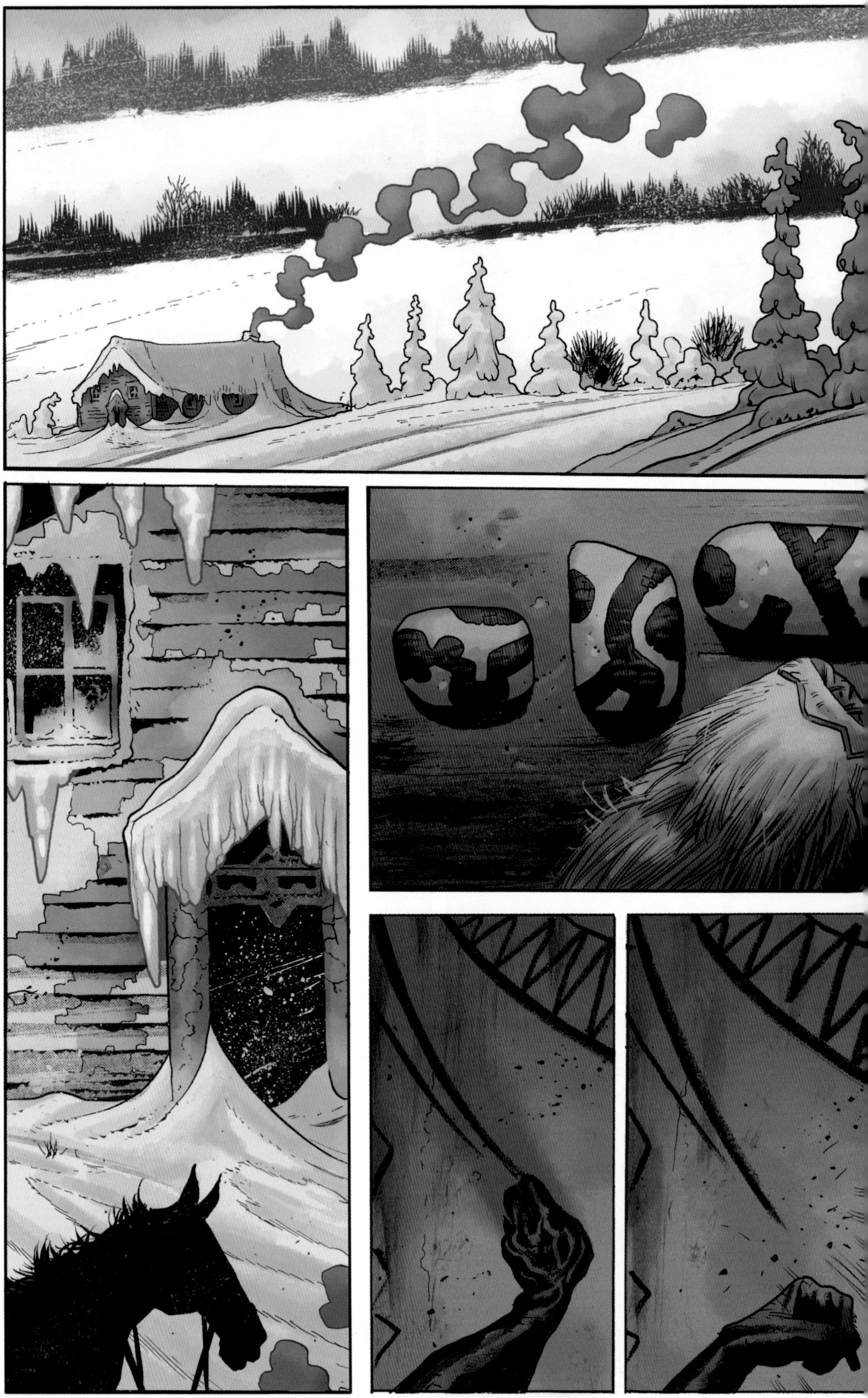

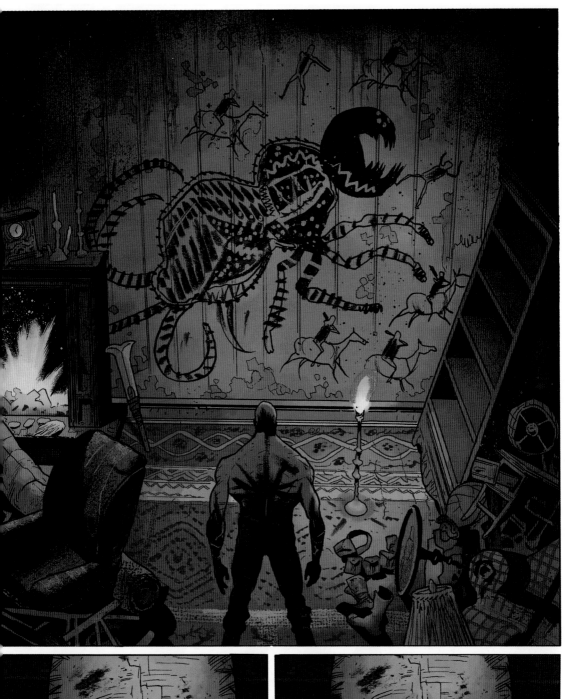

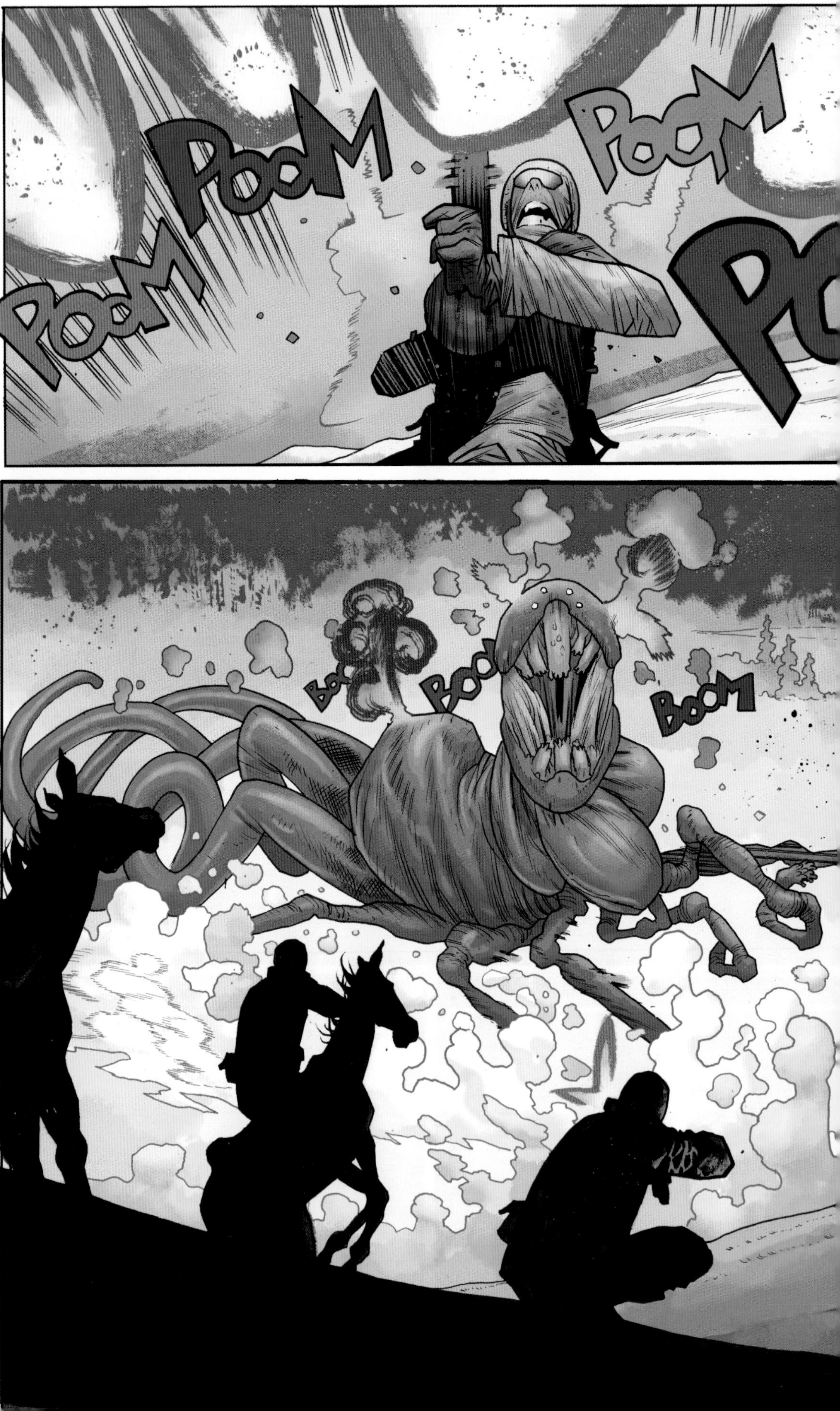
POOM
POOM
POOM
POOM
POOM
PO
BOO
BOO
BOOM

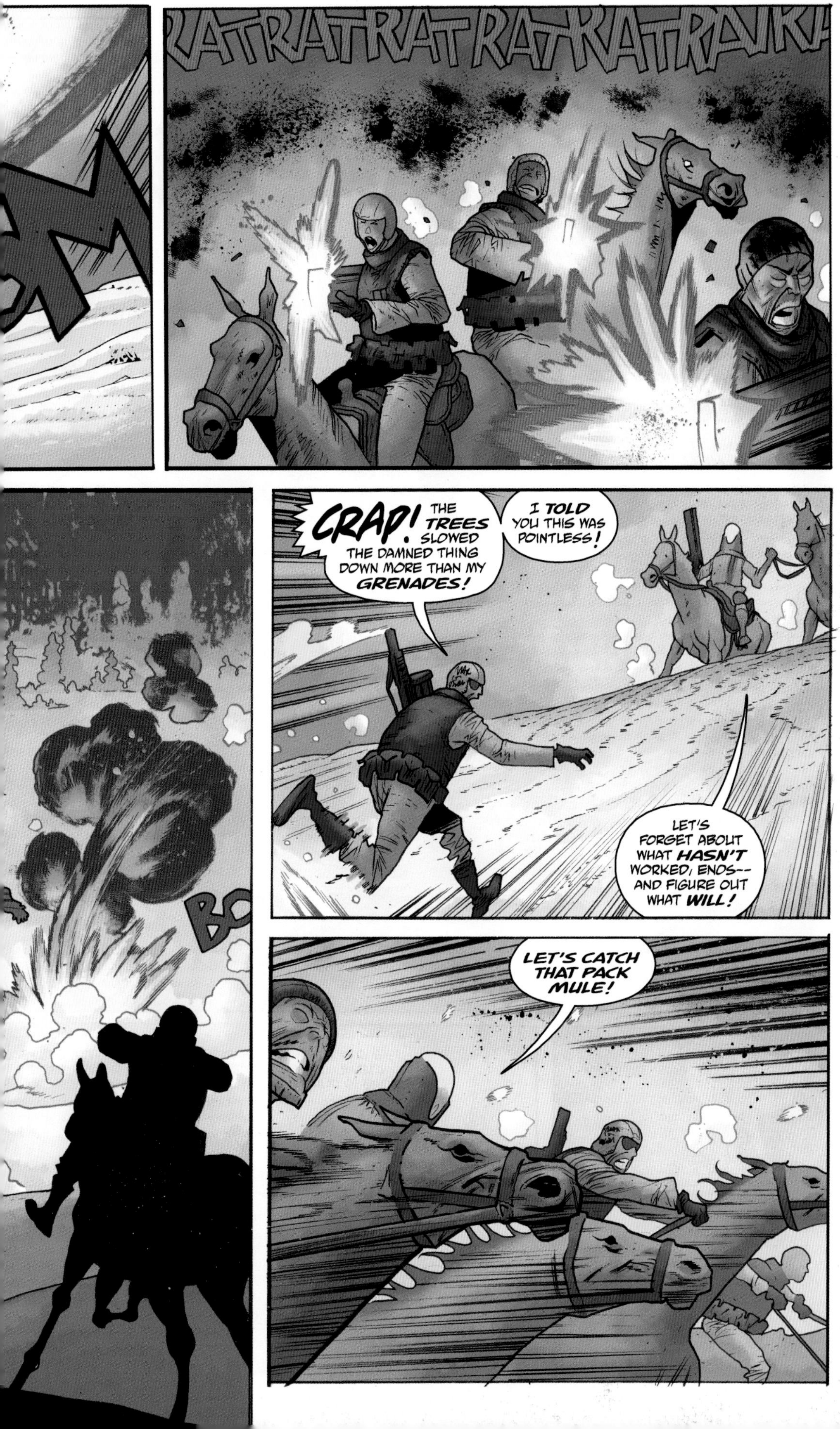
RATRATRATRATRATRATRA
CRAP! THE TREES SLOWED THE DAMNED THING DOWN MORE THAN MY GRENADES!
I TOLD YOU THIS WAS POINTLESS!
LET'S FORGET ABOUT WHAT HASN'T WORKED, ENOS-- AND FIGURE OUT WHAT WILL!
LET'S CATCH THAT PACK MULE!

THERE! RIDE HIM DOWN!

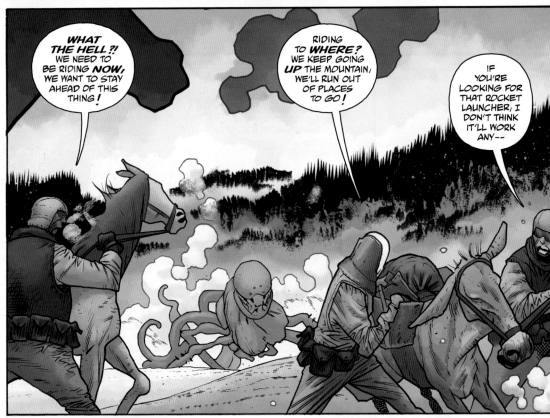

WHAT THE HELL?! WE NEED TO BE RIDING NOW, WE WANT TO STAY AHEAD OF THIS THING!

RIDING TO WHERE? WE KEEP GOING UP THE MOUNTAIN, WE'LL RUN OUT OF PLACES TO GO!

IF YOU'RE LOOKING FOR THAT ROCKET LAUNCHER, I DON'T THINK IT'LL WORK ANY--

I'M NOT LOOKING FOR THE ROCKET LAUNCHER.

"WE CAN'T FIGHT IT, THAT'S CLEAR. THE AIR FORCE BOMB IS OUR BEST OPTION.

"BUT WE NEED TO LIVE LONG ENOUGH TO MAKE THE RADIO CALL.

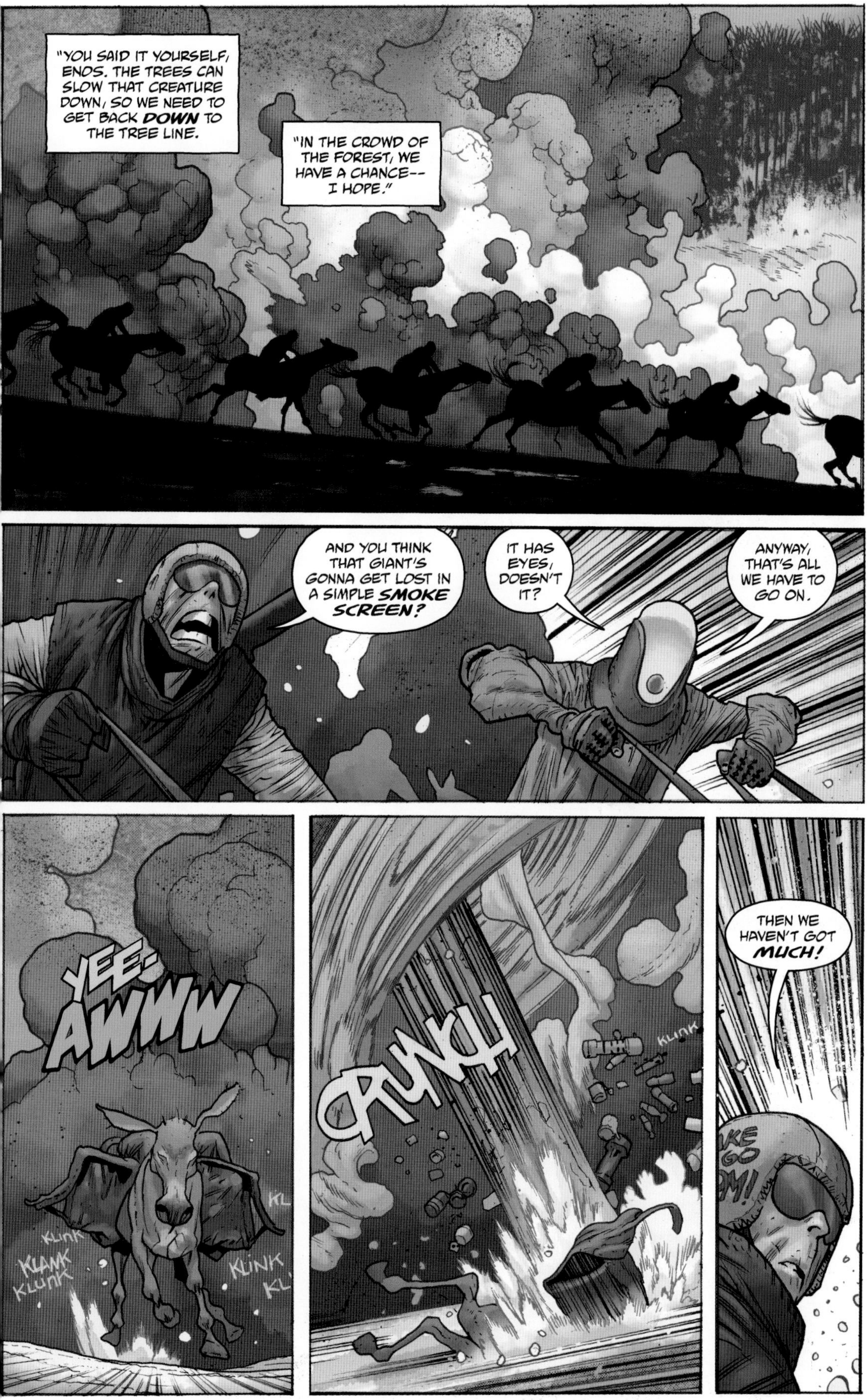
"YOU SAID IT YOURSELF, ENOS. THE TREES CAN SLOW THAT CREATURE DOWN, SO WE NEED TO GET BACK DOWN TO THE TREE LINE.
"IN THE CROWD OF THE FOREST, WE HAVE A CHANCE-- I HOPE."
AND YOU THINK THAT GIANT'S GONNA GET LOST IN A SIMPLE SMOKE SCREEN?
IT HAS EYES, DOESN'T IT?
ANYWAY, THAT'S ALL WE HAVE TO GO ON.
YEE-AWWW
KLINK
KLANK
KLUNK
KLINK
CRUNCH
KLINK
THEN WE HAVEN'T GOT MUCH!

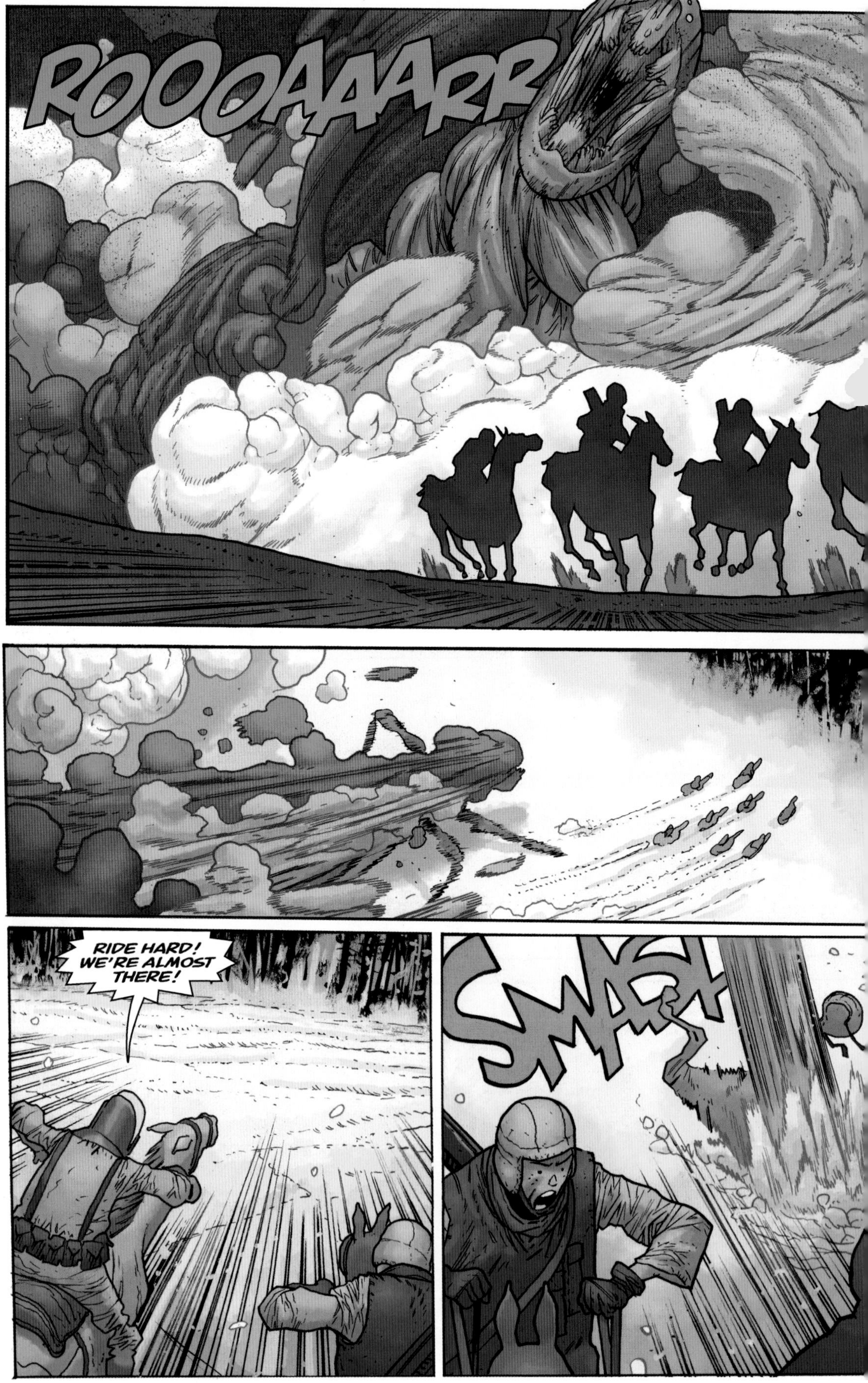
ROOOAAARR
RIDE HARD! WE'RE ALMOST THERE!
SMASH

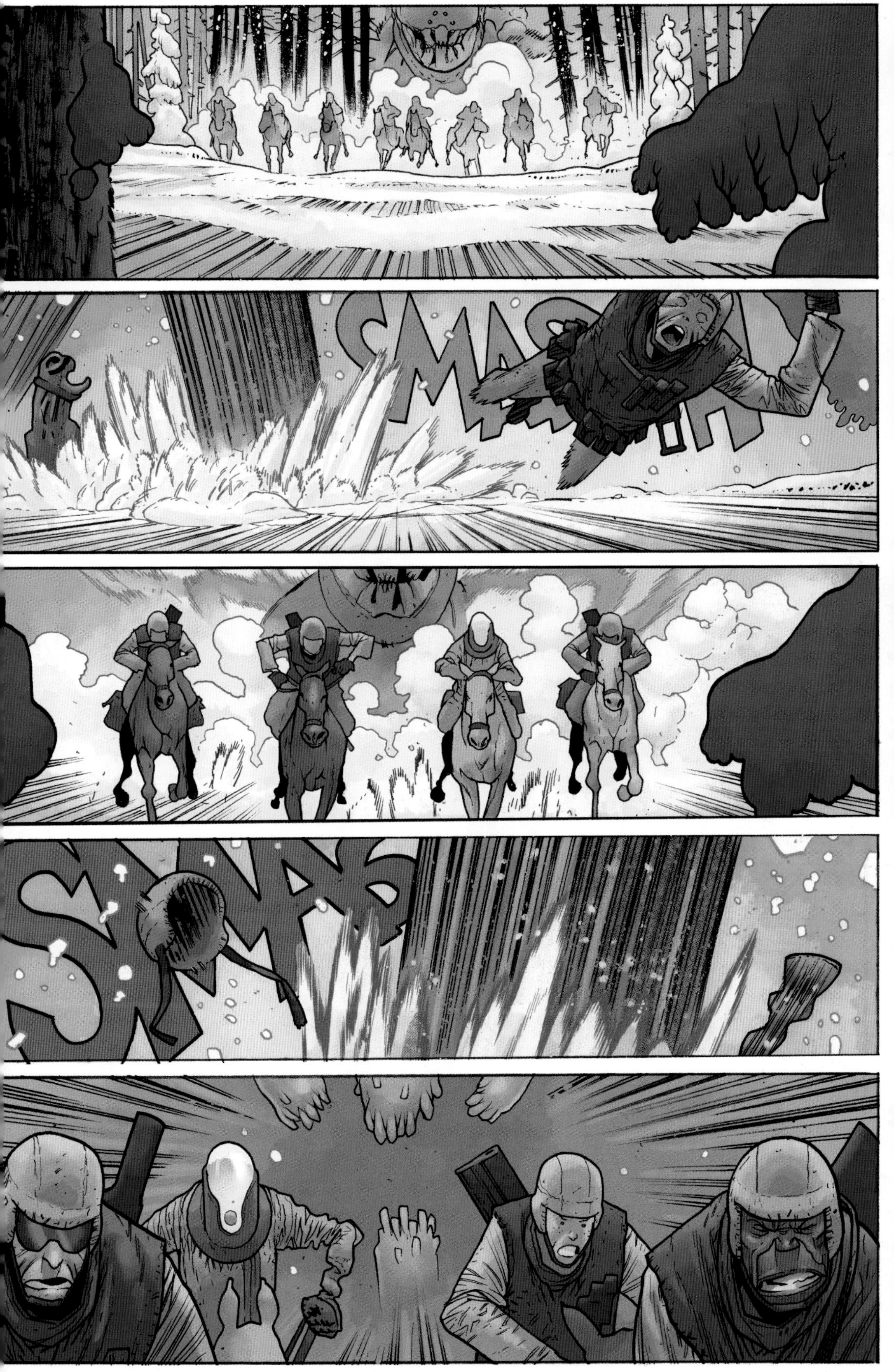

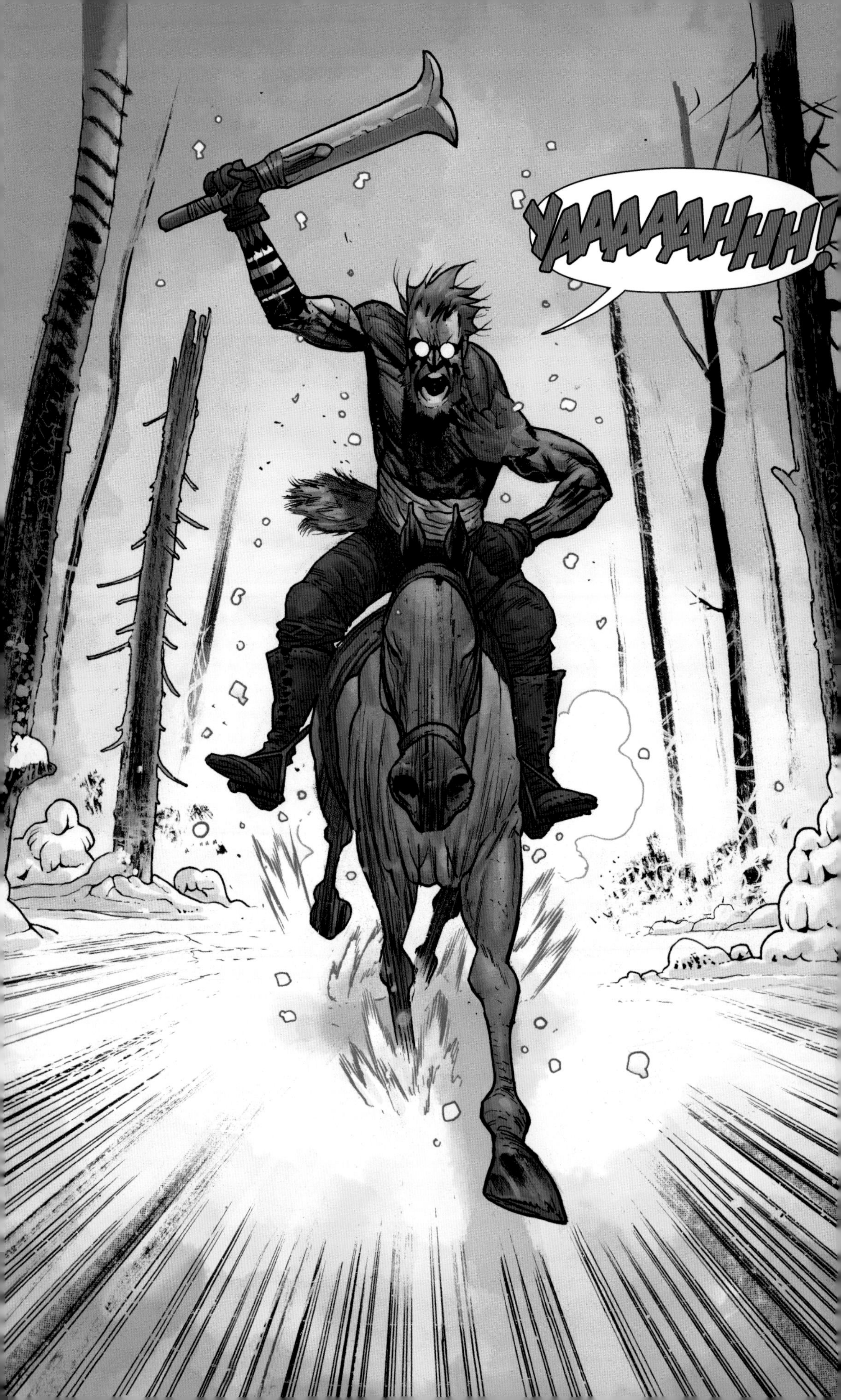
YAAAAAHHH!

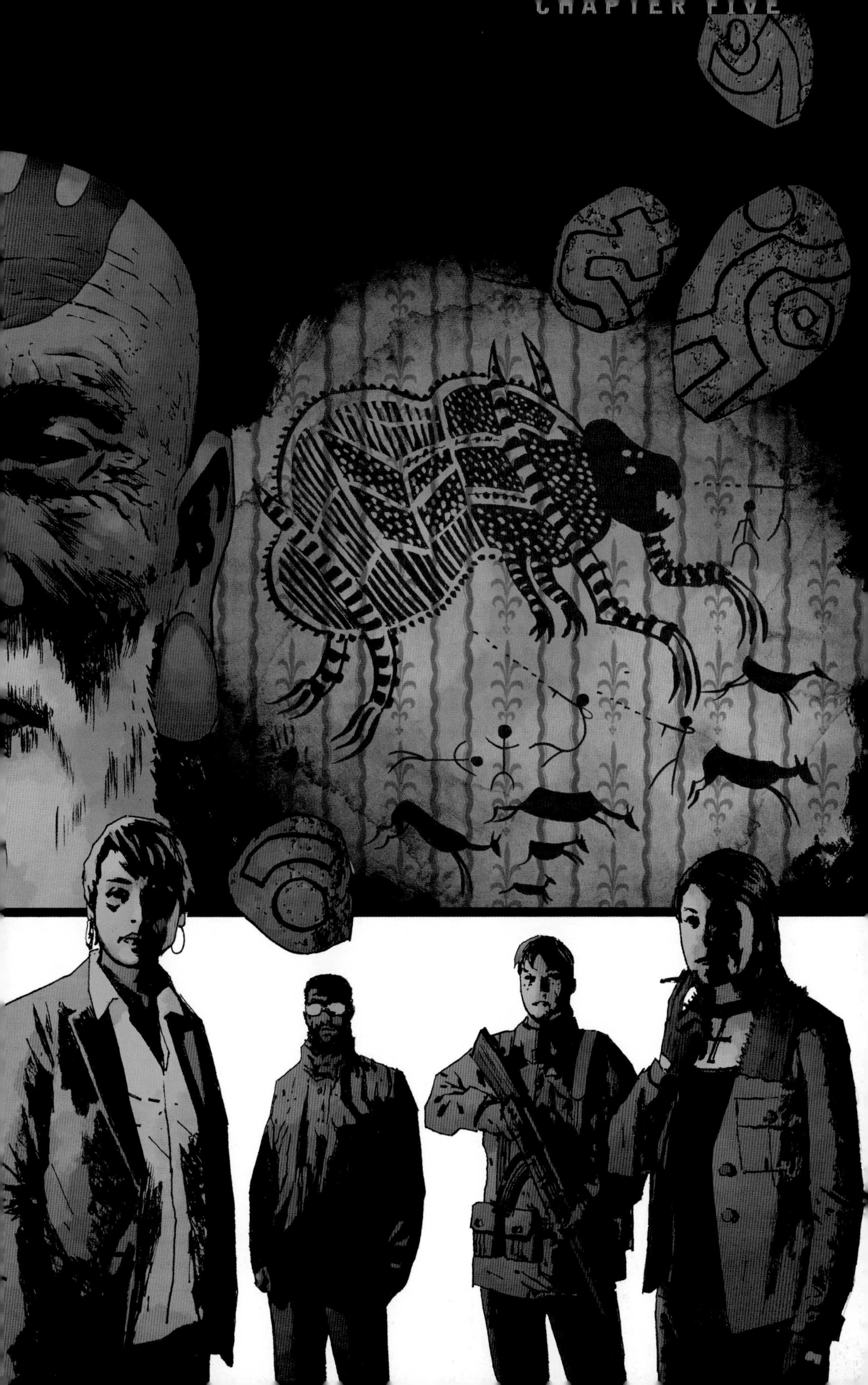
CHAPTER FIVE

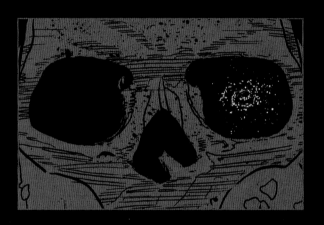

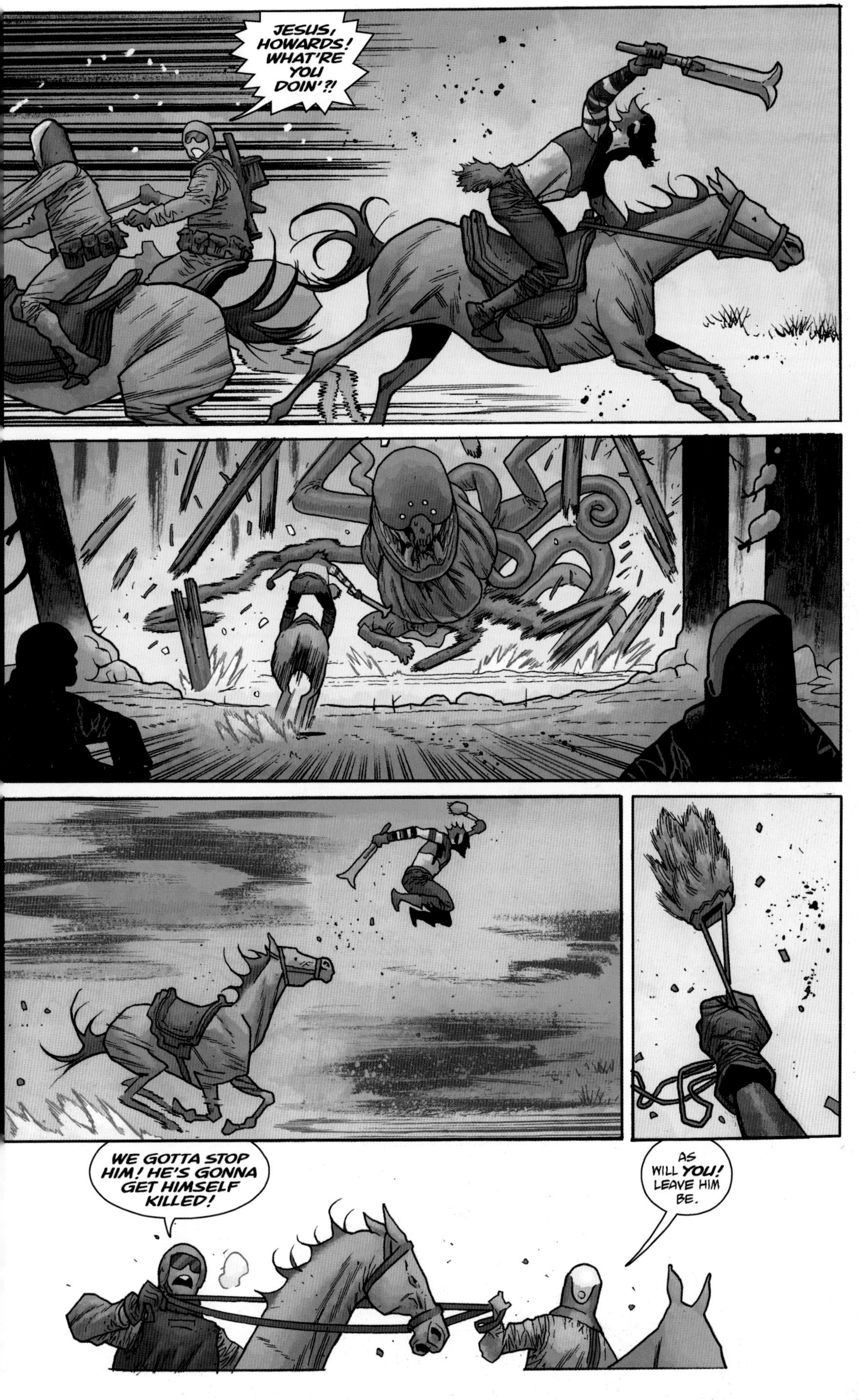
JESUS, HOWARDS! WHAT'RE YOU DOIN'?!
WE GOTTA STOP HIM! HE'S GONNA GET HIMSELF KILLED!
AS WILL YOU! LEAVE HIM BE.

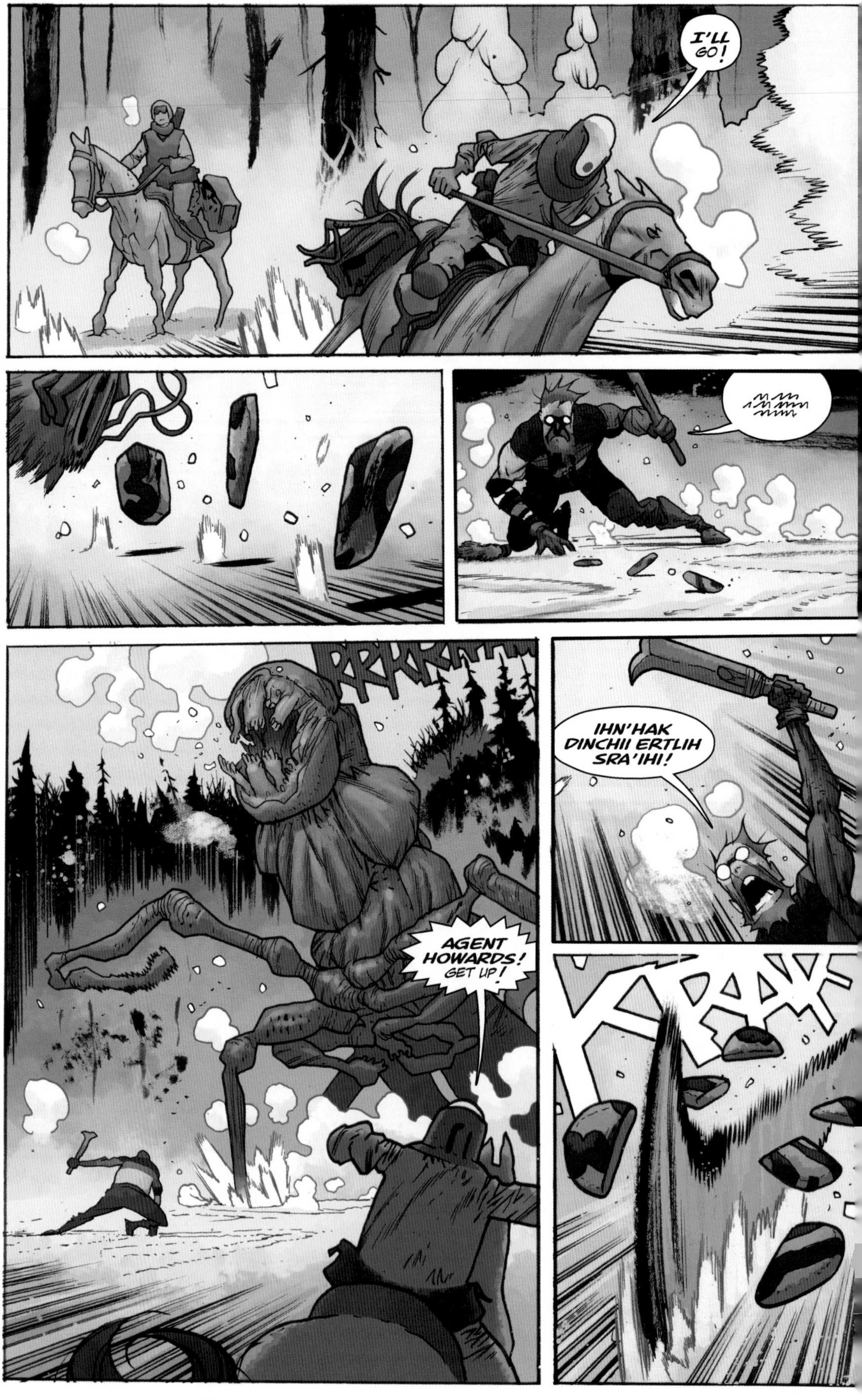
I'LL GO!
RRRRRAHH
IHN'HAK DINCHII ERTLIH SRA'IHI!
AGENT HOWARDS! GET UP!
KRAAK

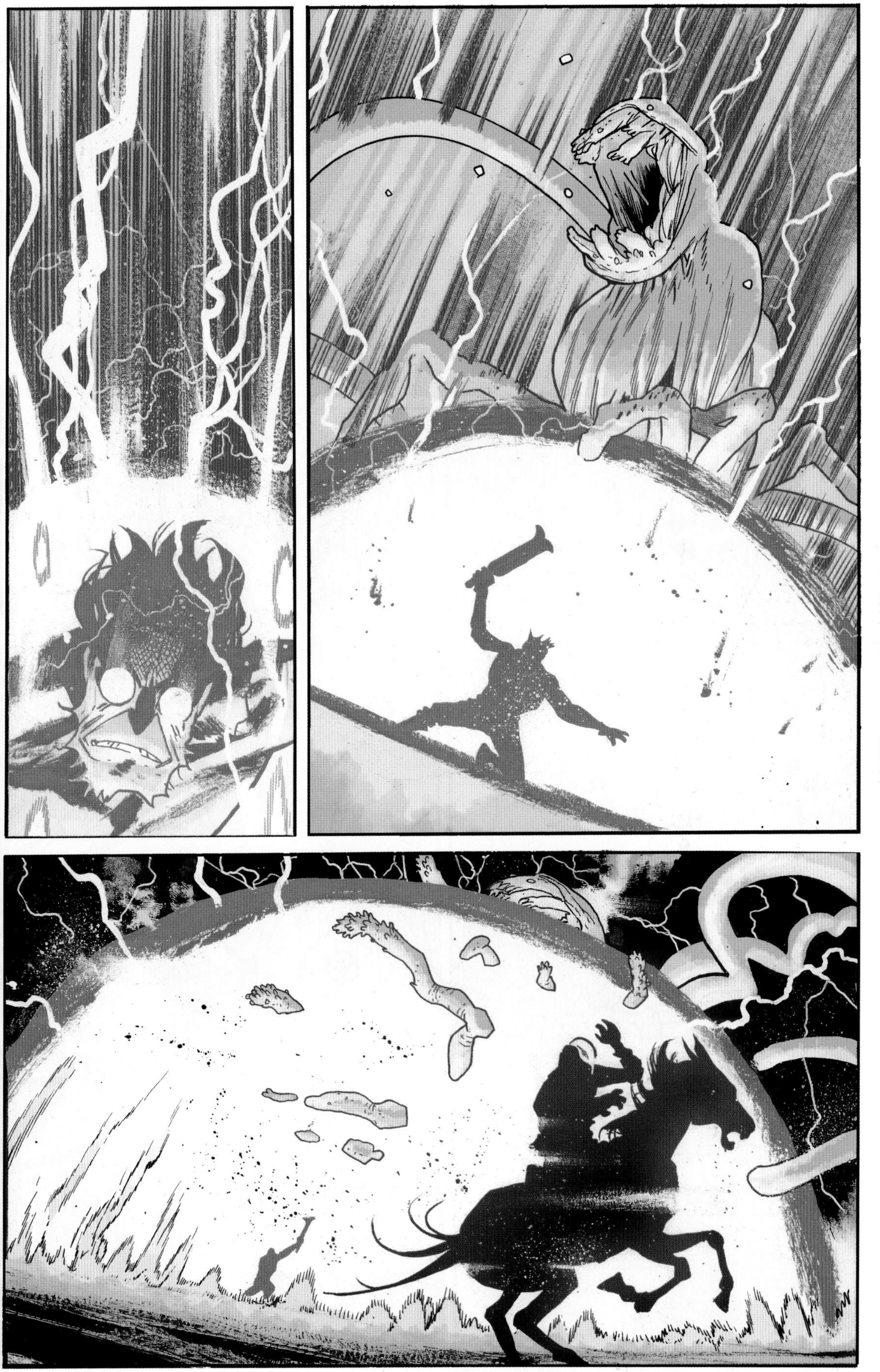

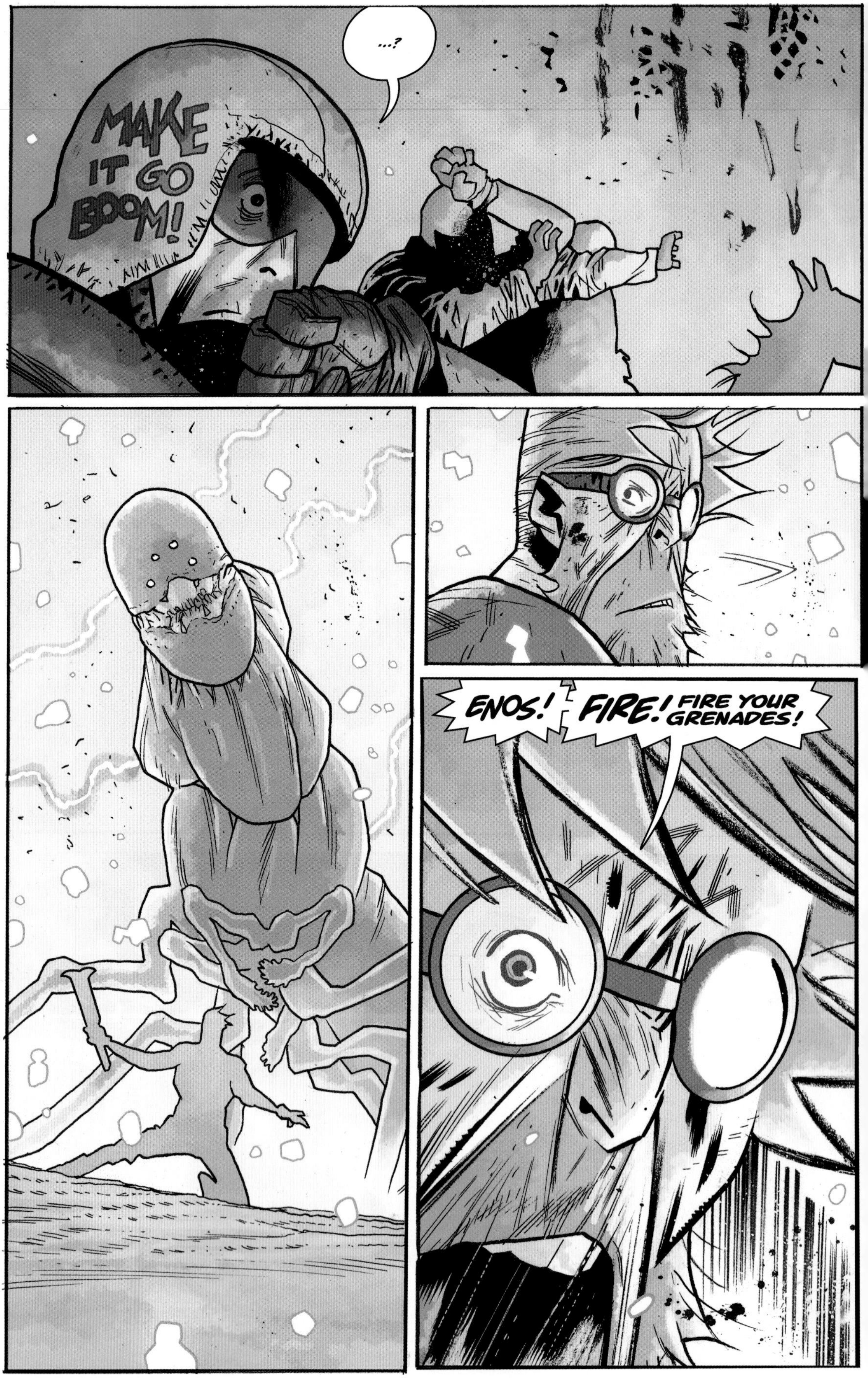
MAKE IT GO BOOM!
...?
ENOS!
FIRE! FIRE YOUR GRENADES!

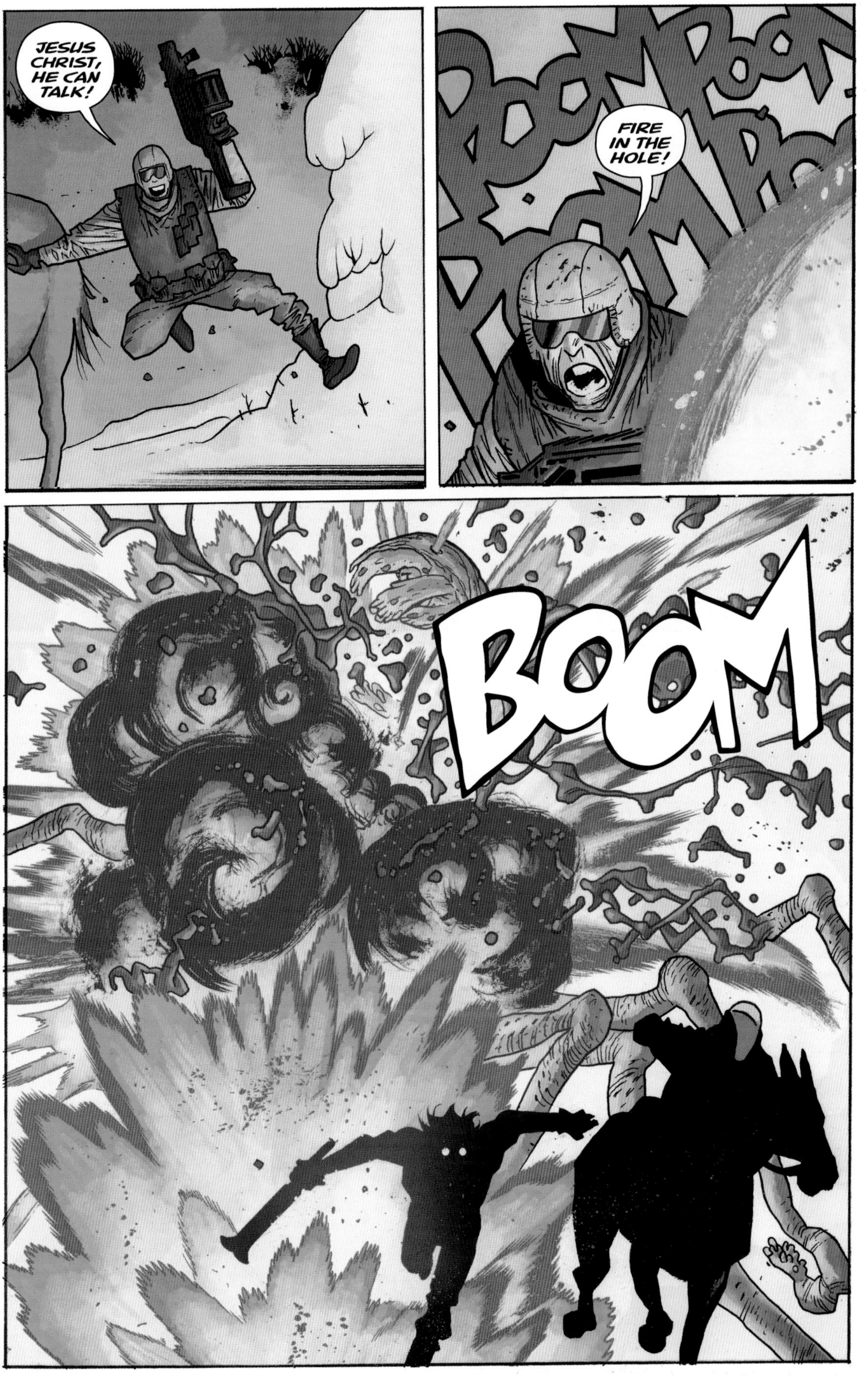

JESUS CHRIST, HE CAN TALK!
FIRE IN THE HOLE!
BOOM

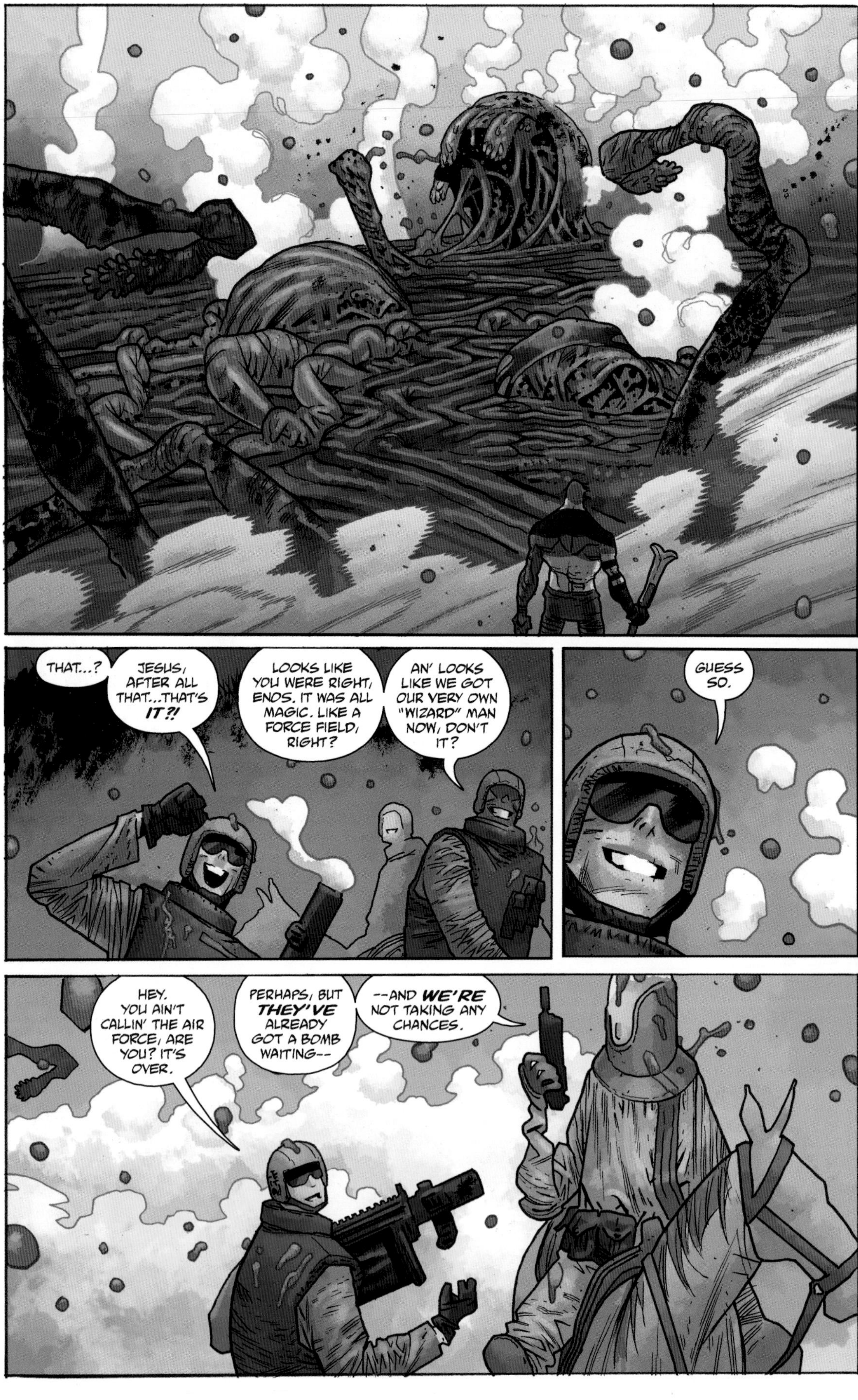
THAT...?
JESUS, AFTER ALL THAT...THAT'S *IT?!*
LOOKS LIKE YOU WERE RIGHT, ENOS. IT WAS ALL MAGIC. LIKE A FORCE FIELD, RIGHT?
AN' LOOKS LIKE WE GOT OUR VERY OWN "WIZARD" MAN NOW, DON'T IT?
GUESS SO.
HEY. YOU AIN'T CALLIN' THE AIR FORCE, ARE YOU? IT'S OVER.
PERHAPS, BUT ***THEY'VE*** ALREADY GOT A BOMB WAITING--
--AND ***WE'RE*** NOT TAKING ANY CHANCES.

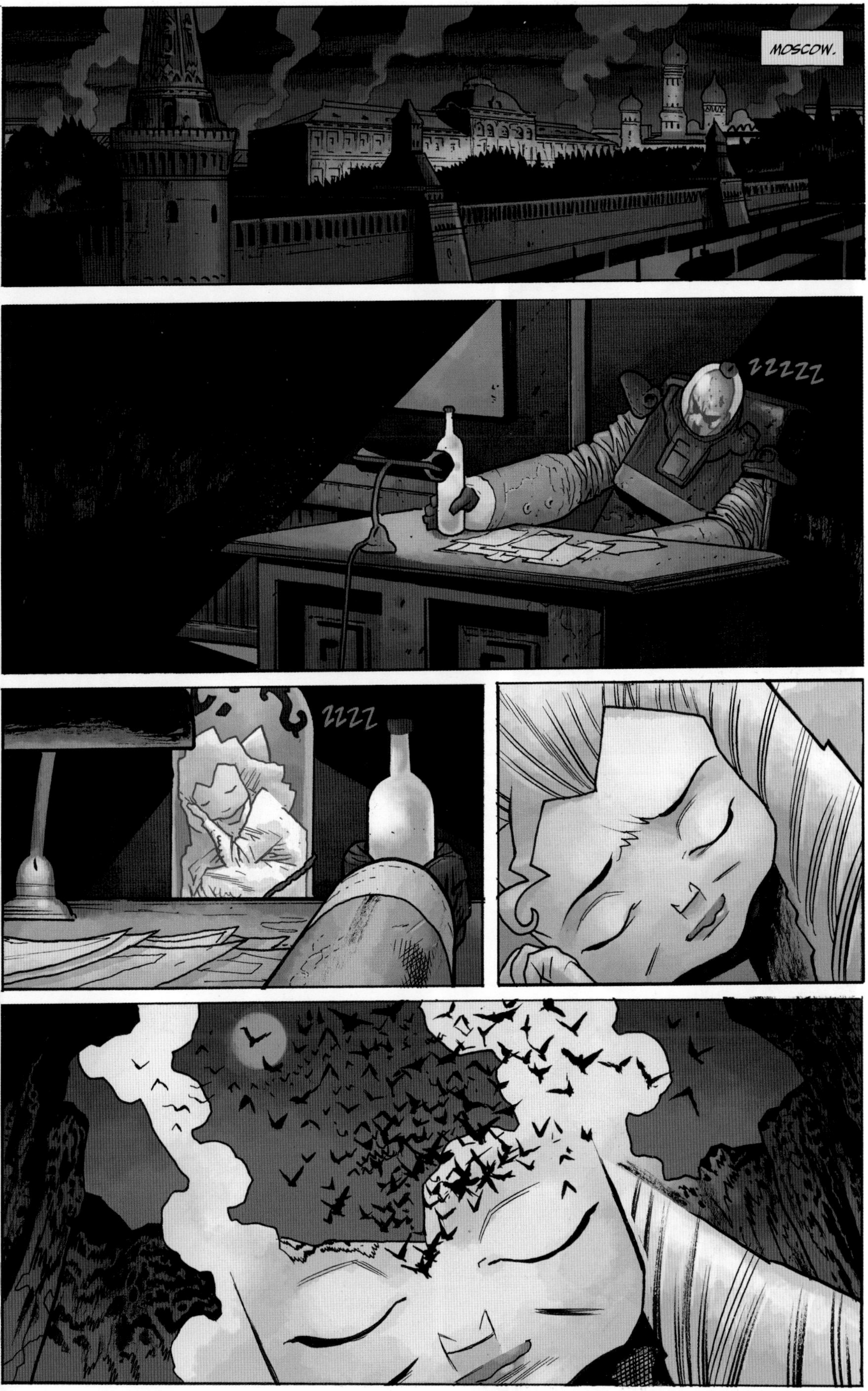
MOSCOW.
ZZZZZ
ZZZZ

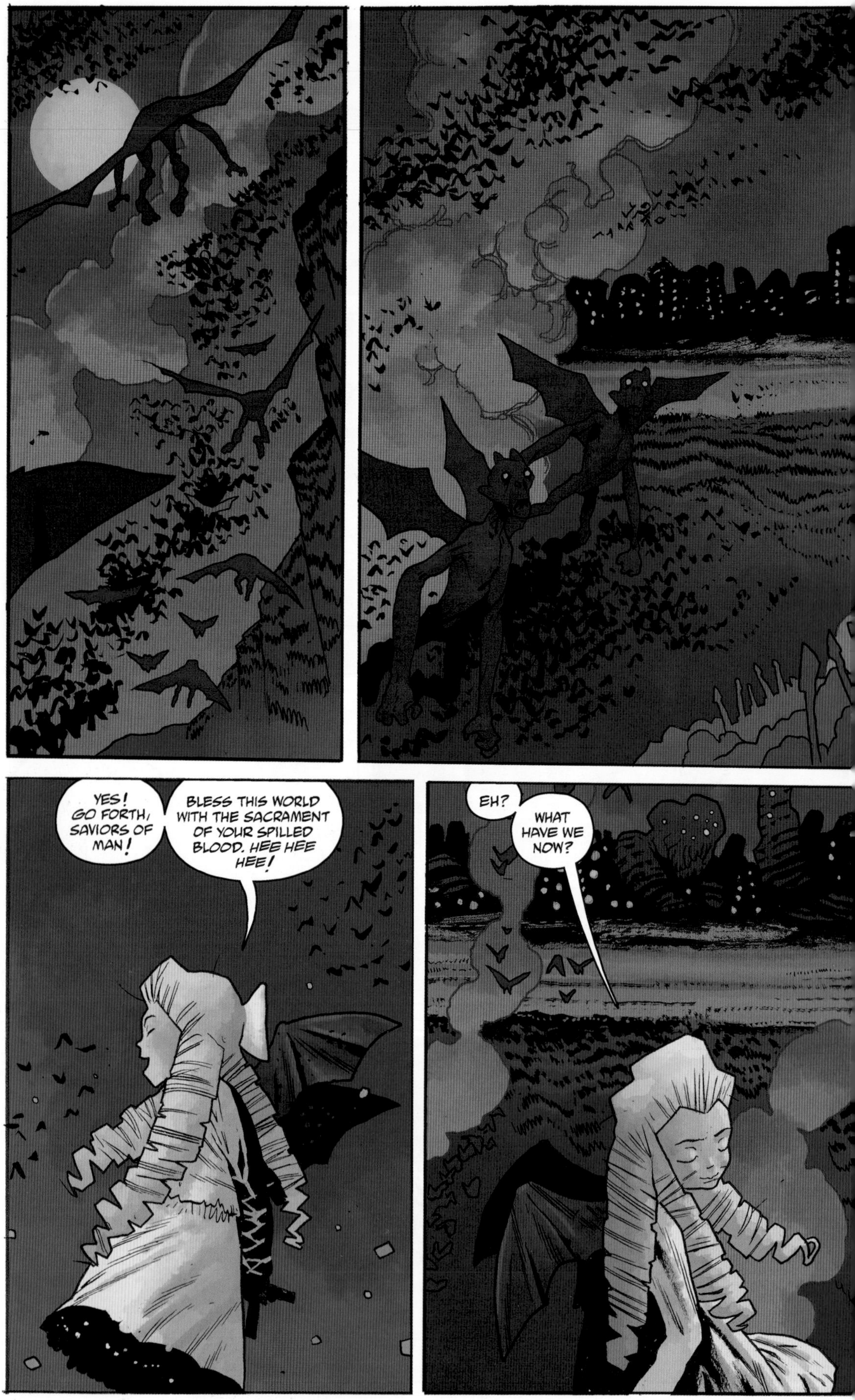
YES! GO FORTH, SAVIORS OF MAN!
BLESS THIS WORLD WITH THE SACRAMENT OF YOUR SPILLED BLOOD. HEE HEE HEE!
EH?
WHAT HAVE WE NOW?

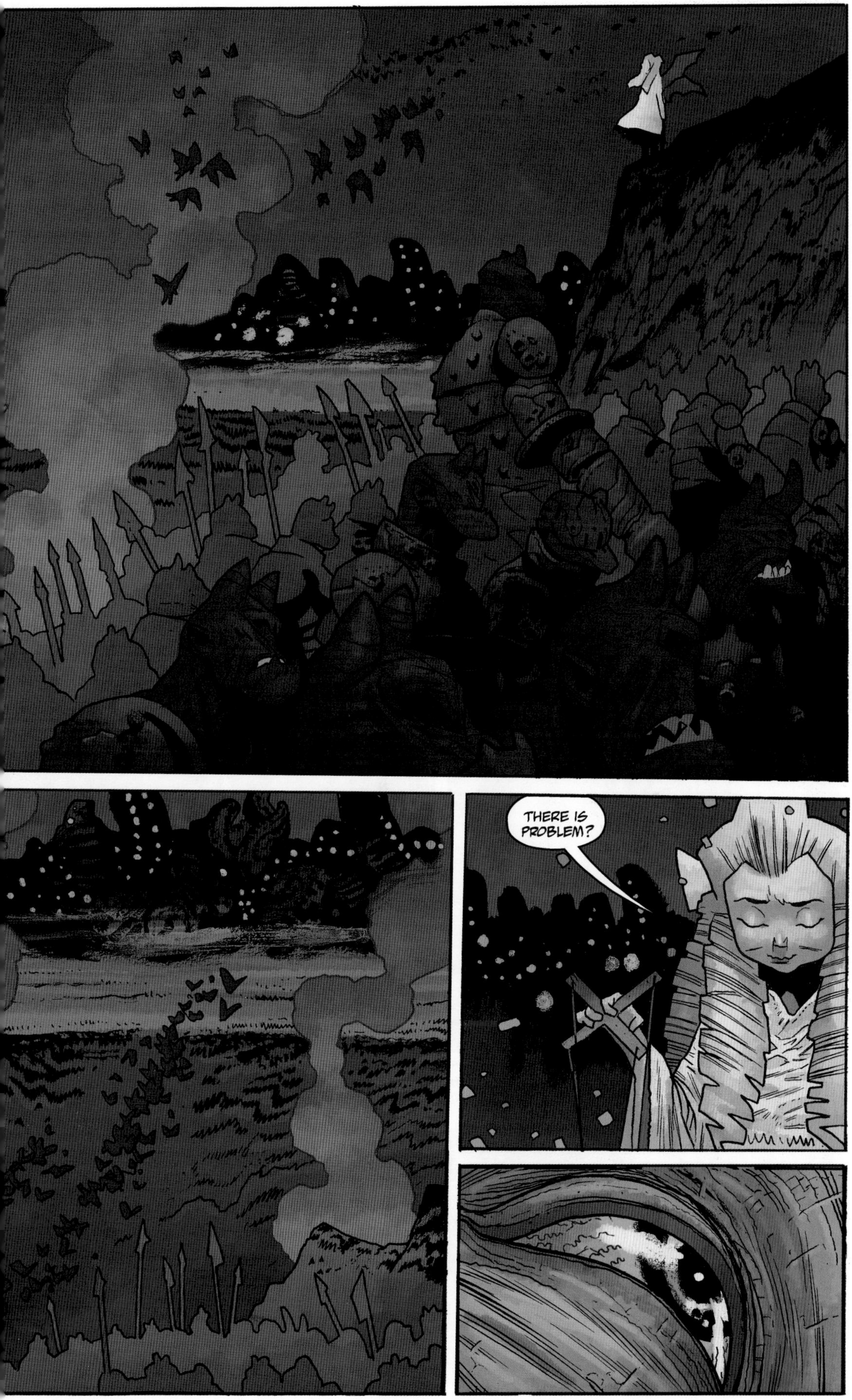
THERE IS PROBLEM?

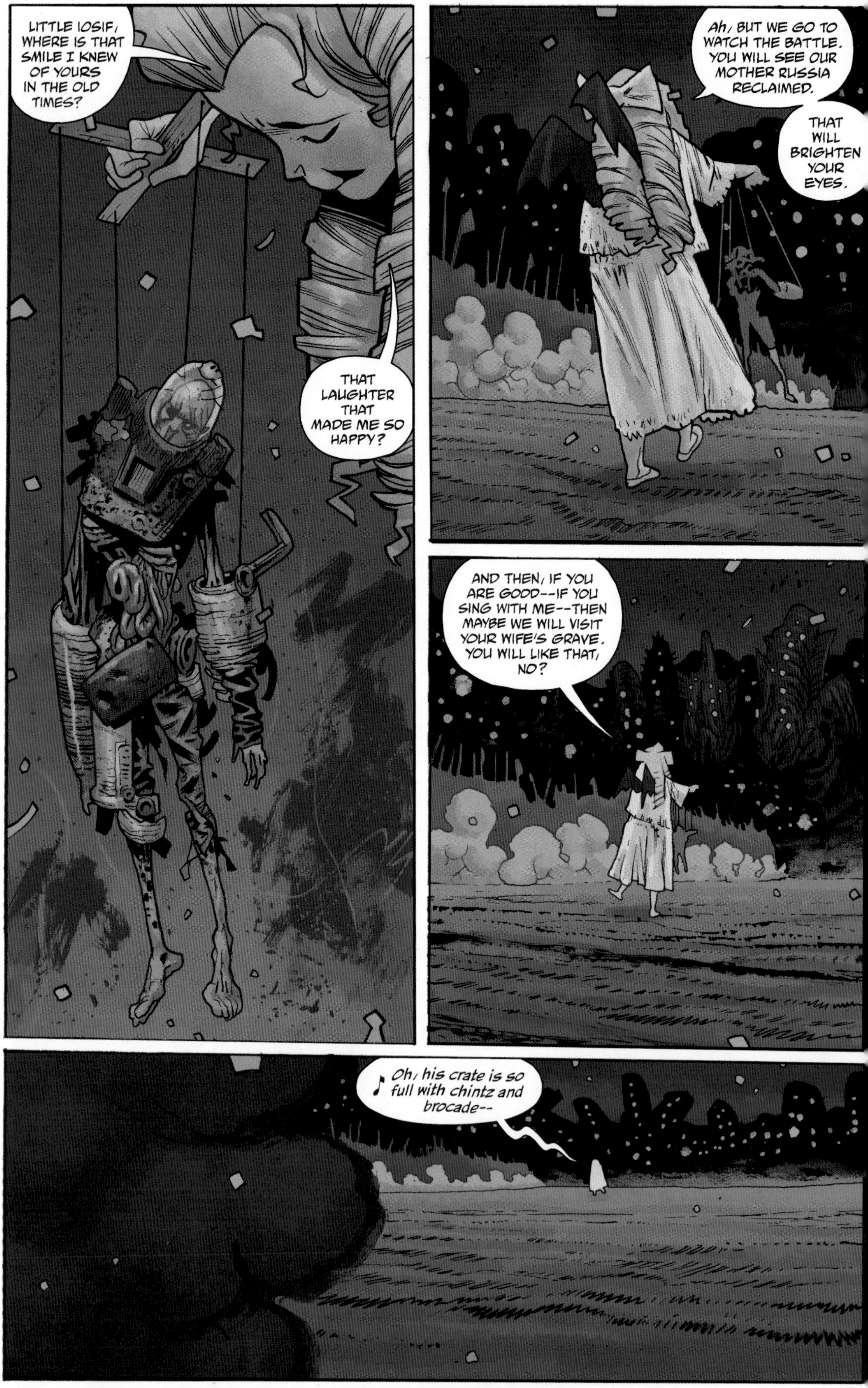
LITTLE IOSIF, WHERE IS THAT SMILE I KNEW OF YOURS IN THE OLD TIMES?
THAT LAUGHTER THAT MADE ME SO HAPPY?
Ah, BUT WE GO TO WATCH THE BATTLE. YOU WILL SEE OUR MOTHER RUSSIA RECLAIMED.
THAT WILL BRIGHTEN YOUR EYES.
AND THEN, IF YOU ARE GOOD--IF YOU SING WITH ME--THEN MAYBE WE WILL VISIT YOUR WIFE'S GRAVE. YOU WILL LIKE THAT, NO?
♪ Oh, his crate is so full with chintz and brocade--

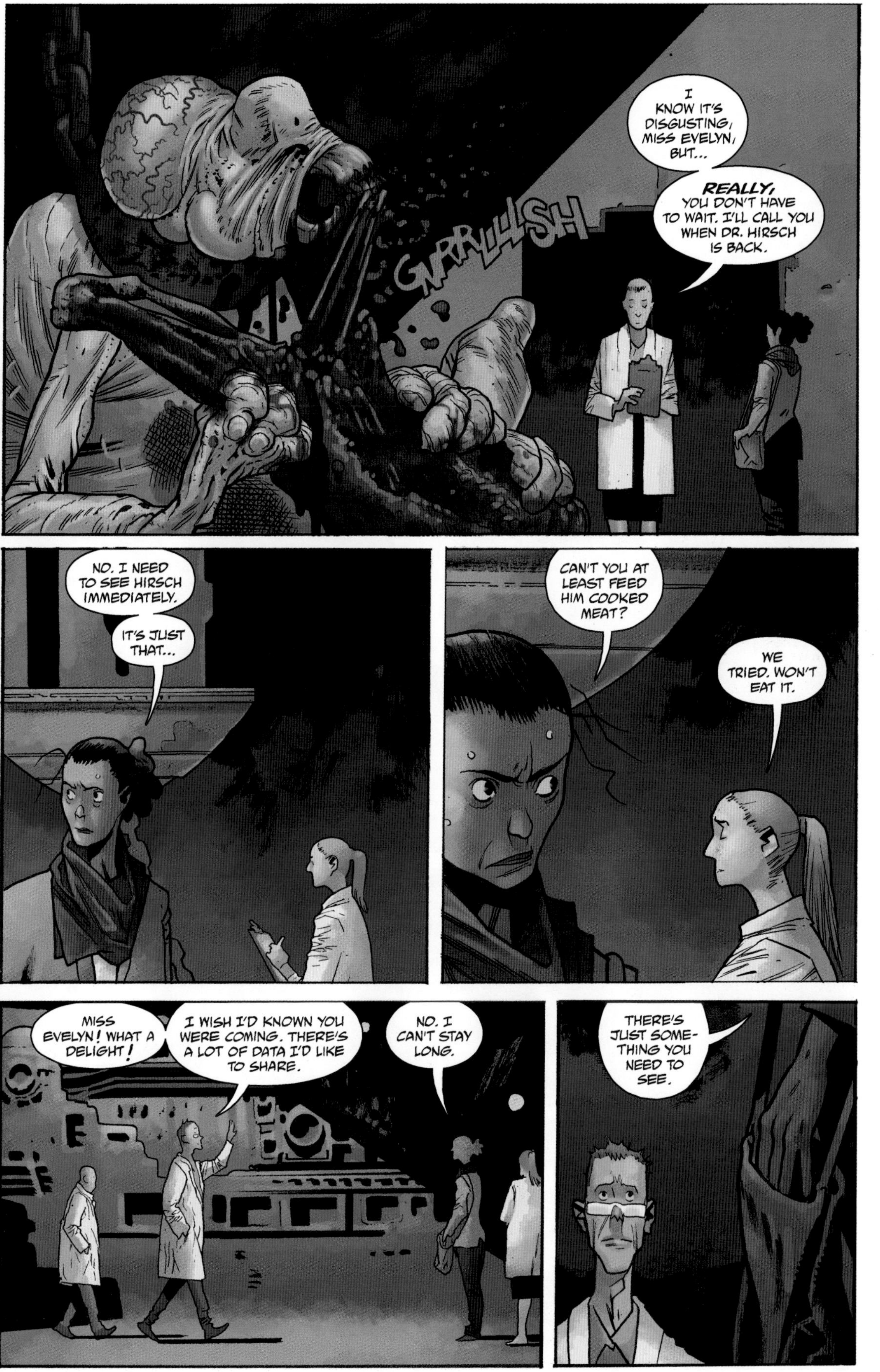
I KNOW IT'S DISGUSTING, MISS EVELYN, BUT...
REALLY, YOU DON'T HAVE TO WAIT. I'LL CALL YOU WHEN DR. HIRSCH IS BACK.
GNRRLLLSH
NO. I NEED TO SEE HIRSCH IMMEDIATELY.
IT'S JUST THAT...
CAN'T YOU AT LEAST FEED HIM COOKED MEAT?
WE TRIED. WON'T EAT IT.
MISS EVELYN! WHAT A DELIGHT!
I WISH I'D KNOWN YOU WERE COMING. THERE'S A LOT OF DATA I'D LIKE TO SHARE.
NO. I CAN'T STAY LONG.
THERE'S JUST SOME-THING YOU NEED TO SEE.

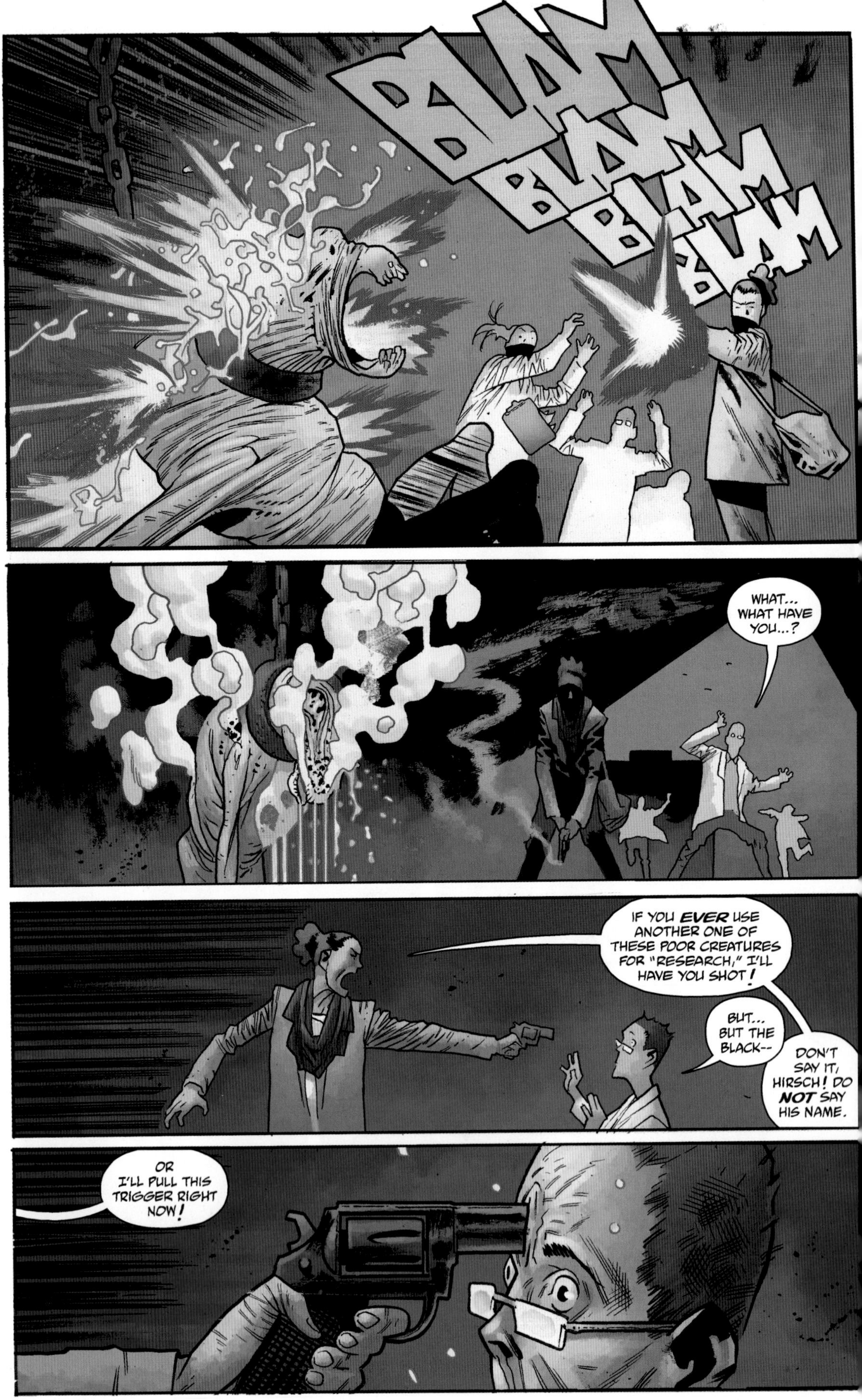
BLAM
BLAM
BLAM
BLAM
BLAM
WHAT... WHAT HAVE YOU...?
IF YOU **EVER** USE ANOTHER ONE OF THESE POOR CREATURES FOR "RESEARCH," I'LL HAVE YOU SHOT!
BUT... BUT THE BLACK--
DON'T SAY IT, HIRSCH! DO **NOT** SAY HIS NAME.
OR I'LL PULL THIS TRIGGER RIGHT NOW!

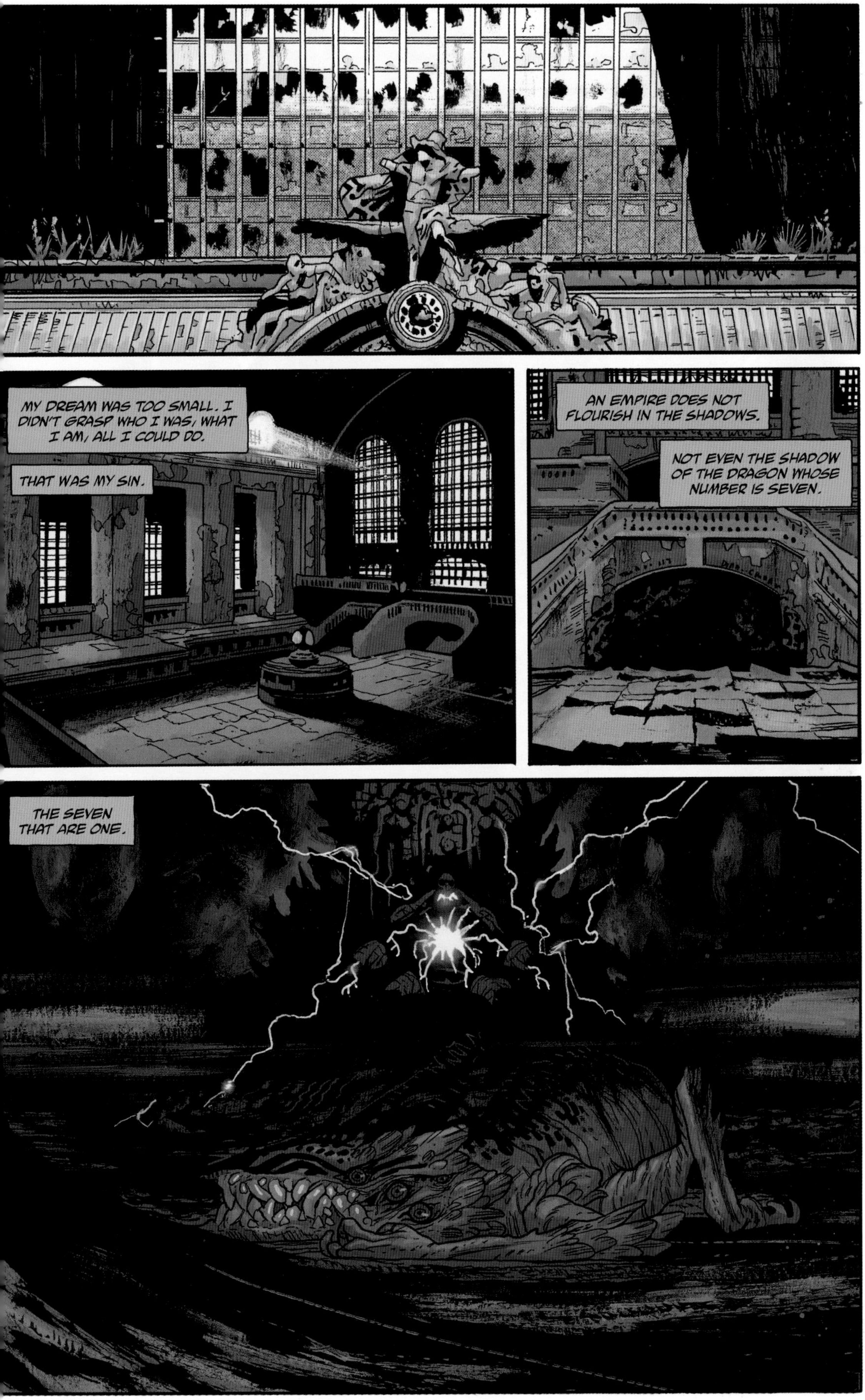
MY DREAM WAS TOO SMALL. I DIDN'T GRASP WHO I WAS, WHAT I AM, ALL I COULD DO.
THAT WAS MY SIN.
AN EMPIRE DOES NOT FLOURISH IN THE SHADOWS.
NOT EVEN THE SHADOW OF THE DRAGON WHOSE NUMBER IS SEVEN.
THE SEVEN THAT ARE ONE.

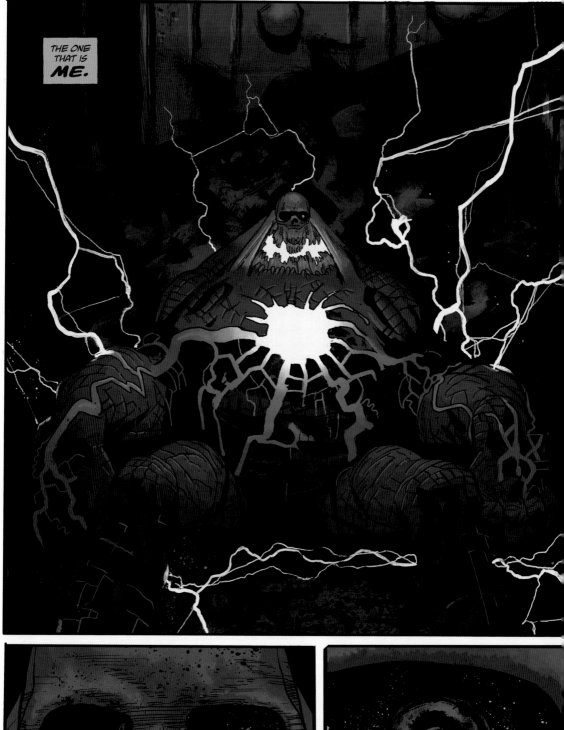

THE ONE
THAT IS
ME.

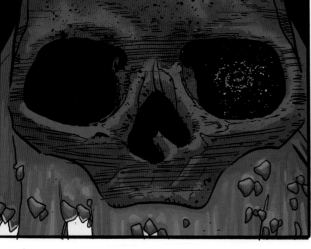

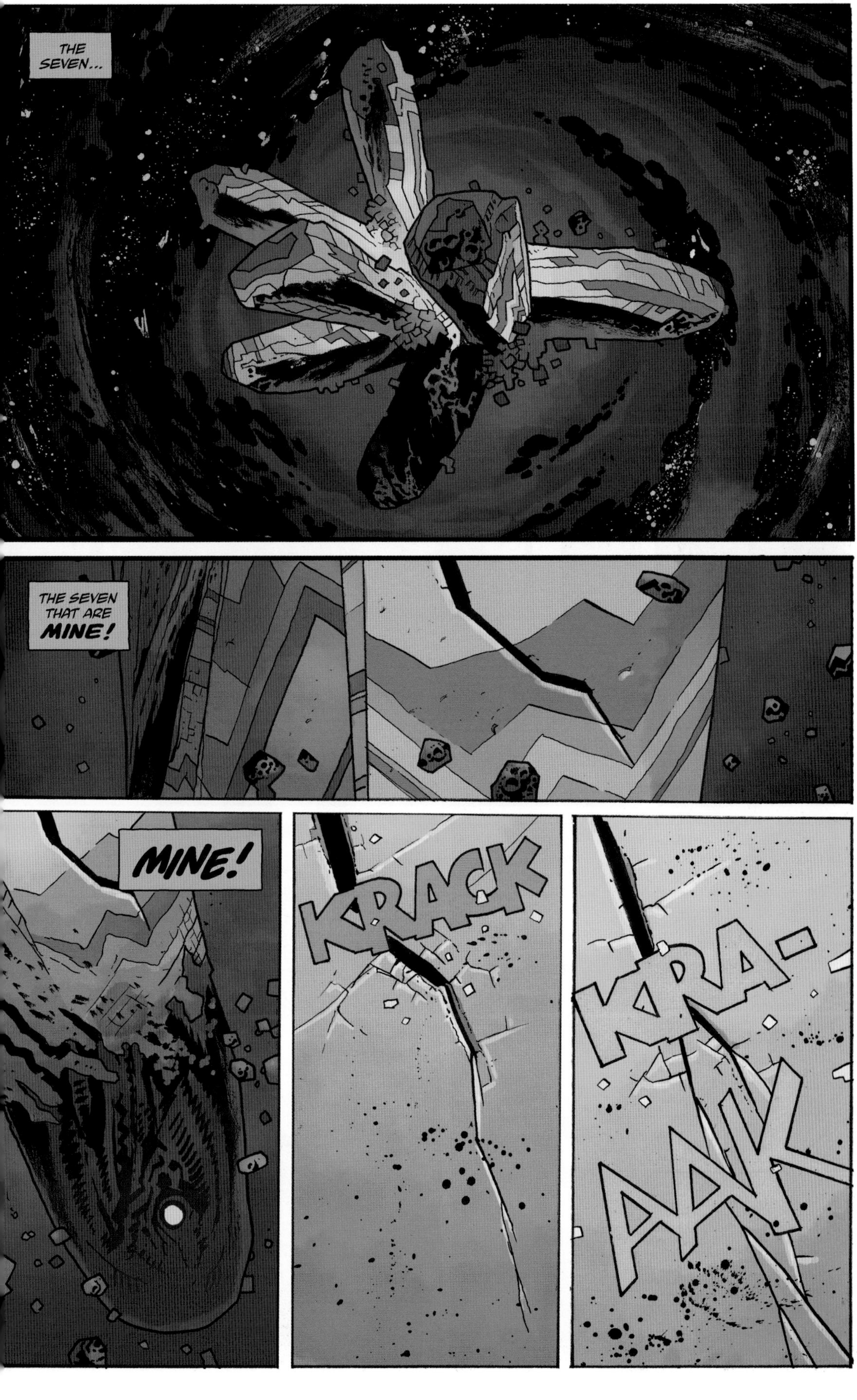
THE SEVEN...
THE SEVEN THAT ARE MINE!
MINE!
KRACK
KRA-AAK

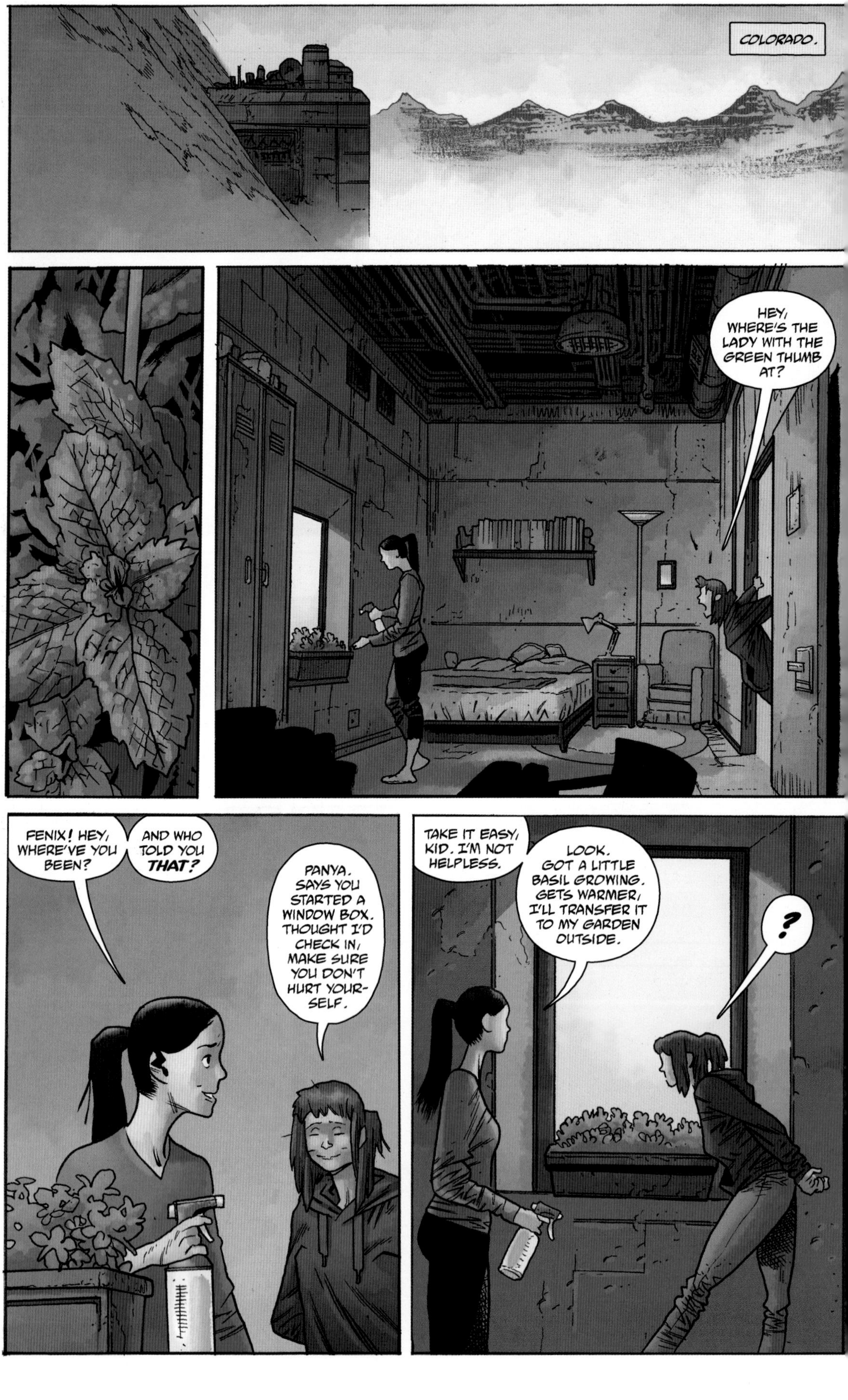
COLORADO.
HEY, WHERE'S THE LADY WITH THE GREEN THUMB AT?
FENIX! HEY, WHERE'VE YOU BEEN?
AND WHO TOLD YOU THAT?
PANYA. SAYS YOU STARTED A WINDOW BOX. THOUGHT I'D CHECK IN, MAKE SURE YOU DON'T HURT YOURSELF.
TAKE IT EASY, KID. I'M NOT HELPLESS.
LOOK. GOT A LITTLE BASIL GROWING. GETS WARMER, I'LL TRANSFER IT TO MY GARDEN OUTSIDE.
?

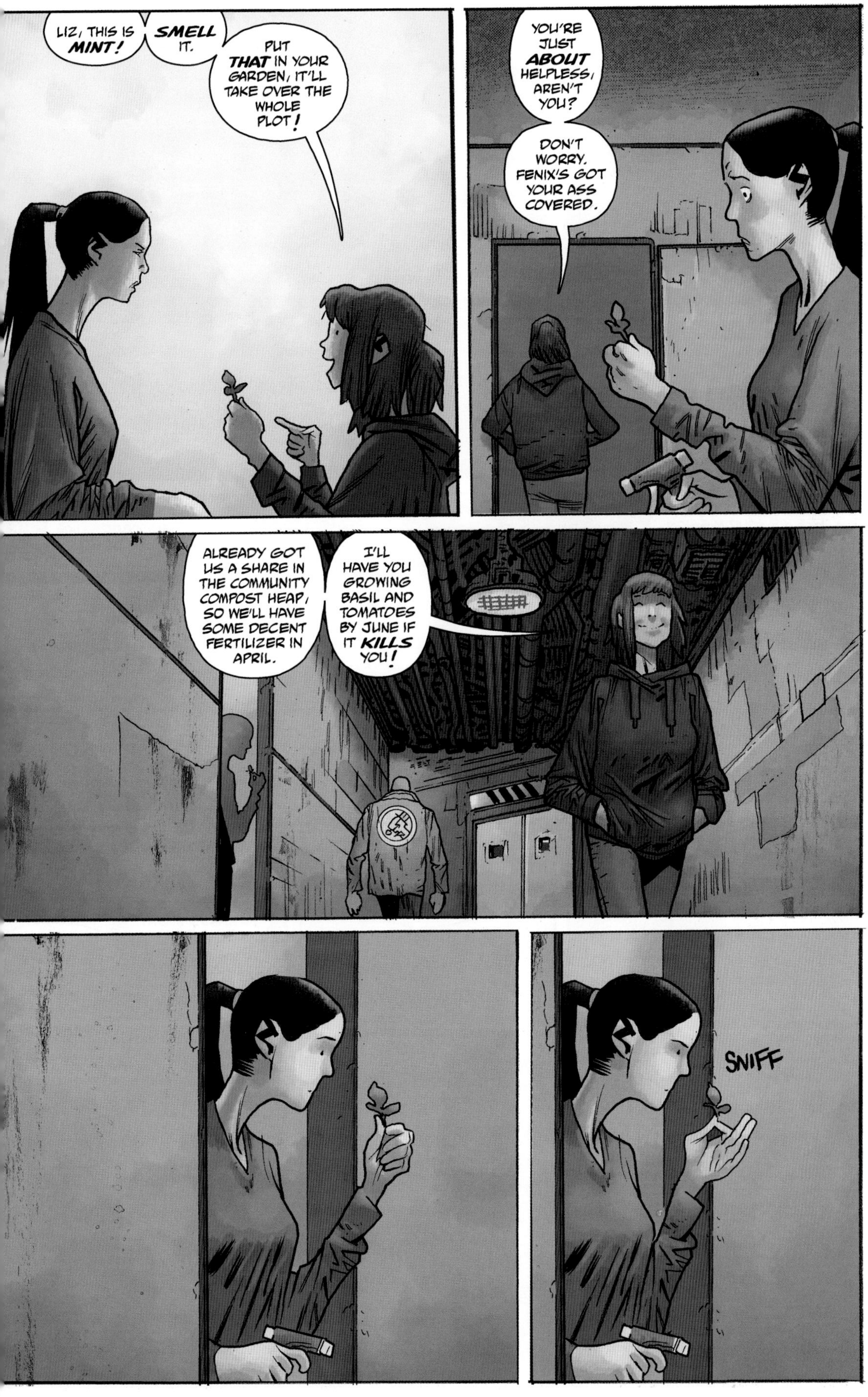

LIZ, THIS IS MINT!
SMELL IT.
PUT THAT IN YOUR GARDEN, IT'LL TAKE OVER THE WHOLE PLOT!
YOU'RE JUST ABOUT HELPLESS, AREN'T YOU?
DON'T WORRY. FENIX'S GOT YOUR ASS COVERED.
ALREADY GOT US A SHARE IN THE COMMUNITY COMPOST HEAP, SO WE'LL HAVE SOME DECENT FERTILIZER IN APRIL.
I'LL HAVE YOU GROWING BASIL AND TOMATOES BY JUNE IF IT KILLS YOU!
SNIFF

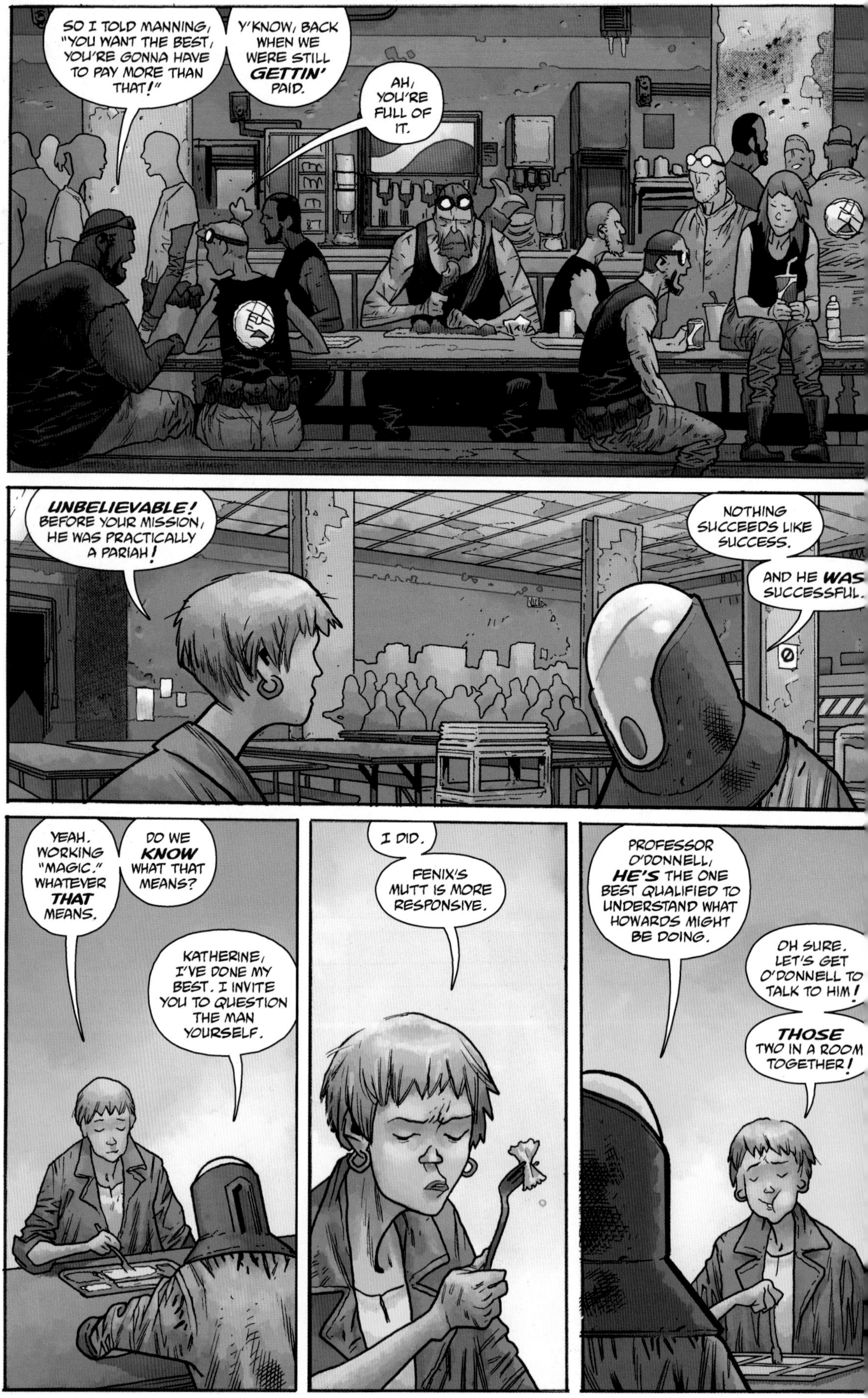

SO I TOLD MANNING, "YOU WANT THE BEST, YOU'RE GONNA HAVE TO PAY MORE THAN THAT!"
Y'KNOW, BACK WHEN WE WERE STILL GETTIN' PAID.
AH, YOU'RE FULL OF IT.
UNBELIEVABLE! BEFORE YOUR MISSION, HE WAS PRACTICALLY A PARIAH!
NOTHING SUCCEEDS LIKE SUCCESS.
AND HE WAS SUCCESSFUL.
YEAH. WORKING "MAGIC." WHATEVER THAT MEANS.
DO WE KNOW WHAT THAT MEANS?
KATHERINE, I'VE DONE MY BEST. I INVITE YOU TO QUESTION THE MAN YOURSELF.
I DID.
FENIX'S MUTT IS MORE RESPONSIVE.
PROFESSOR O'DONNELL, HE'S THE ONE BEST QUALIFIED TO UNDERSTAND WHAT HOWARDS MIGHT BE DOING.
OH SURE. LET'S GET O'DONNELL TO TALK TO HIM!
THOSE TWO IN A ROOM TOGETHER!

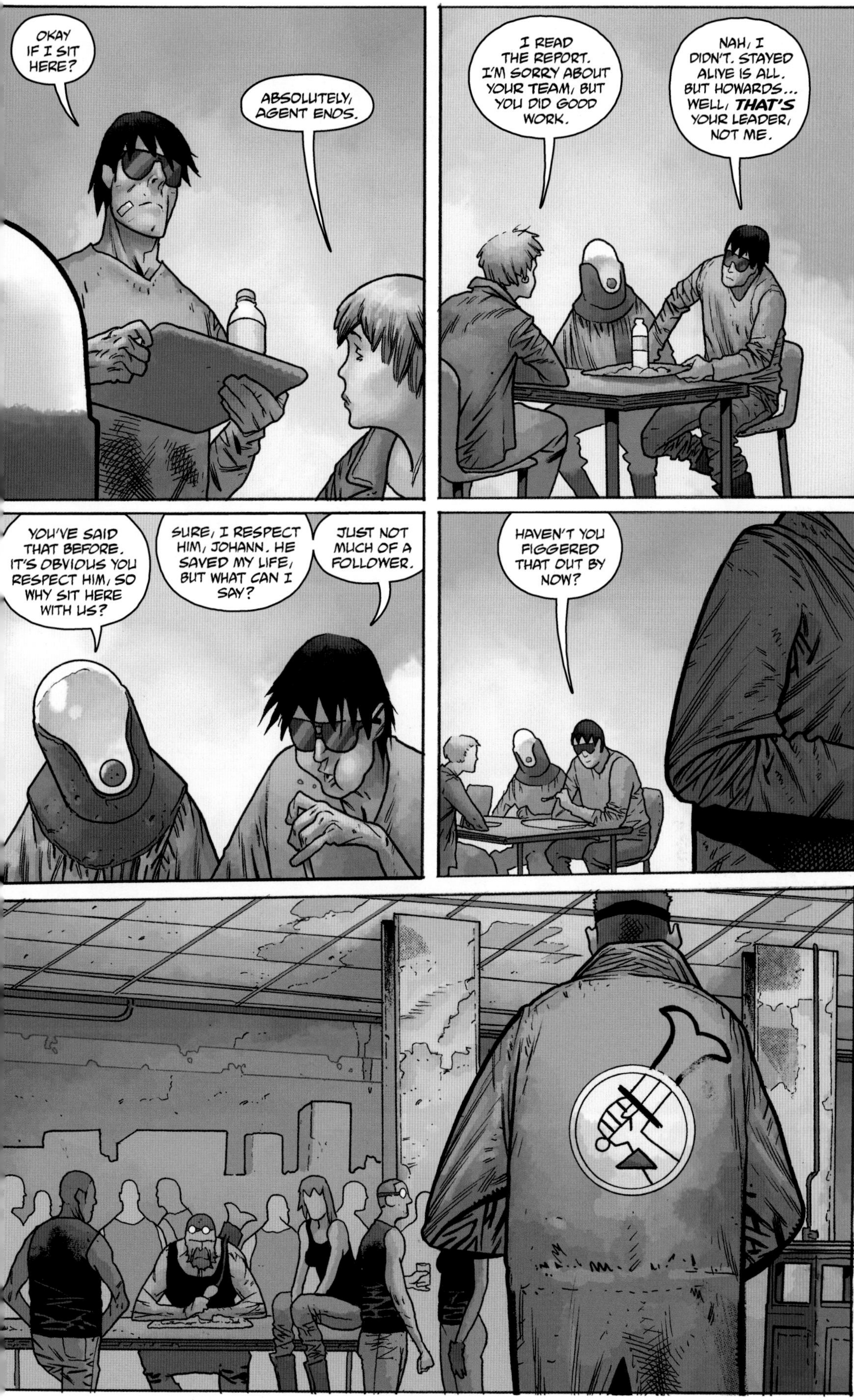
OKAY IF I SIT HERE?
ABSOLUTELY, AGENT ENOS.
I READ THE REPORT. I'M SORRY ABOUT YOUR TEAM, BUT YOU DID GOOD WORK.
NAH, I DIDN'T. STAYED ALIVE IS ALL. BUT HOWARDS... WELL, THAT'S YOUR LEADER, NOT ME.
YOU'VE SAID THAT BEFORE. IT'S OBVIOUS YOU RESPECT HIM, SO WHY SIT HERE WITH US?
SURE, I RESPECT HIM, JOHANN. HE SAVED MY LIFE, BUT WHAT CAN I SAY?
JUST NOT MUCH OF A FOLLOWER.
HAVEN'T YOU FIGGERED THAT OUT BY NOW?

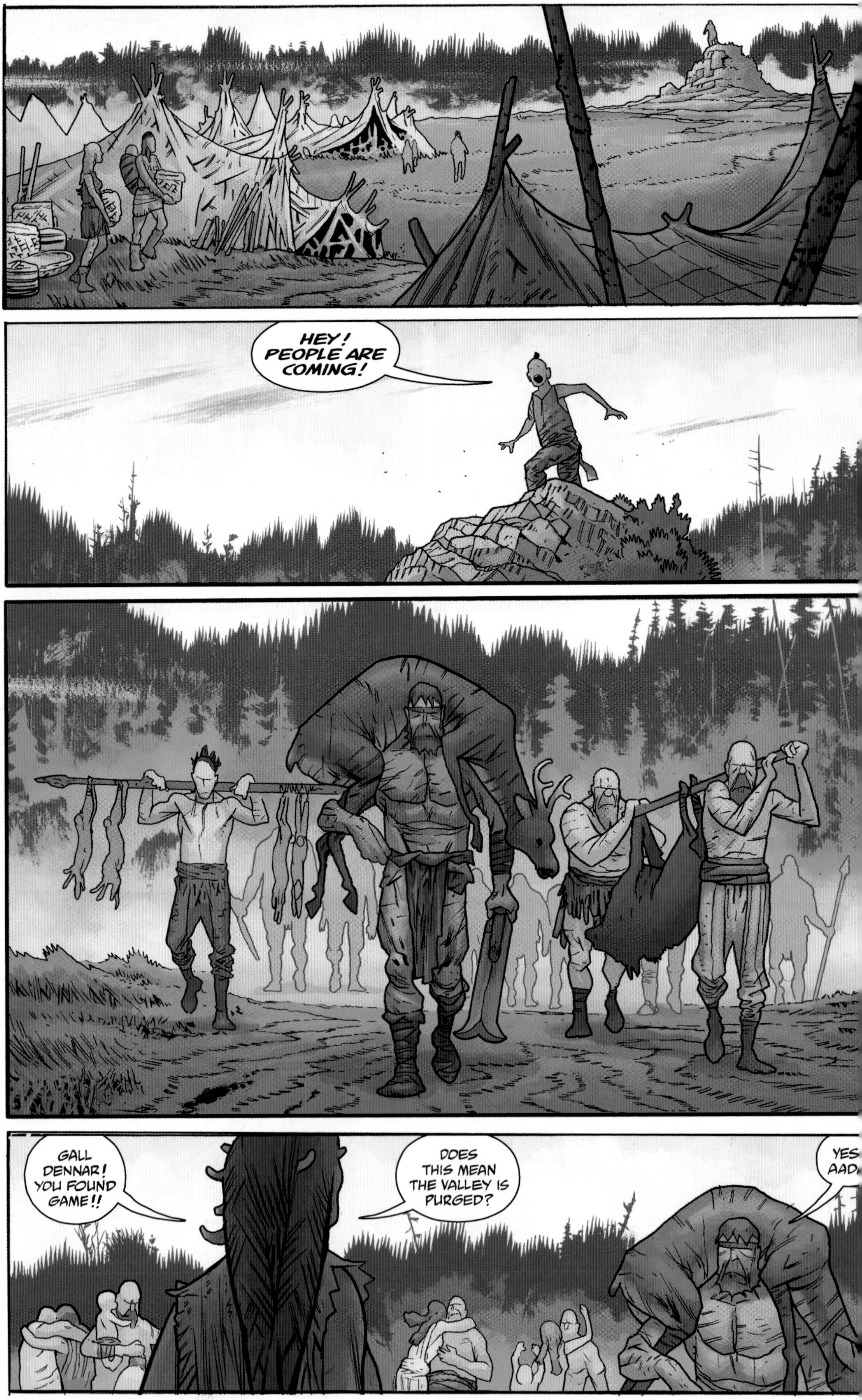
HEY! PEOPLE ARE COMING!
GALL DENNAR! YOU FOUND GAME!!
DOES THIS MEAN THE VALLEY IS PURGED?

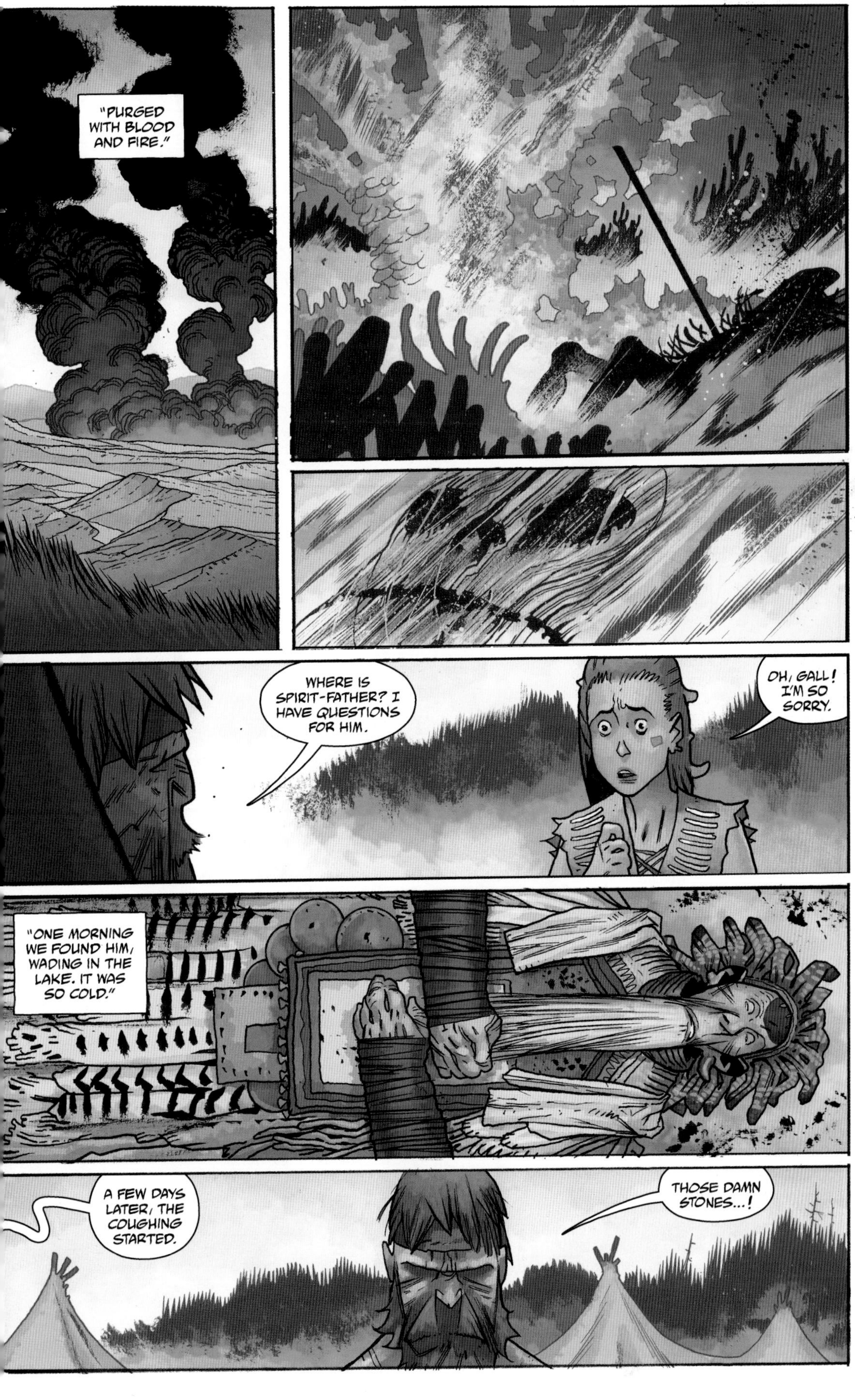
"PURGED WITH BLOOD AND FIRE."
WHERE IS SPIRIT-FATHER? I HAVE QUESTIONS FOR HIM.
OH, GALL! I'M SO SORRY.
"ONE MORNING WE FOUND HIM, WADING IN THE LAKE. IT WAS SO COLD."
A FEW DAYS LATER, THE COUGHING STARTED.
THOSE DAMN STONES...!

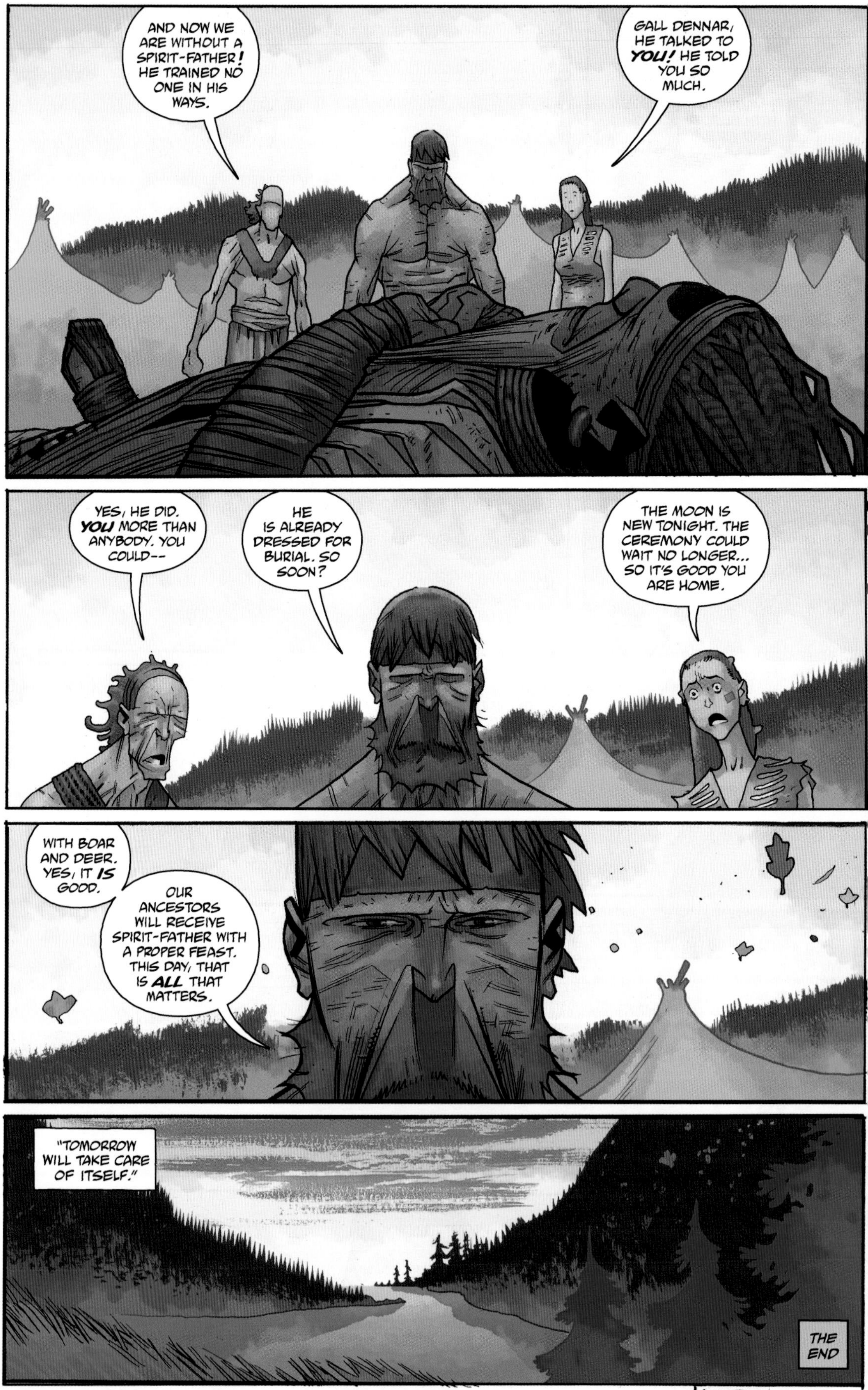
AND NOW WE ARE WITHOUT A SPIRIT-FATHER! HE TRAINED NO ONE IN HIS WAYS.
GALL DENNAR, HE TALKED TO YOU! HE TOLD YOU SO MUCH.
YES, HE DID. YOU MORE THAN ANYBODY. YOU COULD--
HE IS ALREADY DRESSED FOR BURIAL. SO SOON?
THE MOON IS NEW TONIGHT. THE CEREMONY COULD WAIT NO LONGER... SO IT'S GOOD YOU ARE HOME.
WITH BOAR AND DEER. YES, IT IS GOOD.
OUR ANCESTORS WILL RECEIVE SPIRIT-FATHER WITH A PROPER FEAST. THIS DAY, THAT IS ALL THAT MATTERS.
"TOMORROW WILL TAKE CARE OF ITSELF."
THE END
HARREN 2014

B.P.R.D.™

SKETCHBOOK

Notes by James Harren

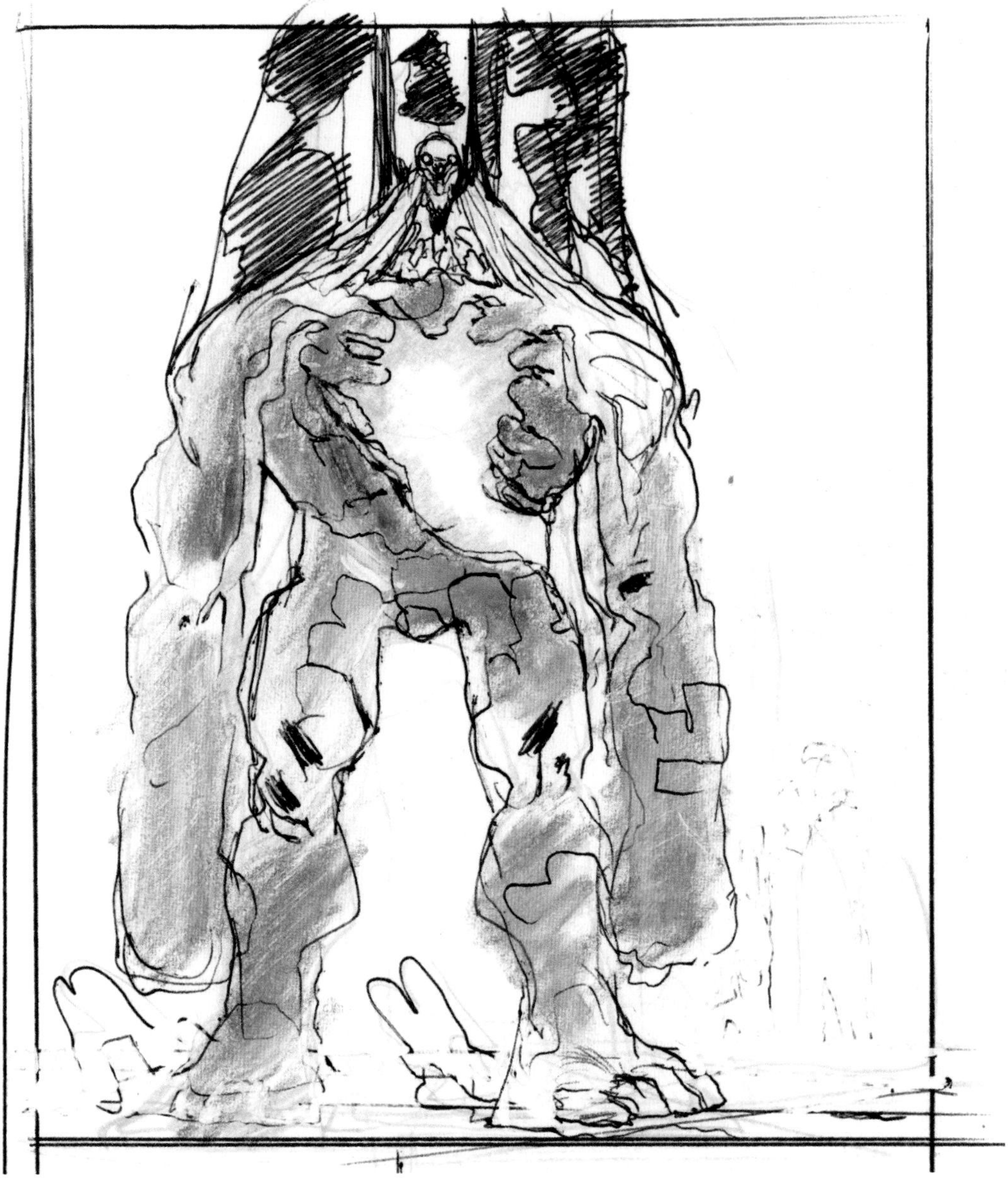

The Black Flame returns! We last saw him blowing up a large portion of Manhattan—I wanted it to look like that took its toll on his body. Either that or there's a natural degradation of his human silhouette from being so gosh-darn evil. Regardless of the why, I wanted him to evolve and change as the series progressed.

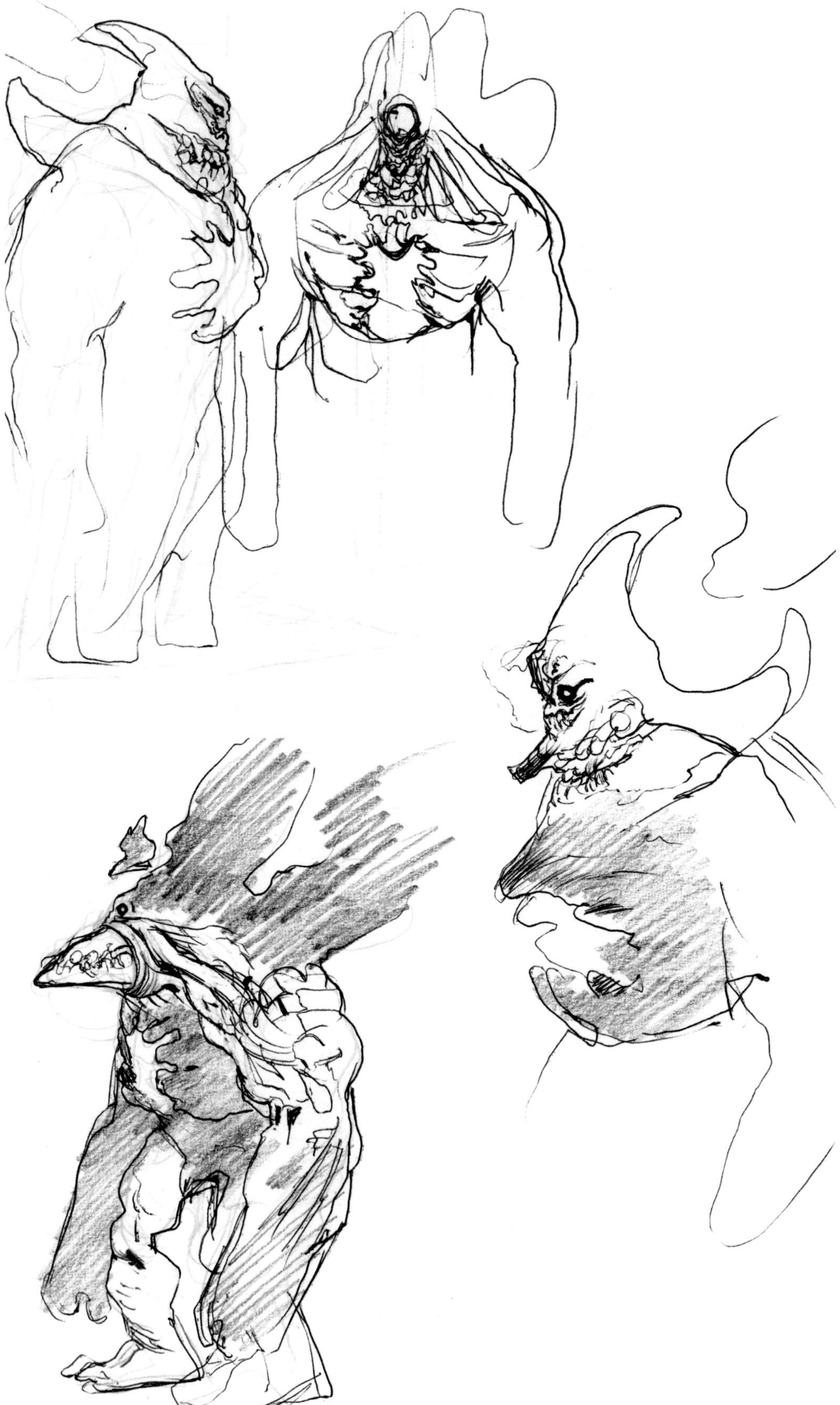

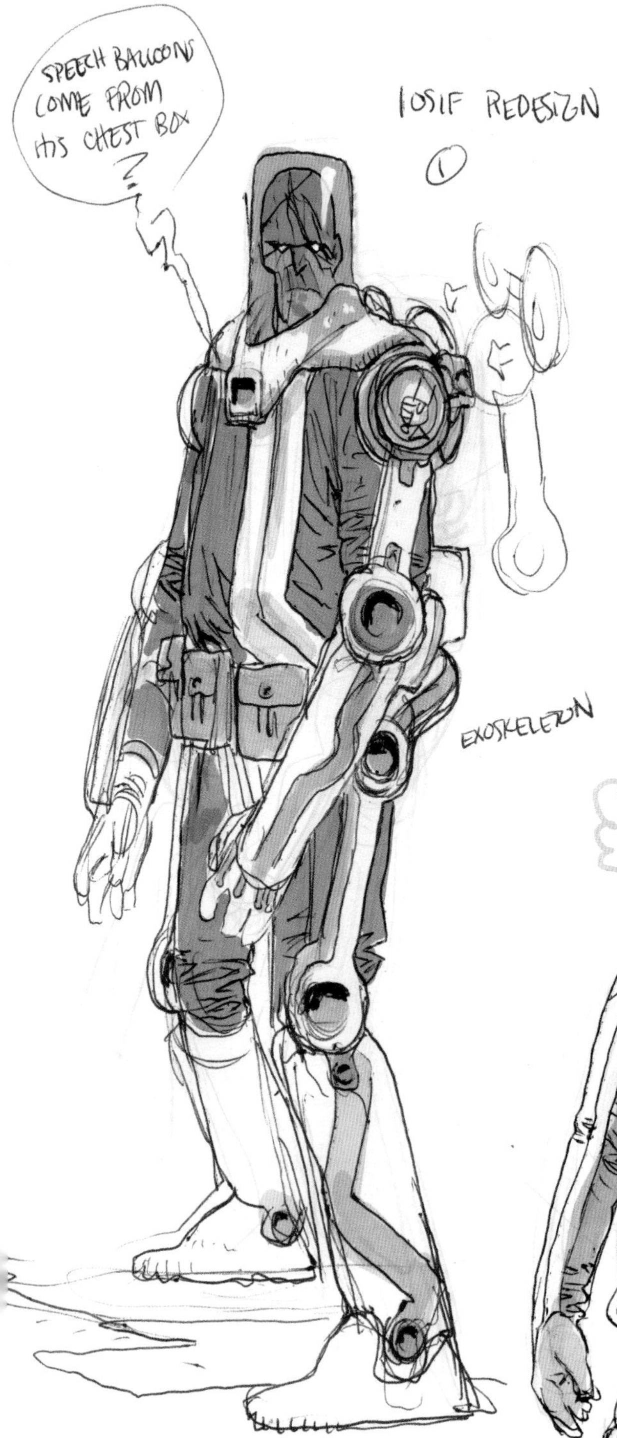

SPEECH BALLOONS COME FROM HIS CHEST BOX ?
IOSIF REDESIGN
①
EXOSKELETON

Iosifs! I tried to give Mike and John as many options as possible so we could pick the one that worked best with the character and the story. We wound up with clunky, early Iron Man/iron lung. I like that he looks cumbersome and as if he is trapped by this thing that's unnaturally extending his life.

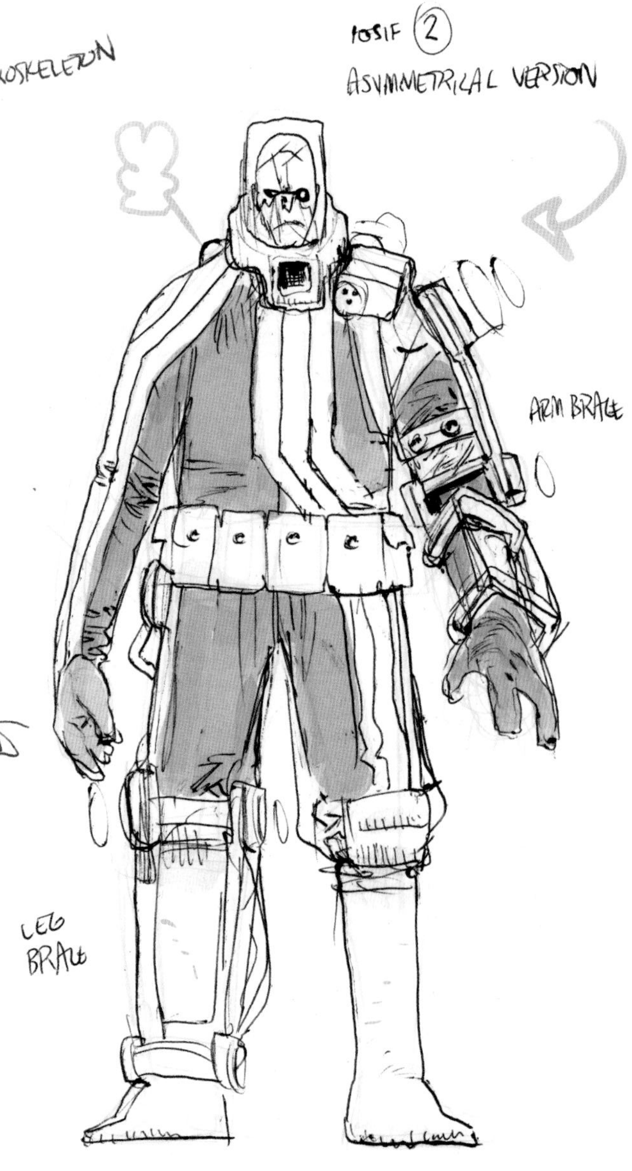

IOSIF ②
ASYMMETRICAL VERSION
ARM BRACE
LEG BRACE

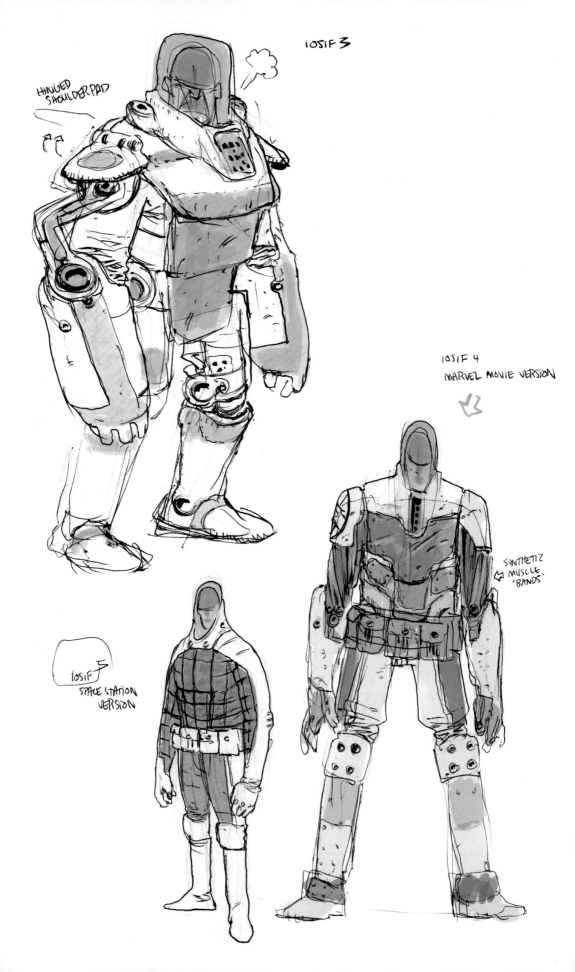

IOSIF 3

HINGED SHOULDER-PAD

IOSIF 4
MARVEL MOVIE VERSION

SYNTHETIZ
MUSCLE
'BANDS'

IOSIF 5
SPACE STATION
VERSION

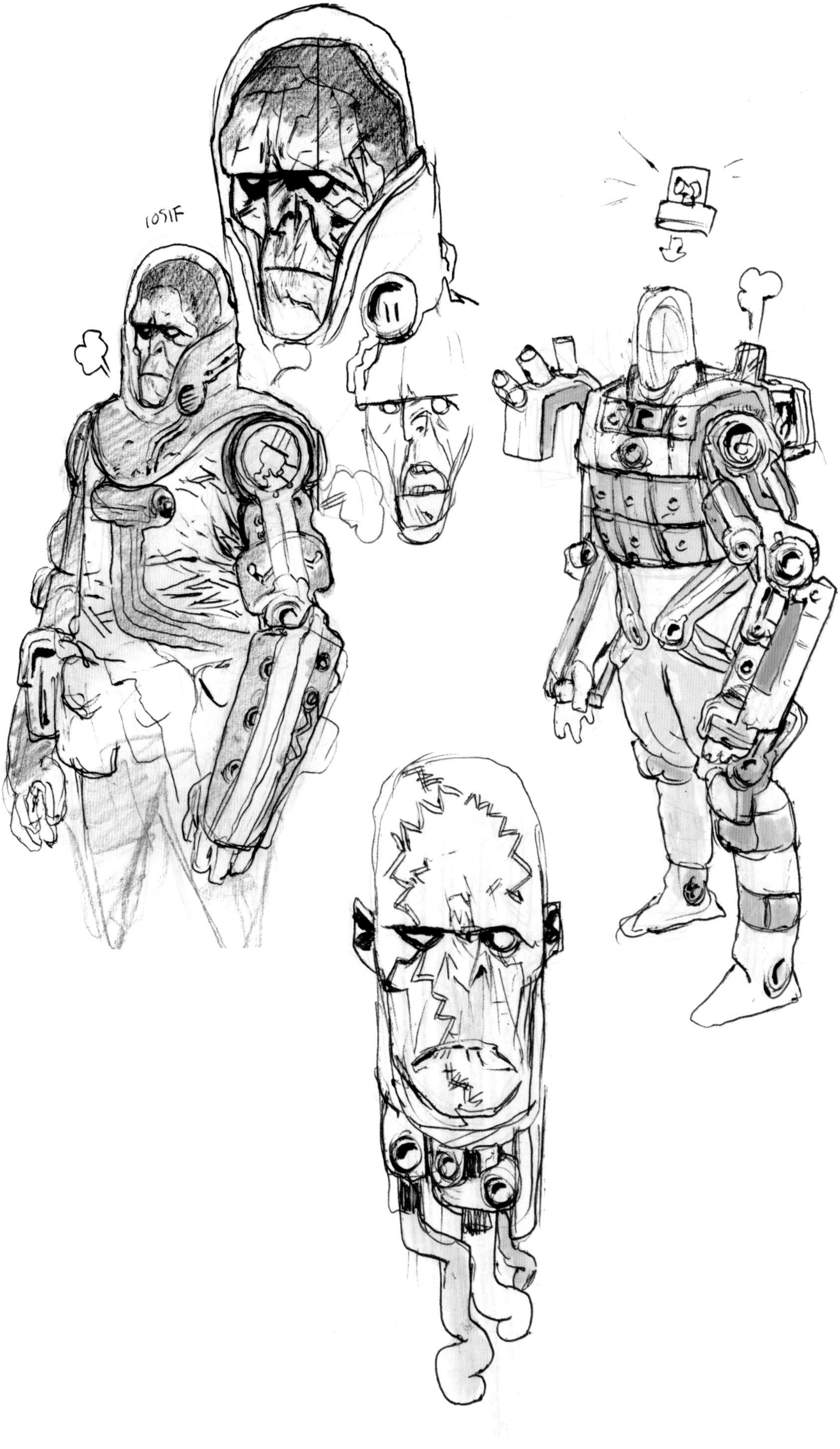
IOSIF

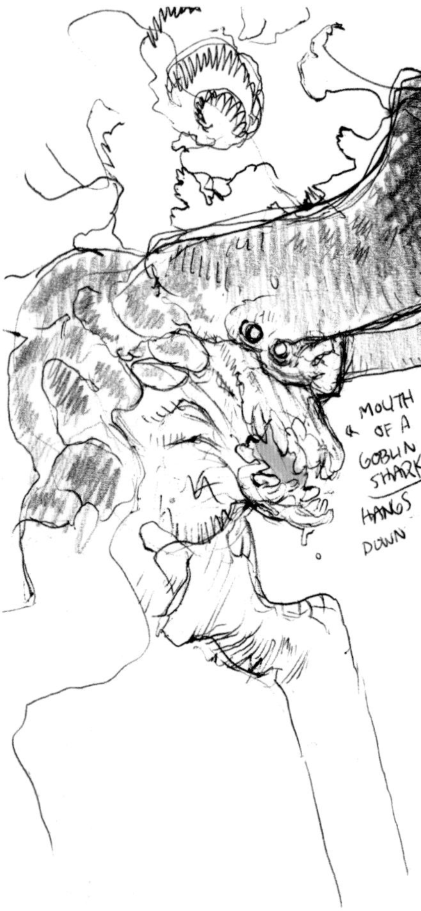
MOUTH
a OF A
GOBLIN
SHARK
HANGS
DOWN

An unused monster design. This is what happens when you don't read the script properly. I designed the wrong monster! I forget how I managed to stray so far from what was actually needed. Probably drugs. I even got to the pencil and inking stage before someone tugged my coat, and I redesigned her to be the tubby tumor monster that we all know and love.

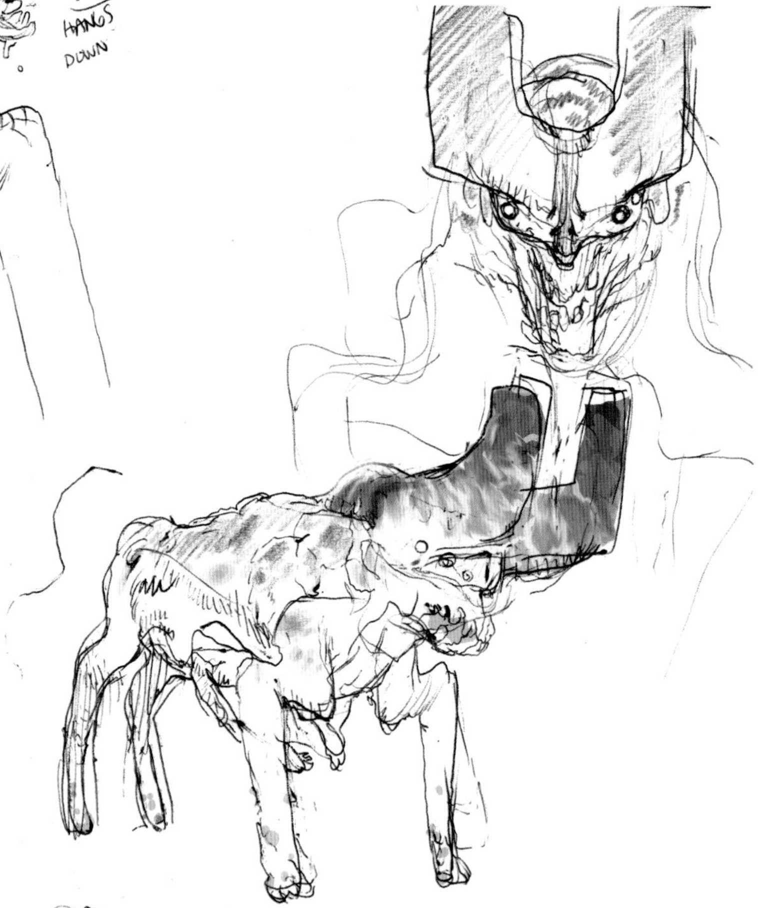

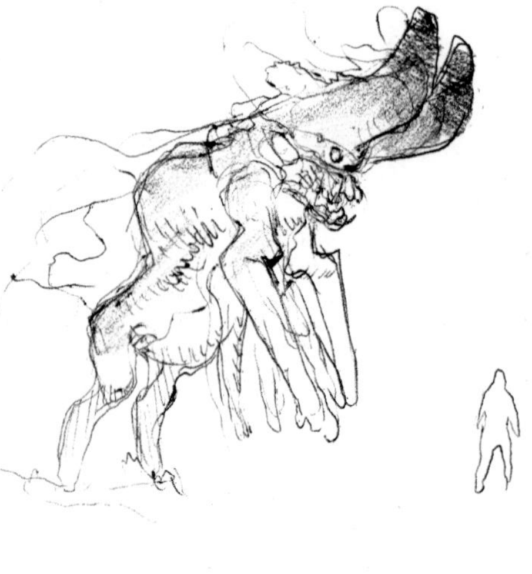

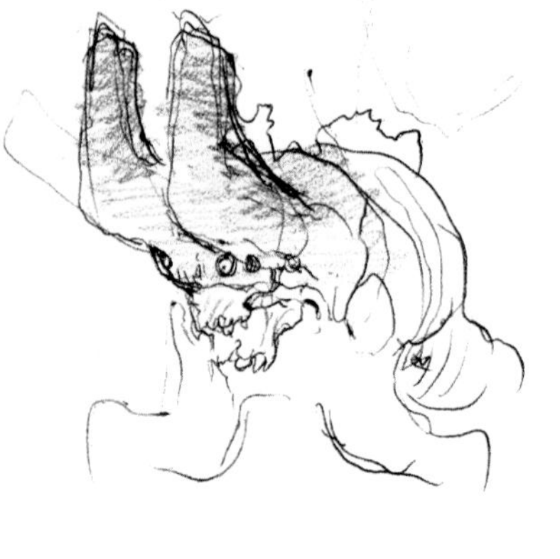

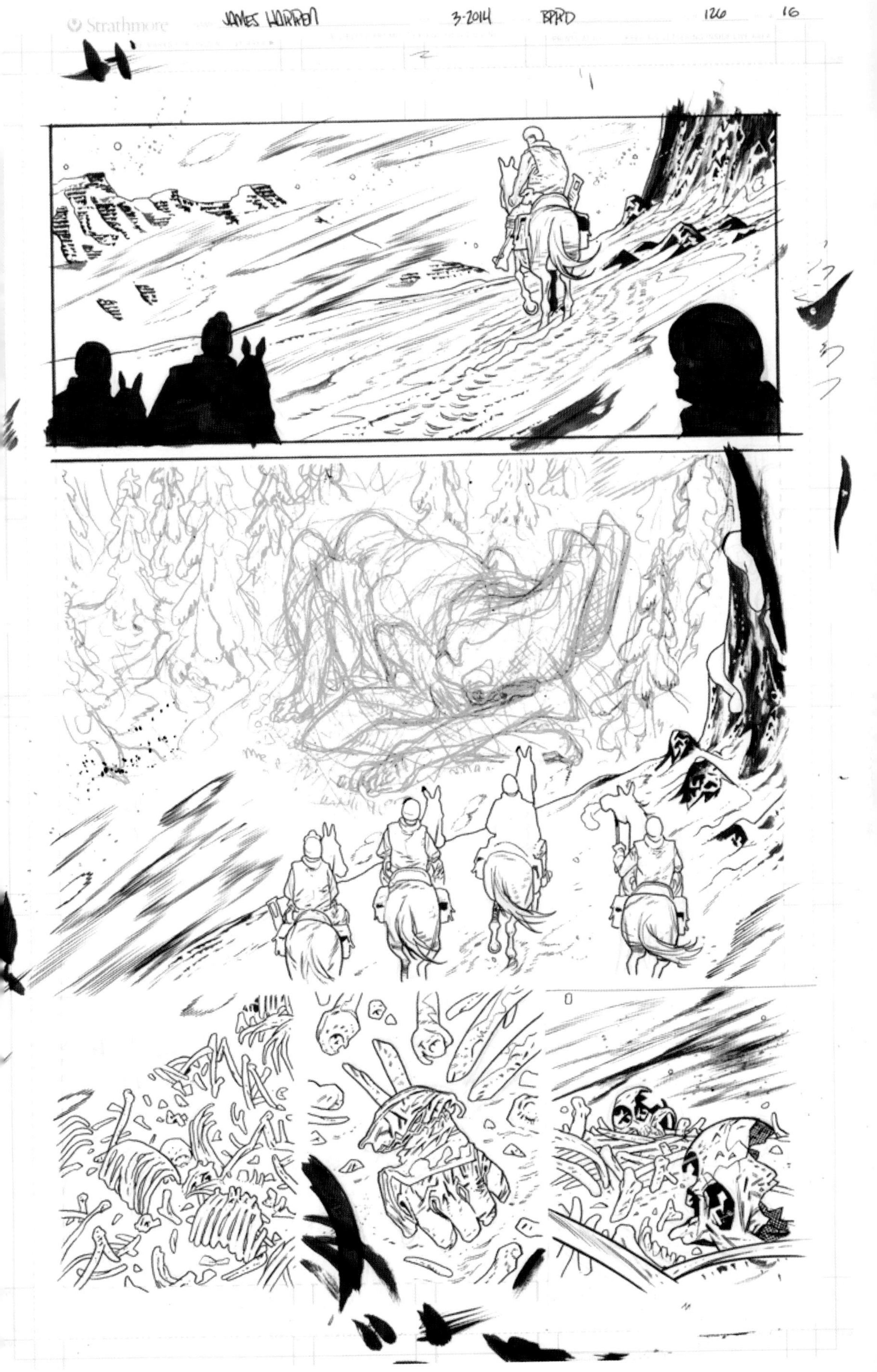
Strathmore
JAMES HARREN
3-2014
BPRD
126
16

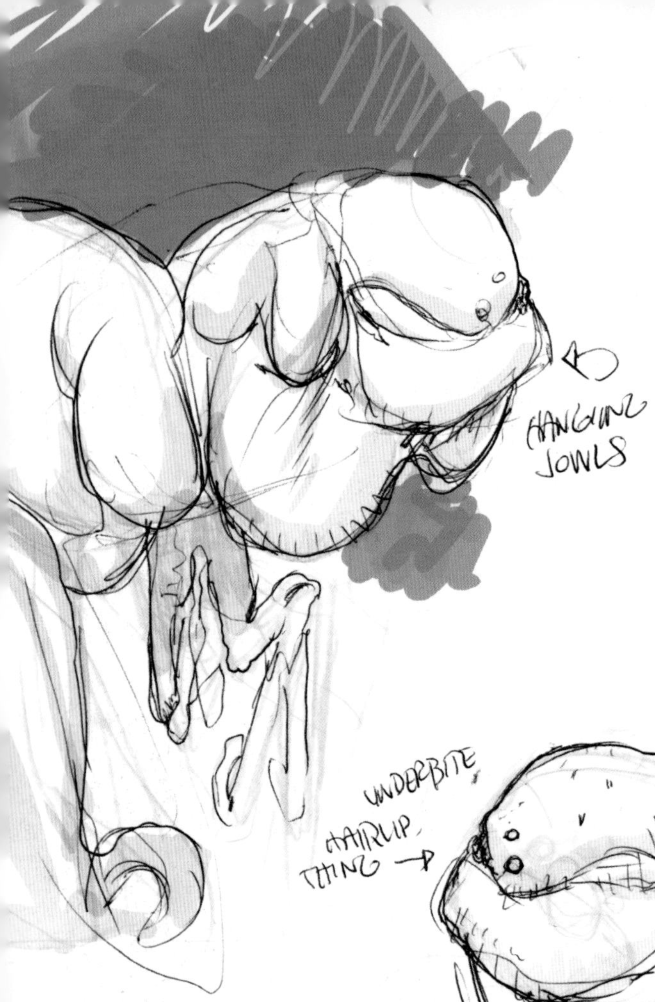

HANGING
JOWLS

Facing: Another blunder (drugs). I drew the wrong Howards. In his shamanic metamorphosis, he was supposed to be beyond his black-ash stage and moving on to his colorful, fully activated shaman-barbarian stage.

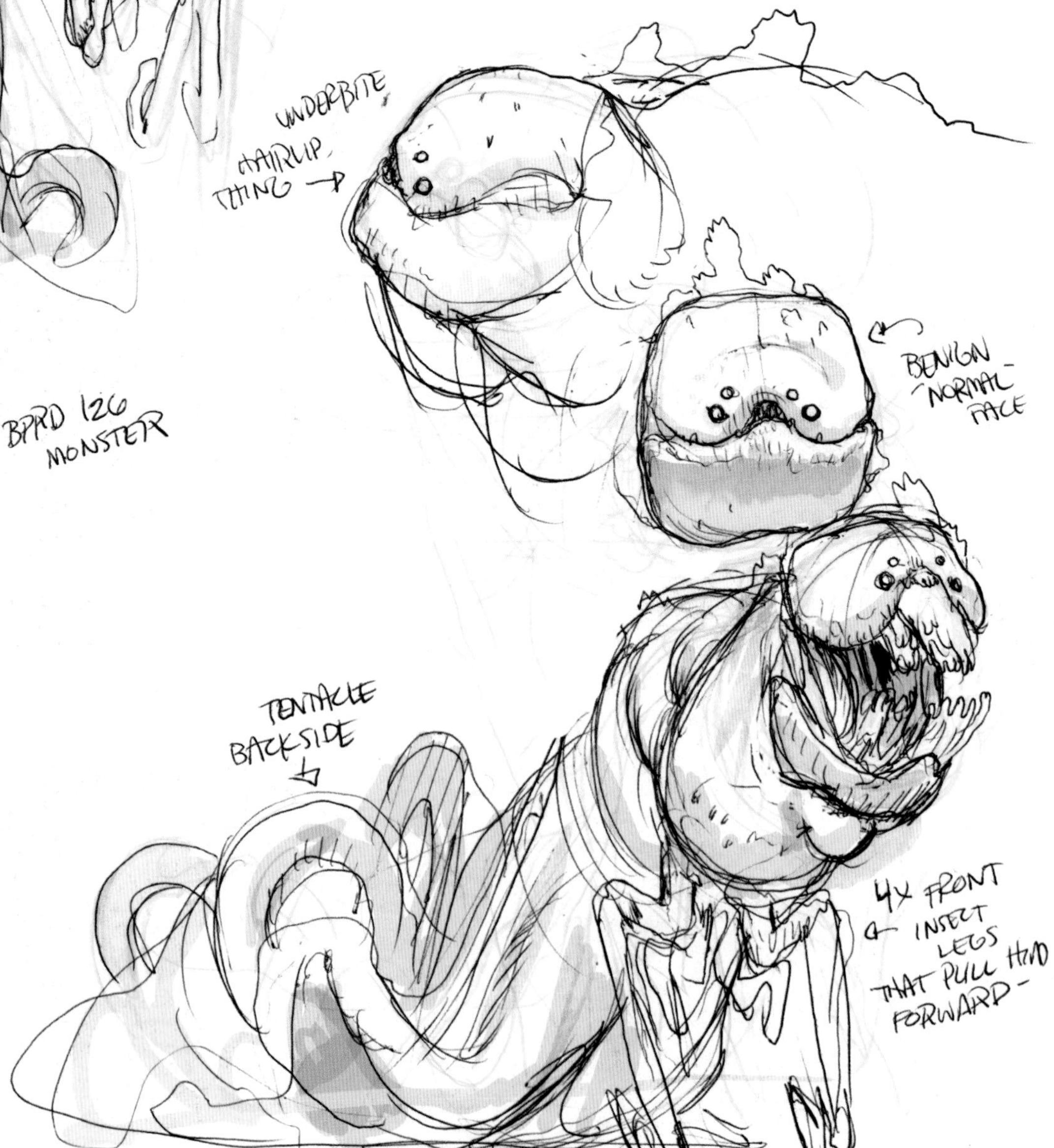

UNDERBITE
HAIRLIP
THING
BENIGN
"NORMAL"
FACE
BPRD 126
MONSTER
TENTACLE
BACKSIDE
4X FRONT
INSECT
LEGS
THAT PULL HIM
FORWARD -

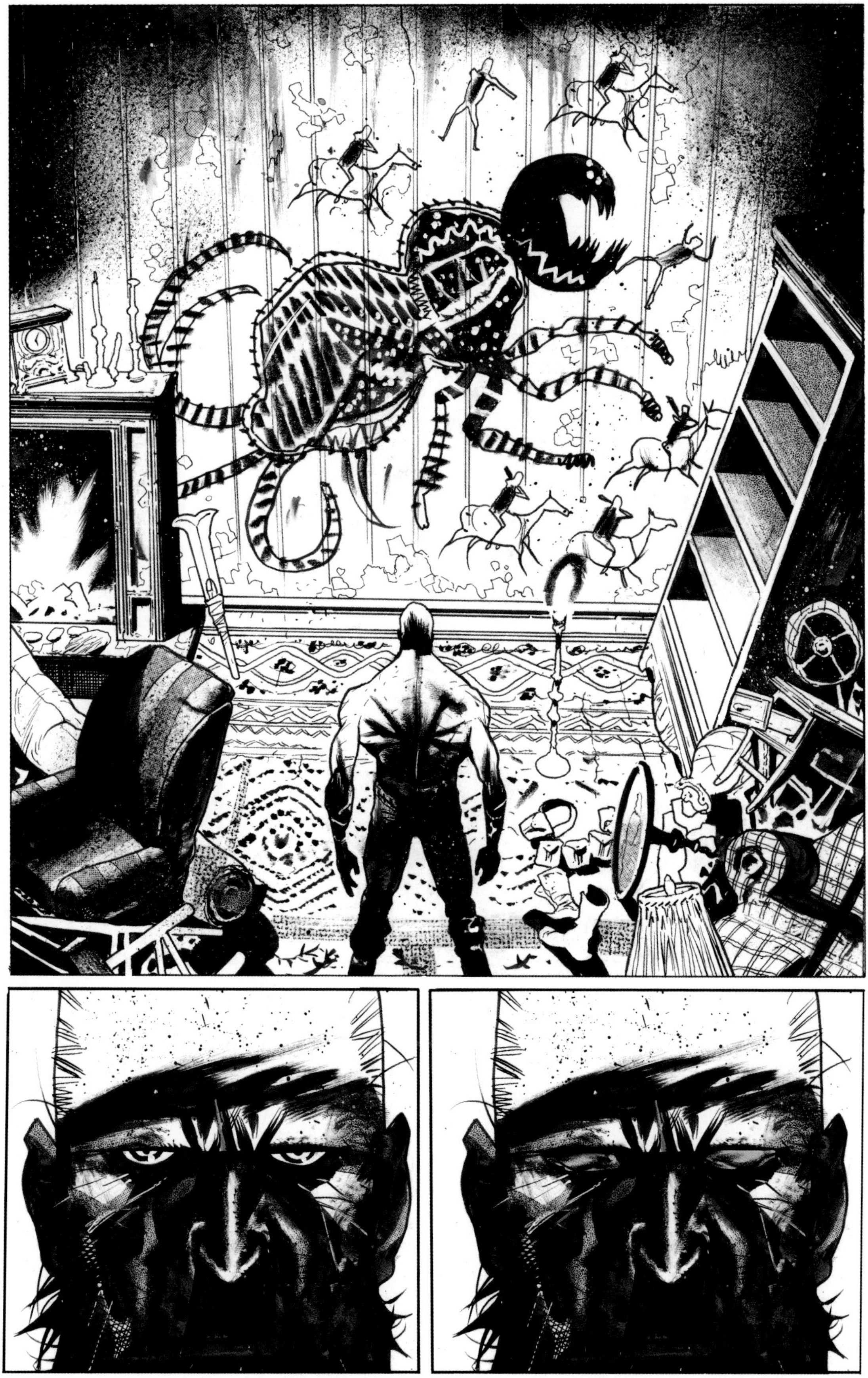

I don't remember having too much trouble with the fungal monster. John's description conjured a pretty specific image. I think we were all in love with the cordyceps mushrooms that take over ants' brains and later grow out of their heads like horns. What's not to love!

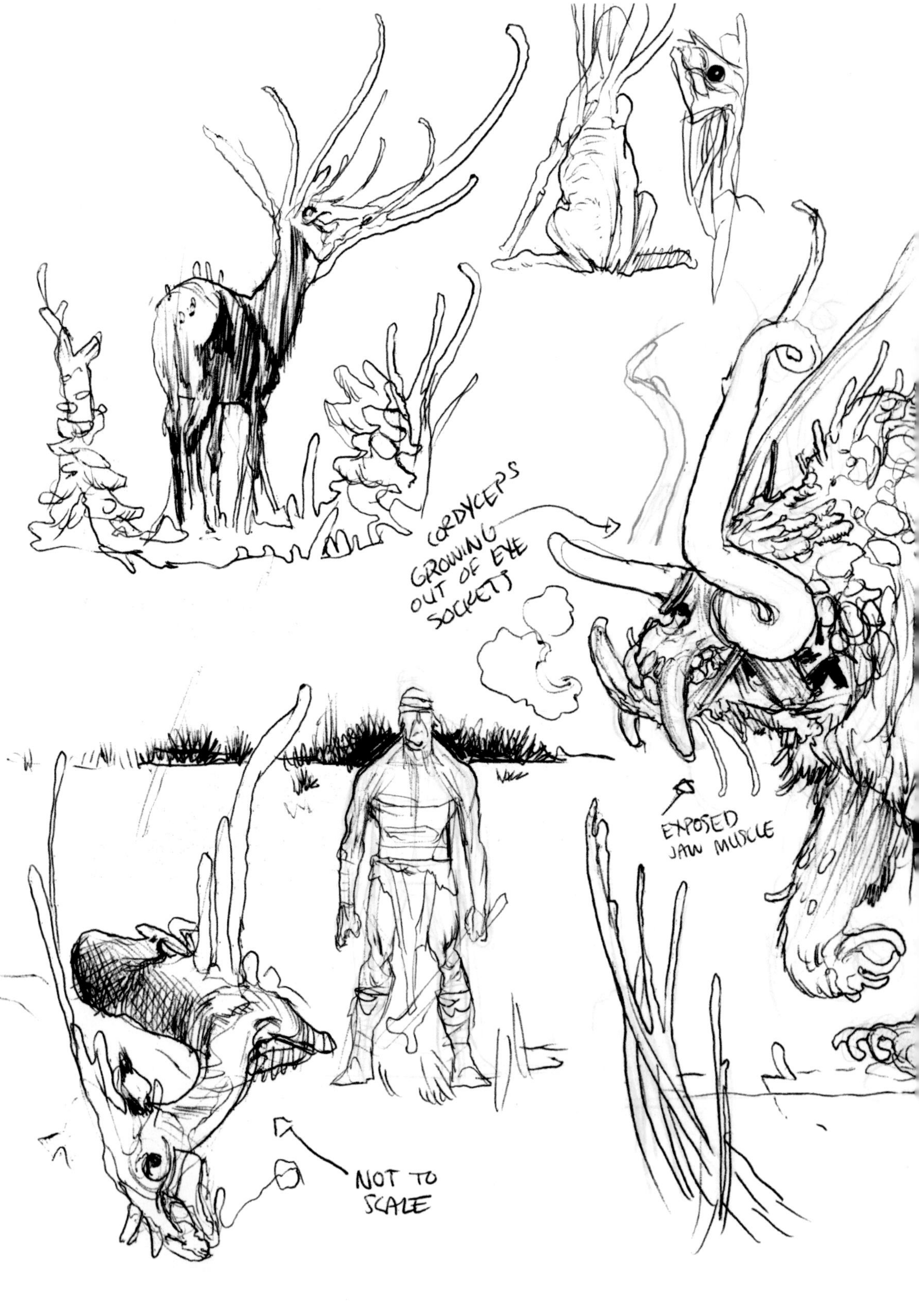
CORDYCEPS GROWING OUT OF EYE SOCKETS
EXPOSED JAW MUSCLE
NOT TO SCALE

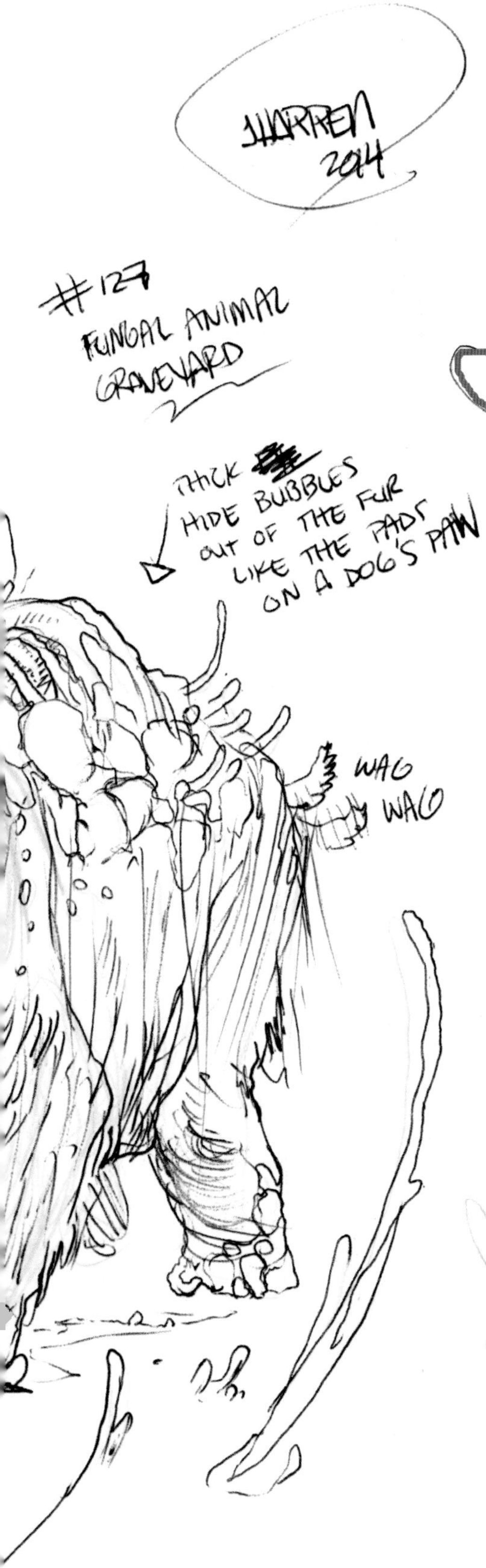

JWARREN
2014
#127
FUNGAL ANIMAL
GRAVEYARD
THICK HIDE BUBBLES
OUT OF THE FUR
LIKE THE PADS
ON A DOG'S PAW
WAG
WAG

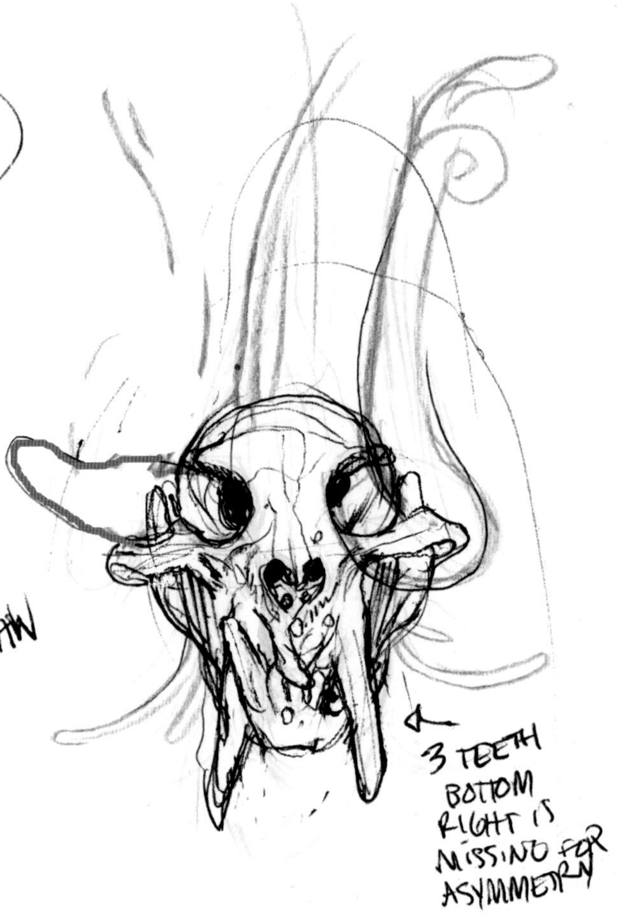

3 TEETH
BOTTOM
RIGHT IS
MISSING FOR
ASYMMETRY

A diagram of the fungal horns for Laurence to work off for his *amazing* cover series.

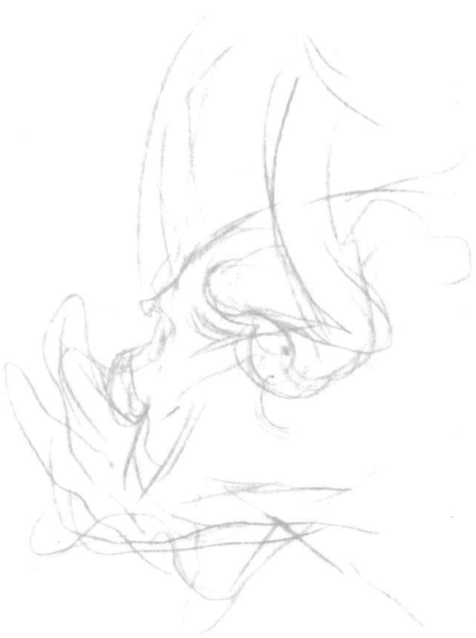

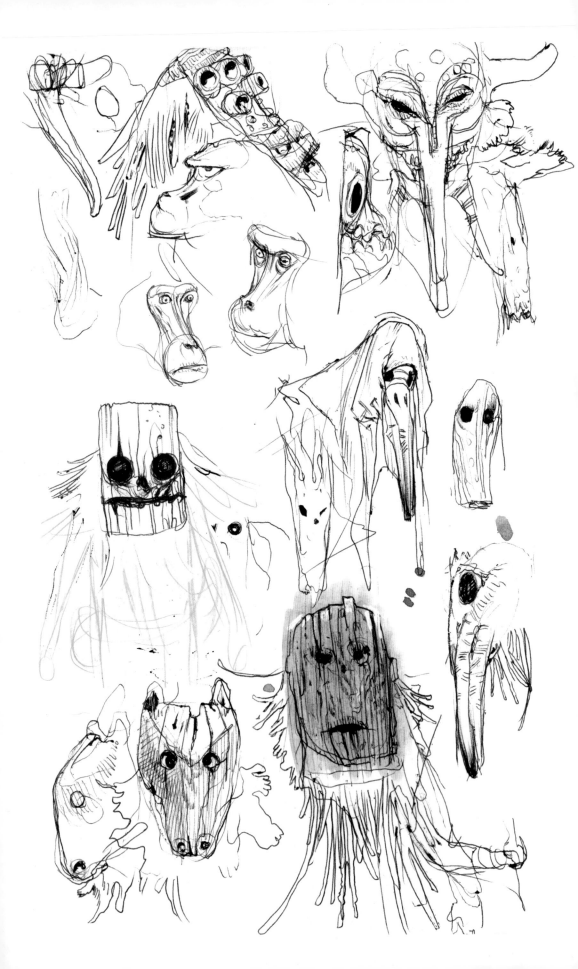

Looking for a sticky-mask idea for our evil fungus shaman. I was playing around with something that looked like a seventeenth-century plague doctor mask. That would've been neat.

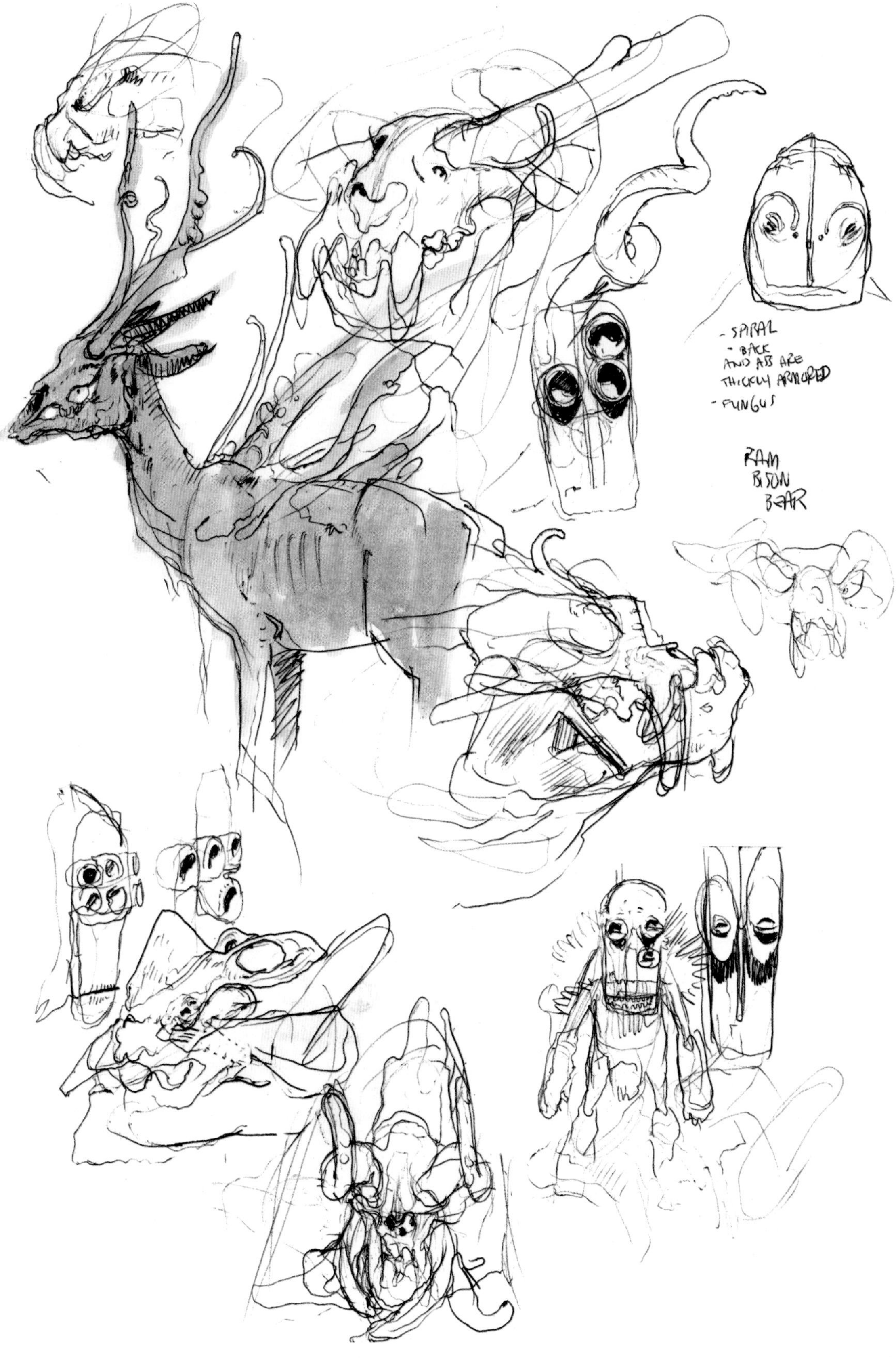
- SPIRAL
- BACK AND ASS ARE THICKLY ARMORED
- FUNGUS
RAM
BISON
BEAR

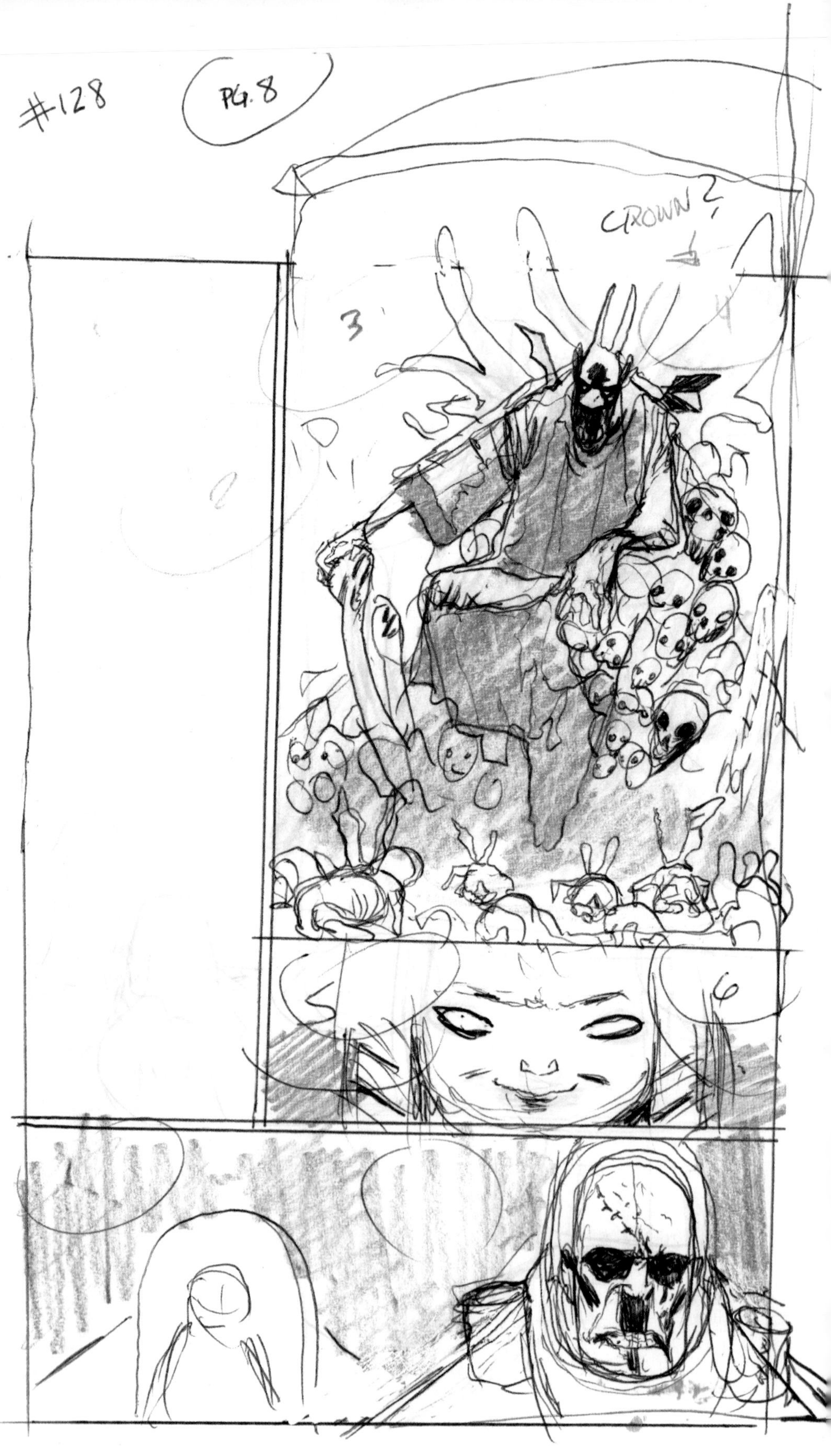

#128
PG. 8
CROWN?
3
6

Sketches and studies to try to get Mike's version of Hell right.

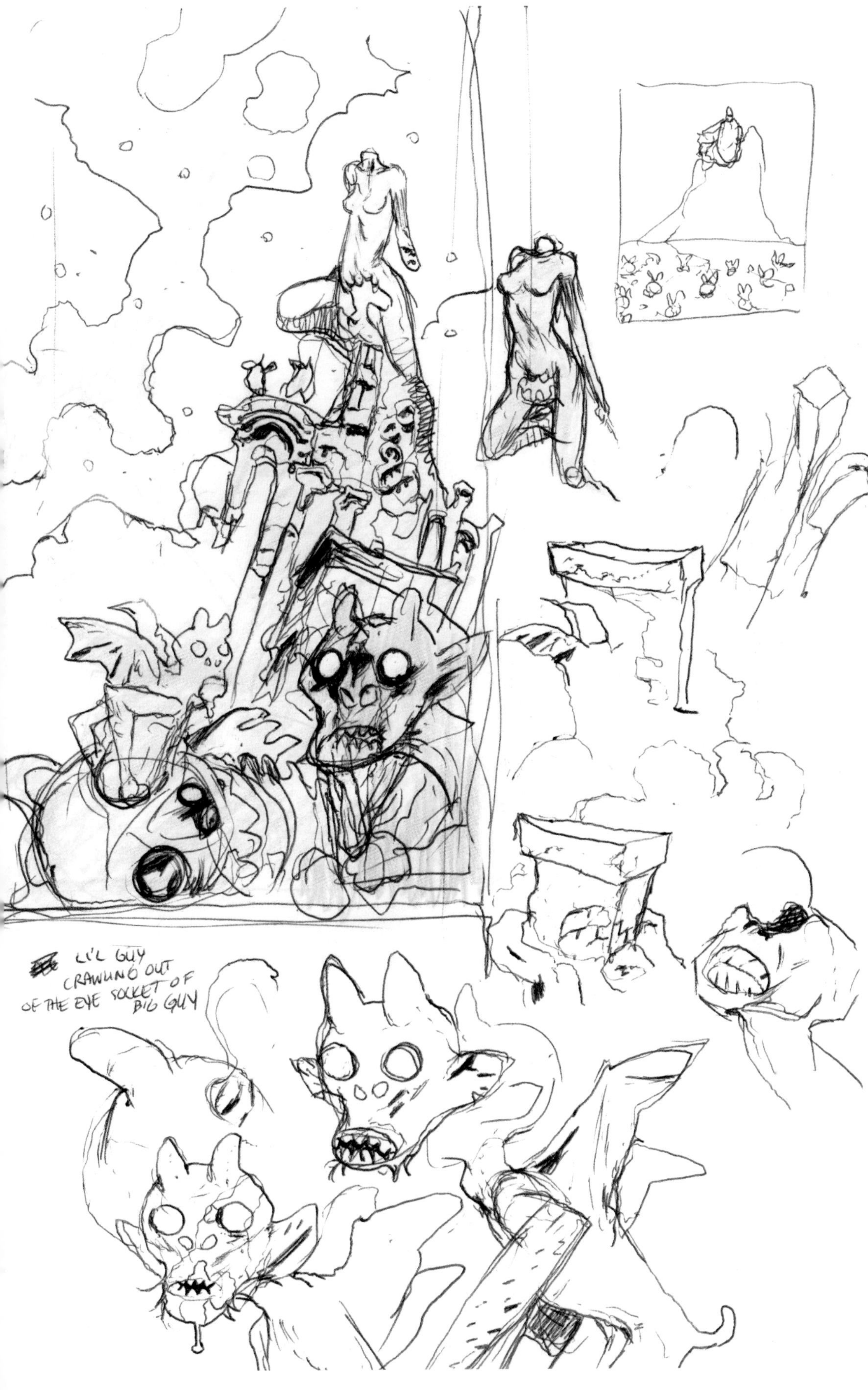
LI'L GUY CRAWLING OUT OF THE EYE SOCKET OF BIG GUY

It was Laurence's idea to do the five covers of the original series as a single piece. Dark Horse produced a free print given away at New York Comic Con in 2014.

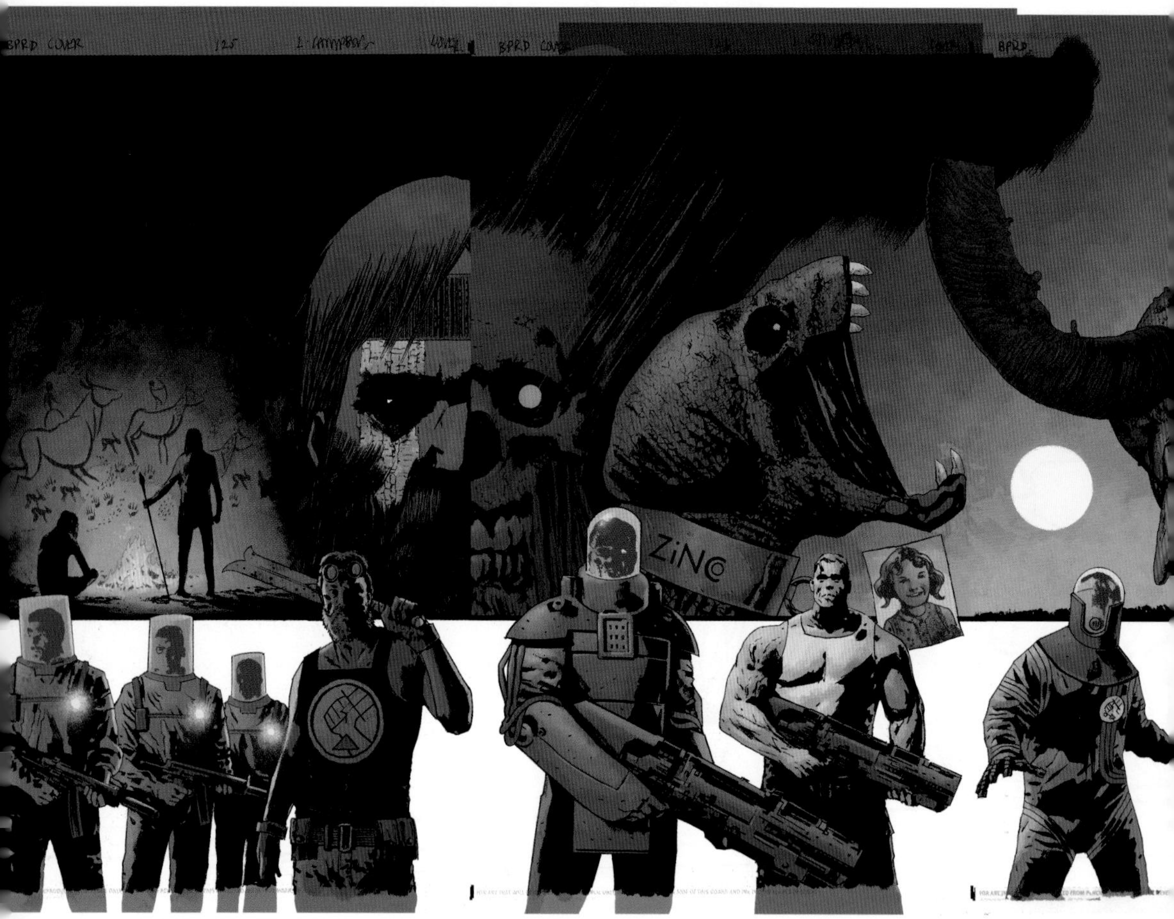
ZiNC

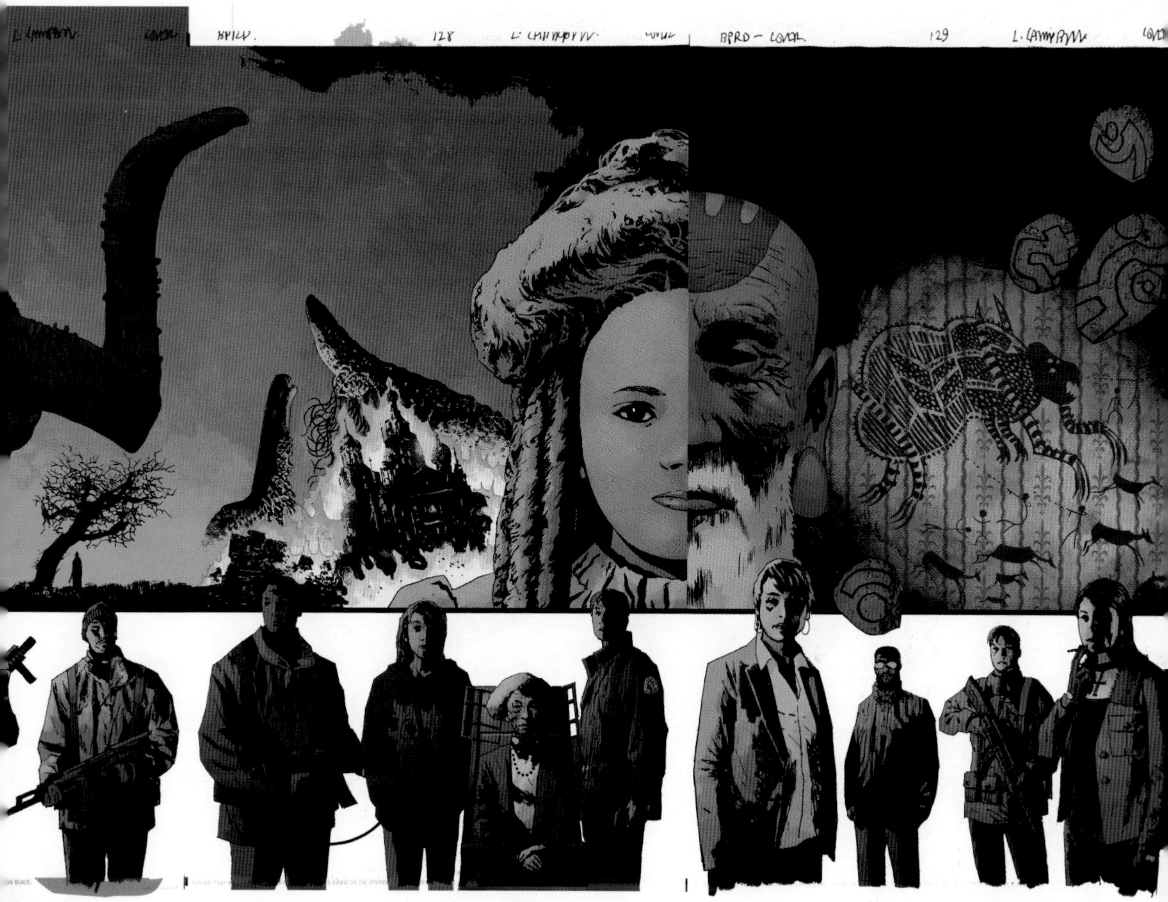
128
BPRD - COVER.
129

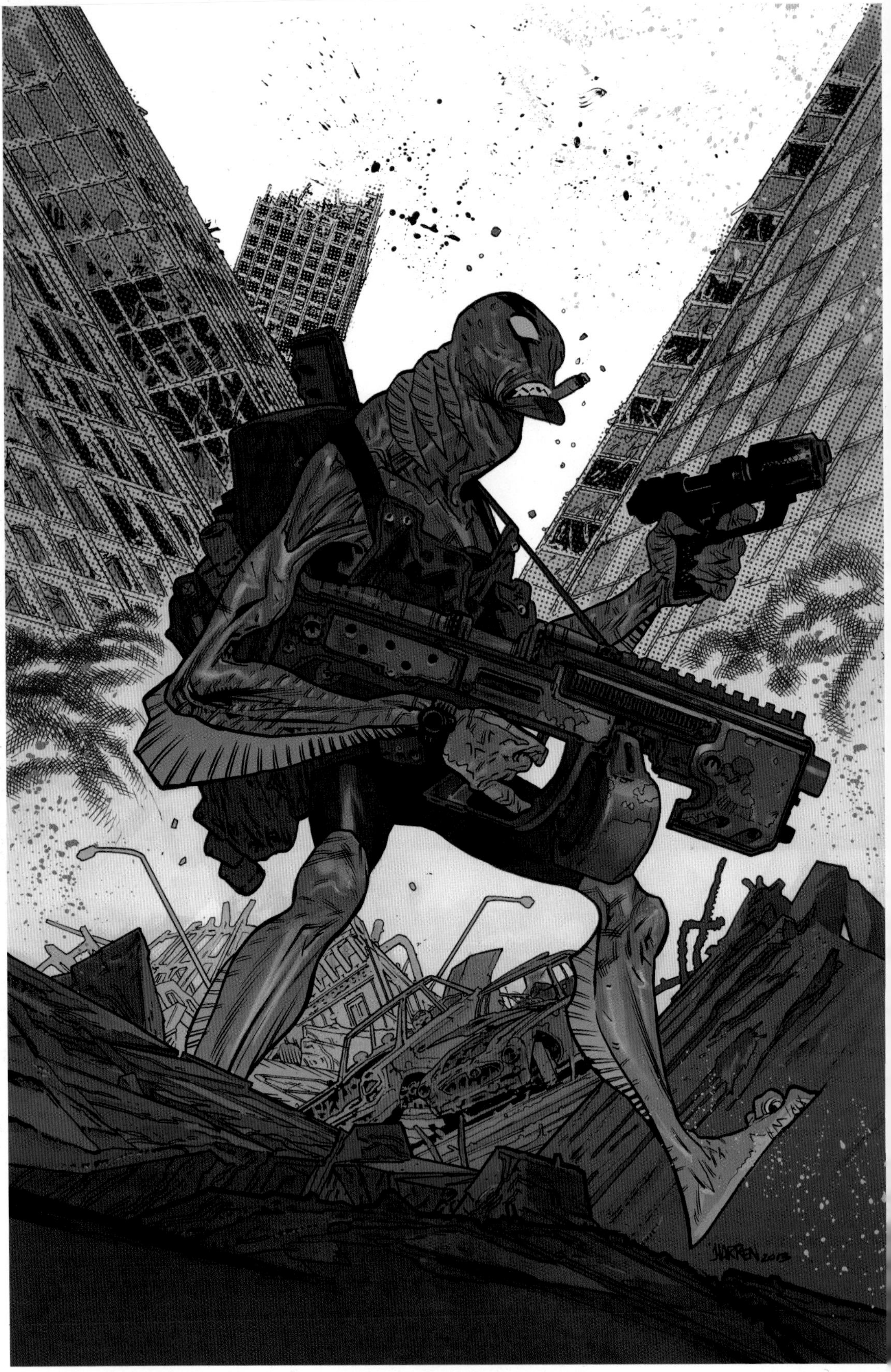

WARREN 2013

James's contribution to the 30 Days of Abe promotion on Multiversity.com in honor of the debut of the monthly Abe Sapien *series.*

Also by

MIKE MIGNOLA

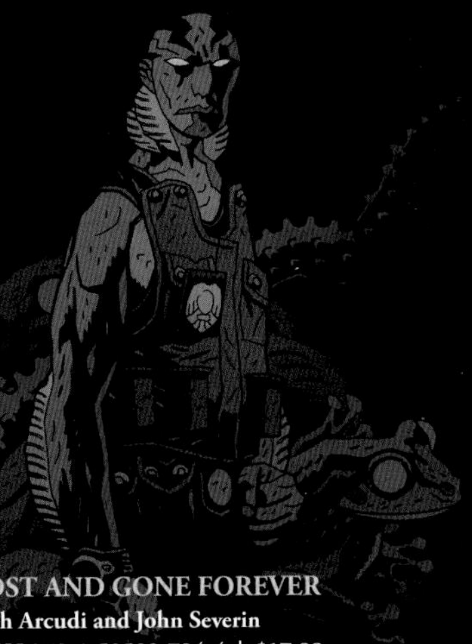

B.P.R.D.

PLAGUE OF FROGS

Volume 1
with Chris Golden, Guy Davis, and others
HC: ISBN 978-1-59582-609-1 | $34.99
TPB: ISBN 978-1-59582-675-6 | $19.99

Volume 2
with John Arcudi, Davis, and others
HC: ISBN 978-1-59582-672-5 | $34.99
TPB: ISBN 978-1-59582-676-3 | $24.99

Volume 3
with Arcudi and Davis
HC: ISBN 978-1-59582-860-6 | $34.99
TPB: ISBN 978-1-61655-622-8 | $24.99

Volume 4
with Arcudi and Davis
HC: ISBN 978-1-59582-974-0 | $34.99
TPB: ISBN 978-1-61655-641-9 | $24.99

1946–1948
with Joshua Dysart, Paul Azaceta, Fábio Moon, Gabriel Bá, Max Fiumara, and Arcudi
ISBN 978-1-61655-646-4 | $34.99

BEING HUMAN
with Scott Allie, Arcudi, Davis, and others
ISBN 978-1-59582-756-2 | $17.99

VAMPIRE
with Moon and Bá
ISBN 978-1-61655-196-4 | $19.99

B.P.R.D. HELL ON EARTH

NEW WORLD
with Arcudi and Davis
ISBN 978-1-59582-707-4 | $19.99

GODS AND MONSTERS
with Arcudi, Davis, and Tyler Crook
ISBN 978-1-59582-822-4 | $19.99

RUSSIA
with Arcudi, Crook, and Duncan Fegredo
ISBN 978-1-59582-946-7 | $19.99

THE DEVIL'S ENGINE AND THE LONG DEATH
with Arcudi, Crook, and James Harren
ISBN 978-1-59582-981-8 | $19.99

THE PICKENS COUNTY HORROR AND OTHERS
with Allie, Jason Latour, Harren, and Max Fiumara
ISBN 978-1-61655-140-7 | $19.99

THE RETURN OF THE MASTER
with Arcudi and Crook
ISBN 978-1-61655-193-3 | $19.99

A COLD DAY IN HELL
with Arcudi, Peter Snejbjerg, and Laurence Campbell
ISBN 978-1-61655-199-5 | $19.99

THE REIGN OF THE BLACK FLAME
with Arcudi and Harren
ISBN 978-1-61655-471-2 | $19.99

THE DEVIL'S WINGS
with Arcudi, Campbell, Joe Querio, and Crook
ISBN 978-1-61655-617-4 | $19.99

LAKE OF FIRE
with Arcudi and Crook
ISBN 978-1-61655-402-6 | $19.99

FLESH AND STONE
with Arcudi and Harren
ISBN 978-1-61655-762-1 | $19.99

ABE SAPIEN

THE DROWNING
with Jason Shawn Alexander
ISBN 978-1-59582-185-0 | $17.99

THE DEVIL DOES NOT JEST AND OTHER STORIES
with Arcudi, Harren, and others
ISBN 978-1-59582-925-2 | $17.99

DARK AND TERRIBLE AND THE NEW RACE OF MAN
with Allie, Arcudi, Sebastián Fiumara, and Max Fiumara
ISBN 978-1-61655-284-8 | $19.99

THE SHAPE OF THINGS TO COME
with Allie, S. Fiumara, and M. Fiumara
ISBN 978-1-61655-443-9 | $19.99

SACRED PLACES
with Allie, S. Fiumara, and M. Fiumara
ISBN 978-1-61655-515-3 | $19.99

A DARKNESS SO GREAT
with Allie and M. Fiumara
ISBN 978-1-61655-656-3 | $19.99

LOBSTER JOHNSON

THE IRON PROMETHEUS
with Jason Armstrong
ISBN 978-1-59307-975-8 | $17.99

THE BURNING HAND
with Arcudi and Tonci Zonjic
ISBN 978-1-61655-031-8 | $17.99

SATAN SMELLS A RAT
with Arcudi, Fiumara, Querio, Wilfredo Torres, and Kevin Nowlan
ISBN 978-1-61655-203-9 | $18.99

GET THE LOBSTER
with Arcudi and Zonjic
ISBN 978-1-61655-505-4 | $19.99

WITCHFINDER

IN THE SERVICE OF ANGELS
with Ben Stenbeck
ISBN 978-1-59582-483-7 | $17.99

LOST AND GONE FOREVER
with Arcudi and John Severin
ISBN 978-1-59582-794-4 | $17.99

THE MYSTERIES OF UNLAND
with Kim Newman, Maura McHugh, and Crook
ISBN 978-1-61655-630-3 | $19.99

FRANKENSTEIN UNDERGROUND

with Stenbeck
ISBN 978-1-61655-782-9 | $19.99

THE AMAZING SCREW-ON HEAD AND OTHER CURIOUS OBJECTS

ISBN 978-1-59582-501-8 | $17.99

BALTIMORE

THE PLAGUE SHIPS
with Golden and Stenbeck
ISBN 978-1-59582-677-0 | $24.99

THE CURSE BELLS
with Golden and Stenbeck
ISBN 978-1-59582-674-9 | $24.99

A PASSING STRANGER AND OTHER STORIES
with Golden and Stenbeck
ISBN 978-1-61655-182-7 | $24.99

CHAPEL OF BONES
with Golden and Stenbeck
ISBN 978-1-61655-328-9 | $24.99

THE APOSTLE AND THE WITCH OF HARJU
with Golden, Stenbeck, and Peter Bergting
ISBN 978-1-61655-618-1 | $24.99

NOVELS

LOBSTER JOHNSON: THE SATAN FACTORY
with Thomas E. Sniegoski
ISBN 978-1-59582-203-1 | $12.95

JOE GOLEM AND THE DROWNING CITY
with Golden
ISBN 978-1-59582-971-9 | $99.99

AVAILABLE AT YOUR LOCAL COMICS SHOP OR BOOKSTORE! • To find a comics shop in your area, call 1-888-266-4226.
For more information or to order direct visit DarkHorse.com or call 1-800-862-0052 Mon.–Fri. 9 AM to 5 PM Pacific Time.
Prices and availability subject to change without notice.

DarkHorse.com

HELLBOY by MIKE MIGNOLA

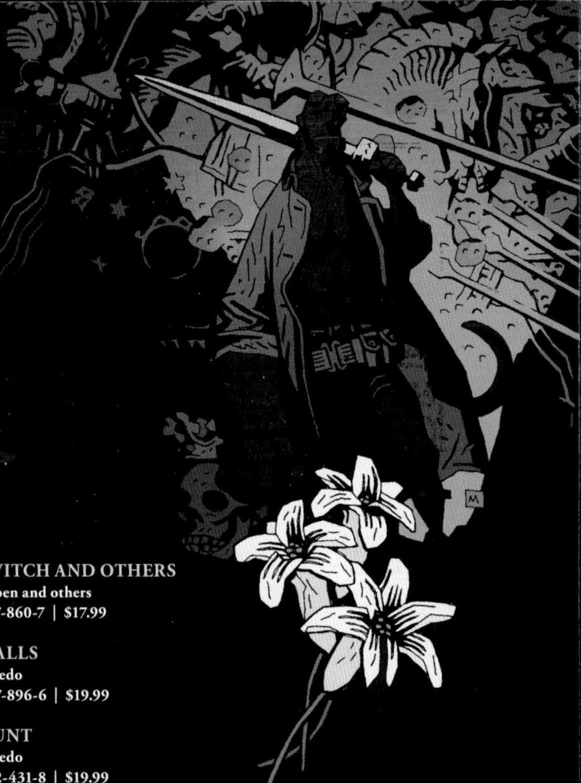

HELLBOY LIBRARY EDITION VOLUME 1:
Seed of Destruction and Wake the Devil
ISBN 978-1-59307-910-9 | $49.99

HELLBOY LIBRARY EDITION VOLUME 2:
The Chained Coffin and The Right Hand of Doom
ISBN 978-1-59307-989-5 | $49.99

HELLBOY LIBRARY EDITION VOLUME 3:
Conqueror Worm and Strange Places
ISBN 978-1-59582-352-6 | $49.99

HELLBOY LIBRARY EDITION VOLUME 4:
The Crooked Man and The Troll Witch
with Richard Corben and others
ISBN 978-1-59582-658-9 | $49.99

HELLBOY LIBRARY EDITION VOLUME 5:
Darkness Calls and the Wild Hunt
with Duncan Fegredo
ISBN 978-1-59582-886-6 | $49.99

HELLBOY LIBRARY EDITION VOLUME 6:
The Storm and the Fury and The Bride of Hell
with Duncan Fegredo, Richard Corben, Kevin Nowlan, and Scott Hampton
ISBN 978-1-61655-133-9 | $49.99

SEED OF DESTRUCTION
with John Byrne
ISBN 978-1-59307-094-6 | $17.99

WAKE THE DEVIL
ISBN 978-1-59307-095-3 | $17.99

THE CHAINED COFFIN AND OTHERS
ISBN 978-1-59307-091-5 | $17.99

THE RIGHT HAND OF DOOM
ISBN 978-1-59307-093-9 | $17.99

CONQUEROR WORM
ISBN 978-1-59307-092-2 | $17.99

STRANGE PLACES
ISBN 978-1-59307-475-3 | $17.99

THE TROLL WITCH AND OTHERS
with Richard Corben and others
ISBN 978-1-59307-860-7 | $17.99

DARKNESS CALLS
with Duncan Fegredo
ISBN 978-1-59307-896-6 | $19.99

THE WILD HUNT
with Duncan Fegredo
ISBN 978-1-59582-431-8 | $19.99

THE CROOKED MAN AND OTHERS
with Richard Corben
ISBN 978-1-59582-477-6 | $17.99

THE BRIDE OF HELL AND OTHERS
with Richard Corben, Kevin Nowlan, and Scott Hampton
ISBN 978-1-59582-740-1 | $19.99

THE STORM AND THE FURY
with Duncan Fegredo
ISBN 978-1-59582-827-9 | $19.99

HOUSE OF THE LIVING DEAD
with Richard Corben
ISBN 978-1-59582-757-9 | $14.99

THE MIDNIGHT CIRCUS
with Duncan Fegredo
ISBN 978-1-61655-238-1 | $14.99

HELLBOY IN HELL VOLUME 1: THE DESCENT
ISBN 978-1-61655-444-6 | $17.99

HELLBOY: THE FIRST 20 YEARS
ISBN 978-1-61655-353-1 | $19.99

THE ART OF HELLBOY
ISBN 978-1-59307-089-2 | $29.99

HELLBOY II: THE ART OF THE MOVIE
ISBN 978-1-59307-964-2 | $24.99

HELLBOY: THE COMPANION
ISBN 978-1-59307-655-9 | $14.99

HELLBOY: WEIRD TALES
ISBN 978-1-61655-510-8 | $24.99

HELLBOY: MASKS AND MONSTERS
with James Robinson and Scott Benefiel
ISBN 978-1-59582-567-4 | $17.99

HELLBOY AND THE B.P.R.D: 1952
with John Arcudi and Alex Maleev
ISBN 978-1-61655-660-0 | $19.99

THE HELLBOY 100 PROJECT
TPB: ISBN 978-1-61655-932-8 | $12.99
HC: ISBN 978-1-61655-933-5 | $24.99

NOVELS

HELLBOY: EMERALD HELL
By Tom Piccirilli
ISBN 978-1-59582-141-6 | $12.99

HELLBOY: THE ALL-SEEING EYE
By Mark Morris
ISBN 978-1-59582-142-3 | $12.99

HELLBOY: THE FIRE WOLVES
By Tim Lebbon
ISBN 978-1-59582-204-8 | $12.99

HELLBOY: THE ICE WOLVES
By Mark Chadbourn
ISBN 978-1-59582-205-5 | $12.99

SHORT STORIES

Illustrated by Mike Mignola

HELLBOY: ODDER JOBS
By Frank Darabont, Charles de Lint, Guillermo del Toro, and others
ISBN 978-1-59307-226-1 | $14.99

HELLBOY: ODDEST JOBS
By Joe R. Lansdale, China Miéville, and others
ISBN 978-1-59307-944-4 | $14.99

DARK HORSE BOOKS

AVAILABLE AT YOUR LOCAL COMICS SHOP OR BOOKSTORE! • To find a comics shop in your area, call 1-888-266-4226.
For more information or to order direct visit DarkHorse.com or call 1-800-862-0052 Mon.–Fri. 9 AM to 5 PM Pacific Time.
Prices and availability subject to change without notice.

DarkHorse.com